Freny Manecksha is an independe
began her journalism career worki
also worked with *The Times of In*
She left mainstream journalism af
her areas of interest which include development, gender and human rights. For the past eleven years, she has travelled and written extensively on people's struggles from Kashmir and Chhattisgarh and has been published in *Himal South Asian*, *TheWire*, *Raiot* and PARI. She is the author of *Behold, I Shine Narratives of Kashmir's Women and Children*.

FLAMING FOREST, WOUNDED VALLEY

Stories from BASTAR and KASHMIR

FRENY MANECKSHA

SPEAKING TIGER BOOKS LLP
125A, Ground Floor, Shahpur Jat, near Asiad Village,
New Delhi 110049

First published by Speaking Tiger Books 2022

ISBN: 978-93-5447-267-1
eISBN: 978-93-5447-251-0

10 9 8 7 6 5 4 3 2 1

For those who dare to tell their stories and for those brave truth-tellers—journalists and human rights activists—who recount them and even go to jail for doing so.

Contents

Preface ix

Part One: FLAMING FOREST: *Stories from Bastar*

1. Forest 3
2. Body 34
3. Court 71
4. Jameen 112

Part Two: WOUNDED VALLEY: *Stories from Kashmir*

5. Siege 131
6. Hospital 168
7. Home/Homeland 194
8. Nyabar/Outside 218
9. Spaces of Dissent 251

Acknowledgements 275
Notes 277

Preface

In 2010, I began a series of journeys to various parts of India to try and understand peoples' uprisings and movements. I had moved out of mainstream media and, as an independent journalist, was keen to visit the hinterlands where crucial struggles for survival were taking place. My visits to Bastar in Chhattisgarh, Odisha and Kashmir brought about a tectonic shift in my ways of seeing. They set me on a learning course, and over the years, as I continued my journeys, I saw the horrific consequences of State repression in the name of 'national interest': death, dispossession and routine violation of human rights. I saw the numbing tragedies that result from the vicious cycle of militarism and militancy and are dismissed as 'collateral damage'.

From the Adivasis of Bastar, who were squatting in the forests of adjoining Telangana, I heard accounts of killings, beatings and razing of homes because they were reluctant to relocate to the camps the government had set up for them. There was no one whom they could turn to for redressal. This violence was emanating from the police and largely from the Salwa Judum, a militia, initiated by the state and corporate interests who wanted to clear forest lands for mining. Adivasis who resisted could also be hauled away to jail and labelled 'Naxali'. In Odisha, which

I visited two months later, the betel leaf growers of Dhinkia who had protested against the acquisition of their lands by the Odisha government and a South Korean steel company had been jailed in similar fashion. One thousand villagers had false cases foisted on them. The Korean company gave up its bid years later but the struggle is not yet over. There are new moves to acquire lands, this time by an Indian company.

I arrived in Kashmir in October at the tail-end of the summer uprising of 2010, following encounter killings of three Kashmiri civilians by the Army in Kupwara. There had been massive protest marches, and people had been killed in firing by the police and security forces. The armed struggle of the 1990s had waned, militancy was down. It had been replaced by an unarmed mass civil disobedience movement. But the number of troops on the ground had not been reduced and the Valley remained one of the most heavily militarized regions in the world. Some 110 people, including an eleven-year-old boy, were killed in the face-off that took place on the streets that summer of 2010. Visual images captured the contrast between boys with stones in hand protesting against heavily armed troops. Pellet guns were being deployed, a weapon seldom used elsewhere. Militarization, I learnt, has an added dimension in Kashmir. Not only is it a deterrence against Pakistan in the territorial wars but it is also a weapon to quell Kashmiri dissidence and exercise control over the political aspirations of its people. These aspirations existed even before Partition. Dissent against the Hindu Dogra rulers had been openly manifested in an uprising in 1931. Military strength is bolstered by extraordinary security legislation like the Armed Forces Special Powers Act (AFSPA). It provides blanket immunity to the security forces against crimes like unlawful detentions, torture and custodial killings. My travels to all these regions were a revelatory exercise on the ways in which the state uses nomenclatures like 'development', or concerns of 'national security' or 'securing the sovereignty of the nation' to wage war on citizens and hold in contempt their basic rights.

I returned again and again to Kashmir and then Chhattisgarh and saw how the conflict and the imposition of authoritarian rule permeate every aspect of life. Militarism spreads and enters every nook and crevice of everyday living. No space is left untouched.

I learned how merely failing to stop at a check-post barrier can get you shot in Kashmir. Or then, as a lawyer in Mumbai explained, how even routine activities become dangerous for Adivasis living deep in the forests of Bastar. He spoke about an incident in which seventeen Adivasis were shot one night as they sat in their fields discussing the impending celebrations for Beej Pandum (a festival before the sowing of seeds). They were labelled as dreaded Maoists by the Central Reserve Police Force (CRPF) who came upon them during a night march. I remember him saying that as middle-class urban Indians we were insulated from this violence and have very little inkling of how life can be in other places.This gave me the seedling for the book: how places and spaces are impacted by the politics of a nation and how people fight to reclaim them.

For Adivasis, the forest has shaped their entire culture and ecosystem and produced what a researcher in development, Arunopol Seal, calls an ethics of reciprocity. This deals with how indigenous peoples live in harmony with the trees, waterbodies and earth. What happens to this construct when Adivasis are ordered to leave the forests they have lived in all their lives and are 'settled' in makeshift camps by the side of busy roads? How did that impact their right to life? The government ordered the move on the pretext that it was for the people's safety against attacks by the Naxalites but intimidatory tactics made it clear it was the concerns of corporate firms, with whom it had drawn up memorandums of understanding, that was paramount. It was not as if the Adivasis had other choices: anyone who chose to ignore the Chhattisgarh government's diktat was outlawed.

In Kashmir, Bakarwals and other pastoral communities have traditionally used the meadows as grazing grounds for their animals in the summer months. Increasing militarization and the army's takeover of lands put their livelihood and their own lives at risk. One example was when the Jammu & Kashmir government in 1964 leased out the vast meadow, known as Tosamaidan, to the army for use as an artillery field. Firing exercises began in the morning and coincided with school hours: children cowered in fright as guns boomed and sometimes the school building shook. The army continued to use the beautiful meadow as a firing range until 2014. Unexploded shells lying around in the area have killed at least 65 people, including children, and injured and disabled almost 300. In June 2009, two people who were collecting iron scrap in the meadow were killed when an old shell exploded. In 2020, three people were grievously injured, including fifteen-year-old Muhammad Asif Wani, who was playing in the meadow.

In Chhattisgarh, schools were taken over by security forces and were often blown up by the Maoists. Sometimes school buildings became informal interrogation and torture centres with the police holding Adivasis there in unlawful custody. One of the cases I heard about from lawyers was the story of Arjun (told later in the book). It was Arjun's desire to get an education that became the very reason for him to be cruelly targeted and killed. The security forces were irked because he was "*padha, likha aur sawal karta tha.*" He could read, write and questioned them when they made unlawful arrests of people in the village.

The concept of home as a safe inviolate space does not exist in Kashmir where AFSPA empowers security troops to enter at any hour and where 'night raids' have staged a big comeback. Troops can force their way into homes at any hour, deploy a male member as a 'human shield' or decoy and search the rooms. Even the aged are not spared. In one case, security forces did not hesitate to drag an elderly woman in poor mental health out of her room, with scant regard to the fact that she did not have her salwar on. Nor was she given time to cover her head.

In Chhattisgarh, the CRPF troops on combing missions camped in hamlets for days, sexually assaulting the women even as the children wailed in terror. The forces then decamped with the families' meagre possessions of poultry and bags of coins which represented their entire savings.

How does one access justice and lodge a complaint against those who are meant to be enforcing the law? How does one fight when the law that has been applied is a 'lawless' one? How does one counter official narratives that leave no room for others?

Besides trying to understand the ways spaces are impacted I also began hearing about ways people fought to maintain and reclaim them.

I was reminded of renowned sculptor Auguste Rodin's set of statues, 'The Burghers of Calais', conceived as a way of paying tribute to the idea that heroic deeds may be performed by ordinary people. The story goes that in 1346 CE, King Edward III laid siege to the French city of Calais. He agreed to spare the people if six citizens offered to surrender, presumably to be then executed. The faltering steps, despairing gestures and inner turmoil is powerfully captured by Rodin to depict a group of men, who must struggle with the fears of imminent death and devotion to the cause of saving their people. It is said that their lives were eventually spared because of a plea for mercy by Edward's pregnant wife Queen Philipa. For me 'The Burghers of Calais' draws its power from the way the brute force of any regime demands a sacrifice from those they consider as different, as inferior. And yet here are heroes, six people who are willing to stand up for the rest.

*

Over several field trips, I came upon stories of the resilience shown by ordinary people. In Jagdalpur, Chhattisgarh, where a commission of hearing was taking place into the killings of Adivasis, one villager was asked why he had refused compensation. Was it at the dictates of the Maoists, asked the counsel for the state. His reply was out of a Greek tragedy. 'We have sold our goats and cattle. We do not seek money. That would be akin to selling our dead,' he said. He did not want compensation; he wanted something much larger and much more difficult: he wanted justice.

In 2020, a fifteen-hour-long gun battle took place in Srinagar's Nawakadal area, between two militants and security forces. Since the AFSPA, 1959, empowers security forces to do pretty much as they please in 'disturbed areas', explosives are used freely and homes are blown up regularly. As many as twenty-two houses were blown up or gutted in a fire during the gun battle. Many of the houses belonged to daily wage earners. Over just a few days, an appeal made by the Mohalla Committee and community initiative managed to raise around three crore rupees to rebuild the houses. This was during the time of the Covid pandemic with all its attendant economic hardship but the crowdfunding effort was a moving illustration of how shared suffering can generate empathy.

This book has been written during the Coronavirus surges and lockdowns which restricted my travel. I wonder how much harder the lives of ordinary people in Chhattisgarh and Kashmir must have become during this time. And indeed there is evidence that the pandemic and often arbitrary lockdowns have been used to legitimize authoritarianism.

Even during these hard times the silences are being broken. Somewhere in the jungle a troupe dances, the cries of *'Jal, jungal, jameen hamara hai...'* (The water, the forest and the land is ours) rings out as Adivasis resist land grabbing. Somewhere in the Kashmir mountains, the quest for freedom still rings out. The question is roared: *'Hum kya chaahate...?* The answer: *'Azadi'* has not been quite muffled.

Part One

FLAMING FOREST

Stories from Bastar

Photo credit: Sakhi

1

Forest

Why can he not live in peace anywhere? However remote the place he travels to, something will come out from underground, immediately a big settlement will grow there.

Mahasweta Devi, *Chotti Munda and His Arrow*, translated by Gayatri Chakravorty Spivak

After all these years, I try to conjure up those fleeting moments that created lasting memories. Why did the sight of Adivasis, gathering up their belongings of bamboo baskets, gourd bottles containing mahua liquor, live chickens, wooden sticks, sacks of provisions and then slipping into the forest, turn into such an arresting image for me and my friend Suchitra?

It had been a long, hot, frustrating day. M Suchitra, a journalist from Kerala, and I had planned our visit to the troubled region of Bastar, Chhattisgarh, in the March of 2010, blissfully unaware of the challenges we were going to face. We were armed with telephone numbers of a few contacts and the naïve foolhardiness and determination of first-time journalists to Bastar.

On that particular morning, we had risen early and set out from the Circuit House in Konta, the Bastar frontier town adjoining Andhra Pradesh, to visit the camps at Konta to which Adivasis had been forced to shift, as part of the state's strategic hamletting policy. The Chhattisgarh government had ordered Adivasis in the forests to leave and be resettled in the makeshift camps that were constructed for them, ostensibly for their safety, but believed to be part of a plan to clear the forests for mining operations.

Two youths, who were our local contacts, seemed edgy that morning, belying the enthusiasm they had displayed the night before. Just outside the camp, a car drew up and the police town inspector in mufti, who had met us the previous day, got out and announced no one could visit the camps without the official permission of the Collector. He then peremptorily ordered us to go back across the border, if we wanted to proceed to Dantewada, and make the journey via Visakhapatnam. A detour of more than 500 km.

Why couldn't we use the bus on the direct route along the highway? 'The Naxalites,' he answered. 'They will bomb your bus. They will attack you. It is not safe.'

Hadn't a bunch of tourists from the Circuit House, taken a vehicle on the very same highway bound for Ma Danteshwari's temple in Dantewada? I argued. He remained adamant and Suchitra was forced to use her cell phone to call SRP Kalluri, then the Senior Superintendent of Police (SSP) of Dantewada, to check if it was true that people from outside the state were forbidden to travel in the buses.

Kalluri denied having given any such order but there was more bathos ahead. The youths came and told us the Inspector was pleading with them not to let us board the bus. '*Naukri ka sawaal*' (It's a question of his job), they said.

It was outlandish to believe that two freelancers with no clout, without even a newspaper or magazine to write for should pose a real threat to anyone. We consulted a middle-aged gentleman, whose name had been recommended as a guide. He explained quietly this was Chhattisgarh, the most 'lawless' state in India where the police functioned as arbitrarily as they chose.

On his suggestion, we decided on tactical subterfuge. The youths would tell the Inspector we had retraced our steps, gone back to Chatti in Andhra, where the buses came from and, with his honour and job intact, he could leave. Meanwhile we would be free to take a bus from Konta.

But of course, it wasn't so easy. The bus we boarded was not a direct one. It stopped at Sukma where we waited for more than three hours for a connecting bus. We drank sickly sweet bottled beverages and tried unsuccessfully to contact the Adivasi leader with whom we had tried to set up a meeting for weeks. He had stopped answering our calls. Over the next few days, evasive tactics such as switching off one's mobile or simply maintaining an uneasy quiet in the face of outsiders' questions, would become a familiar trope. It was only years later that I came to understand just how palpable the fears of the people in Bastar were and how I should have interpreted those sounds of silence.

At dusk, the bus to Dantewada came and we boarded along with Adivasis returning from a weekly *haat* or market. The journey was interrupted by gunny bags of rice falling off the top carrier and having to be retrieved.

I had been half dozing, numbed by the heat, when the bus stopped in what appeared to be the middle of the forest. The Adivasis stepped out and joined several others waiting on the roadside. In the light of a faint moon, they found their path among the trees, imperceptibly merging with the landscape.

It was poignant because they were manifesting a feeling of familiarity with the terrain, of belongingness. It was in total contrast to their fellow Adivasis, who had fled across the borders to Andhra Pradesh.

We had met some of them from this very district, just two days earlier, when we had stopped over at Bhadrachalam and gone into the forests of Khammam district of what was then Andhra Pradesh. They displayed a sense of unbelonging, of Internally Displaced People, as they had been officially designated.

Exodus: Fleeing from Judum's Terror

Escorted by a volunteer from a civil society organization, Suchitra and I had bumped along tarred roads and dirt tracks in an autorickshaw. Hot winds swirled around us and the acrid smell of chillies stung our nostrils, burnt our cheeks and we pulled our dupattas around our faces in a tight embrace. This was chilli country, fields upon fields where Adivasi labourers from Bastar came in search of work.

At the edge of a scraggly forest were a few bamboo huts of a small settlement of some twenty families of Adivasis, known as Gotti Koyas or Murias from Amapenta of the Konta block of Chhattisgarh. We dismounted from the rickshaw and walked up to the huts. A soft cloth swing, cocooning a baby, swung from the rafters of a home and a hen sat broodily on a bamboo basket above. The villagers gathered slowly, squatting on the ground, 'like a mini-gram sabha,' Suchitra observed. One of the women nursing a baby, sat a little distance away. With the volunteer translating, we tried to piece together accounts of why they had fled their homes.

Judum, was the reply.

The Salwa Judum to be precise.

Begun in 2005, this group was described by the state and the media as a popular spontaneous people's uprising against the Maoists. In practice it was a group of vigilantes, acting on behalf of politicians, cutting across party lines. Members of the Judum, entrusted with the responsibility of forcing people to leave their forest homes and live in the roadside settlements, unleashed terrible violence. Villagers who resisted the evictions were beaten and killed. Children were not spared. Many women were raped.

One of the men, Vaikosukda, told us some people had come into the village and tried to drag him away but he had managed to escape. He did not know them personally but believed it was this same outfit that had killed two women and three men in the neighbouring village of Ghasanpalli. The Salwa Judum, he said were accompanied by Special Police Officers (SPOs).

This category of foot soldiers was created from untrained cadres of the Salwa Judum in 2005. Under the pretext of a temporary supplementary force, the police recruited hundreds of Adivasis who received a monthly salary of Rs 1500 for counter-insurgency operations. SPOs were not given any official uniform or weapons but later, some of them began wearing camouflage fatigues and acquired sophisticated weapons. In 2011, the Supreme Court ruled that the state must disband and disarm all SPOs and the Union of India was ordered to stop funding these poorly paid, untrained SPOs for Maoist operations.

Another man, Madvi Deva, recalled the horror and coercion that these SPOs and Judum members wreaked when they came into his village. 'Three of us from our family ran away, because they were rounding up people, beating them and taking them away to Dantewada.

'Some of our people are in Dantewada jail. We don't know why they are doing this to us. They don't interrogate us or make any inquiries. They just pick us up and take us away.'

Murkum Ayeta from the Sukma block said he fled in terror when his twenty-year-old son was forcibly taken to jail. Huts were razed and sixty homes destroyed in his village near Itarajpada. He told us he made a journey back to his home in Chhattisgarh, walking through the forest trails for about a month, but did not stay long. He picked up his frugal possessions and came back to Andhra. The district was familiar to him because, like other Adivasis, he had often worked for the famers of the Khammam district. Although the panchayat officials were sympathetic and said he could resettle, the forest officials had been harassing them and often broke down his bamboo hut.

Muchatri Desa of Velpocha village had witnessed the tragic killing of his younger brother, Marakum Sana, in 2005. The eighteen-year-old youth had been fishing in the local pond with others when the Salwa Judum surrounded them and killed him and another youth. 'They used their phone and a helicopter arrived with security forces to take away the dead bodies and also one person held as captive.' The Salwa Judum later claimed there was an encounter with Naxalites and Marakum Sana was described as one, he said.

At the Kondapalli settlement that we next visited, it was the women who poured out their stories, as the men had gone into the forest. Replete with details it was a similar pattern of forced arrests, razed homes and killings. They were hesitant though to speak about the sexual violence.

One particularly searing tale, told in just a few staccato sentences, still haunts. An old woman pleading desperately with the attackers. 'Take my cows, take the bullock, spare my son.' But she was beaten mercilessly and the men were taken away and killed in the dense jungle on the road towards Golapalli.

Only the elderly, who could not have made the arduous exodus, had chosen to stay behind. Now perched on the edge of precariousness in the forests of Andhra, the Adivasis faced further displacement by forest officials. Vaikosukda told me, 'I have *pattas* (land titles) back home. But I am not going back to die. I will do coolie work here.'

Did they file complaints? 'How could we? It was the police along with the Judum who were the perpetrators. We have no trust in the *sarkar* (government).'

How did home and the forest become such a dangerous place? Who were these members of the Salwa Judum? What complex factors could explain why people were being hounded to go into special camps or then face heinous violence? Why did fellow Adivasis want them displaced, to become fugitives from a state that had been carved out in their name? What were the latest intrusions in Adivasi history that had so violently torn the very fabric of their society and their ecosystem?

*

Bastar, a former princely state, traces its history back to the early fourteenth century when it was ruled by Annama Deva, brother of the Kakatiya king Prataparudra. A tributary state of the Marathas, it came under British indirect rule in 1853 as part of the Central Provinces Administration. In 1947, both Bastar and Kanker acceded to the Republic of India and merged to form one of the largest districts of India. It has since been divided.

Bastar lies cradled in a space that, for the Hindu historical imagination, is Dandakaranya or the 'forest of punishment', where the demon Dandaka held sway. The Valmiki Ramayana sites the Dandakaranya as the place where Ramachandra, his wife Sita and brother Lakshman spent years of exile (*vanvaas* or banishment) and mentions demons as well as an indigenous population occupying the territory.

Geographically, Dandakaranya is a continuous area of over

80,000 square kilometres of Central India, encompassing much of Odisha and Chhattisgarh. It is bound by the Abujhmadh Hills with their rich iron ore deposits in the west and in the east by the Eastern Ghats covered with thick forests of teak, sal, bamboo, saja (*Terminalia tomentosa*), bahera (*Terminalia bellirica*) and many others.

This ecosystem has shaped the Adivasi way of life. Its culture emerged, for the most part, in a particular symbiosis of field and forest. They were embedded in a collective vision in which the forest plays a very important part.[1]

Living in relative isolation, the varied tribes of the Murias, Halbis and Durwas of Bastar draw their very identity from their habitat. The Murias, for example, take their name from the word 'mar' or highlands.

Arunopol Seal, a development practitioner, who has lived and worked among Adivasi communities, defines the bedrock of their relationship with the environment as an 'ethics of reciprocity'.

'Animals, plants, birds and insects and humans draw from each other what they need. Each offers themselves to the other for the other's survival around the season.'[2]

Notable Adivasi activist, Soni Sori, told me how Adivasis always leave some corn for the birds to eat when they harvest the crop. Even in semi-urban areas, Adivasis will not milk a cow that is nursing. They would rather buy the milk than 'steal' from the mother.

Their society has been classified and stratified to optimize resource usage through an ethical code whereby totemic species are protected. Hence Mandavis (a gotra) will not kill goats and Anchlas will not kill snakes.[3]

Every season brings changes to the forest, life flows in consonance with these rhythms. Fruit gathering, honey collecting and consuming forest produce are built around this principle of reciprocity. Madhu Ramnath who spent thirty years with the Durwas, writes of how *mutaks* or elders of each village wander around the forest before the mango Pandum or celebration (one among several fruit festivals) and only 'after observing the state of ripeness of the fruit, determine the day when eating wild mango should commence. A delayed date allows the seeds to mature and allows for its regeneration without any other effort, but this reduces the human share as monkeys and other animals are equally fond of the fruit.'[4]

The smallest wedge of development like a pickle industry can disrupt this delicate balance because pickle makers, who want raw fruit, will push for an earlier date of harvest. It is said that the Maoists in their liberated zones would impose fines for early picking of mangoes.

Professor of Sociology, Nandini Sundar, writes how Adivasis have their own notions of property, different from that of the state. 'In Bastar, the Earth, known as Bhum, Jaga or Mati was sovereign, giving permission to certain lineages to settle; if the Earth was unhappy, people fell sick and had to leave. The first founders gave land to others, interceding on their behalf with the Earth. Every village knew where its forest began and that of their neighbours ended; they made sure that each forest spirit got its due.'[5]

Non-Adivasi civilizations do not have such a holistic vision of the forest. They see them as resources and the hierarchies of their products have been derived from their understanding of their 'value', which is essentially based on transaction and exchange. Such a commercial perspective and the logic of economy determines how the forest gets commercially classified and managed.[6]

This rationale identifies timber as a product of primary

importance with the highest 'rate of exchange', hence greater 'exchange value'. The rest of the produce becomes secondary. Whatever else the forest produces is 'non-timber' and is lumped together as minor forest produce (MFP).

For Adivasis, such exchange value is anathema to their way of living. Leaves, flowers, fruits, seeds, stems, bark and even insects—all classified as non-timber forest produce (NTFP)—crucially sustain their livelihood and diet. Much of it, like the mahua flower, the tendu leaf, lac, gum and so on is embedded in their socio-economic and cultural order and is the basis of rituals and festivals. Unlike the trader who was an intruder into the forest, the Adivasis had no control over exchange value, they kept away from circuits of capital and hence did not exploit them.[7]

I can still recall the mahua tree (*Madhuca indica*) in blossom, its aroma pervaded all the journeys Suchitra and I undertook in Dantewada and Bijapur. We saw acres and acres of the earth carpeted in its pale ivory glory. Adivasis squatted on this carpet, patiently picking up the flowers strewn on the ground. The distinctive smell of liquor distilled from it lingered in the nostrils even when we had left the border.

Many years later, I grasped mahua's significance as livelihood. I was part of a small team of journalists rattling along in a trusted old Bolero over forest tracks in the Sukma district. Often, we lost our way, the path petering out and forcing us to retrace. At mid-day with the sun directly overhead, we finally arrived at the village of Godelgudda in which a woman had lost her life in firing by CRPF (Central Reserve Police Force) personnel. The village was eerily quiet with scarcely anyone about but, I was reassured to learn, this was because everyone was out gathering the mahua flowers, even older children. This was the peak harvest season for the Adivasis' chief cash crop and the biggest minor forest produce of Chhattisgarh, earning a revenue of around Rs 200 crore.

Two days later, whilst enjoying a Holi lunch at the home of activist Keshavbhai Sori's home in Kanker, I was shown the mahua tree in the compound. Some blossoms lay scattered on the ground, others had been gathered and spread out to dry. The mahua tree is never cut but handed down from generation to generation. Even on revenue land, a family can lay claim to a particular mahua tree that would have been allocated several decades ago. The fruit and bark are used for medicinal purposes as they are believed to have healing properties. The fruit yields oil. But, it is the flower that is highly valued and even today is part of the barter economy with a bag of flowers being offered for vegetables.

Traditionally boiled and eaten, the mahua flower has been used to stave off hunger and starvation. It is also made into other dishes but its principal use is the distilling of liquor, which fosters conviviality with no gender discrimination, at social gatherings. It is also central to rituals of birth, weddings, death and even sealing a deal. Adivasis consider themselves the guardians of mahua.

According to one story, narrated by Ramnath, it was the mynah bird that taught the Adivasis how to make mel or the mahua liquor. Some flowers that had fallen into the hollow of a tree mingled with rainwater to make a weak mahua infusion. Birds who drank from this hollow, sang happily, attracting the attention of people who followed suit and enjoyed it too. Over time people learnt the art of distillation and mahua, the intoxicant was born.

The brewing of liquor and its consumption has emerged as a major point of friction between Adivasis and traditional Hindu mindsets.

A debate has been raging among India's academics and within struggles and movements on how one can describe Adivasis or tribes in the Indian social and cultural context. Shashank Kela, an author and activist, notes how the current academic consensus on the relationship between Adivasi societies and caste-based agrarian order, can be traced back to G.S. Ghurye, a right-wing nationalist. Ghurye, in response to anthropologist Verrier Elwin's spirited defence of the rights of tribals, argued in the 1940s, that there are essentially no tribal people but only 'culturally backward Hindus'. This argument has gained traction among the current Hindu right-wing outfits, who hold that there is nothing special about Adivasi societies: they just happen to occupy forests. Kela adds that although the exact definitions of the term 'tribal' may not be sharply delineated, there are historians and sociologists who agree there are substantial differences between the Adivasis and the agrarian order based on caste.[8]

Today, among the new generation in particular, there is a rising awareness of a distinctive Adivasi identity. Akash Poyam, journalist and founder editor of the website, Adivasi Resurgence, told me he belongs to the Koitur (Gond) tribe from Balrampur. In an essay, he chronicles the alienation from the clan name with the process of Brahminisation in the nineteenth century and how he acquired the surname of Prasad.

A Gond woman, Rajmohani Devi of Surguja, in 1951 initiated the movement that called for giving up eating meat, for worshipping cows, keeping away from the *devar* or traditional medicine man, wearing *khaddar* and abandoning the consumption of mahua and brewing liquor. She had been influenced by Gandhian ideology, nationalism and support of the Congress party and she claimed she was inspired by a dream. Significantly, it was a period when hunger and starvation was rife because of drought.

Poyam adds that whilst doing his MA he came to interact with Koitur elders. His reading of Adivasi and Ambedkarite literature brought him the awareness of how Adivasi clan names signify social location within the tribe and carry associations of undocumented histories of the community. He dropped his surname of Prasad and says he felt a sense of liberation in asserting his Adivasi ancestry, by taking on the clan name of Poyam, meaning smoke.[9]

There is a growing consciousness that the frowning upon mahua drinking and government policies on prohibition has had a negative impact on Adivasi socio-economic well-being. Although Adivasis of Chhattisgarh are permitted to pick the mahua flowers, there are severe restrictions on transport and trade. The mahua flower attracts 5 per cent GST even if it is being traded or transported by a self-help group at the panchayat level and community access to better markets is hampered.

This example of MFP, the mahua flower, narrated at some length, is to illustrate the huge schism that has developed between the Adivasi vision of a forest as a living community, the distinctive culture that sprang from it as against the opposing notions of market forces, of commerce and 'development' as well as Brahminisation and other intrusions that have been threatening them since the eighteenth century.

The abolition of natural frontiers, after hundreds of years of relative isolation, began with the establishment of colonial rule that brought the trader, forest official, immigrants and moneylenders into spaces that were hitherto the domain of the forest dwellers.

It was under colonial rule that for the first time, direct proprietary rights to the forest were constructed and apportioned. The Indian Forest Act of 1878 empowered the British state to become the conservator of the forest and hundreds of thousands of acres of forest land were suddenly kept in reserve. It was the beginning of Adivasi land displacement and non-Adivasis establishing rights to tax and revenue.

Maoists' Entry into Bastar and 'Janatan Sarkar'

The chief 'outsiders' who exploited the Adivasis were the forest official and the contractor or *thekedar*. Their behaviour alienated the Adivasi from the Indian State and made mobilization that much easier when squads of the People's War Group, one of the factions of the Communist Party of India (Maoists), made inroads into Bastar in the 1980s. The Maoists saw the Dandakaranyas as strategically important because it was easy to manoeuvre across state borders under cover of the forest.[10]

We were given some rudimentary lessons in the political and socio-economic history of Bastar in the house of N.R.K. Pillai, the Vice President of the Working Journalists Trade Union, who hosted us in Dantewada. Originally from Kerala, he has made Bastar his home for many years and is a veteran member of the Communist Party of India (CPI), which has played a prominent role in the electoral politics of this region, often winning many assembly seats.

After a long, anxious ride from Konta, Suchitra and I had been relieved to be met by him at the bus stand and were glad to accept his kind offer to host us. We had heard how the town's only hotel often turfed out journalists in the middle of the night if the police leaned on them and would proffer the excuse that there was a surprise booking of a large wedding party that could not be refused.

That was not the only nasty trick Dantewada town used to spring on outsiders. Although it was the headquarters of the district, it lacked a petrol pump. No autorickshaws plied even though pilgrims flocked to its famed Ma Danteshwari temple.

We would have to walk or hire a car for the entire day. There was no cinema hall. As Pillai joked, the town lacked even the mandatory Sardarji of India's small towns. There was no visible presence of security forces. The seemingly placid nondescript town bore little sign of the region's history of resistance against intrusions.

Tribals of Bastar have a vibrant tradition of rebellions, revolts and uprisings manifested in that of the Halbas (1774–79), Paralkot (1825), Tarapur (1842–54), that of the Murias (1842–63), the Kois (1859), the Muria uprising (1876) and the Bhumkal in 1910.[11]

The varied features of these revolts—ranging from a fight against coercive taxation in the Tarapur revolt or protest against contractors and cutting of sal trees in the Koi revolt and the struggle by the Murias against exploitation by the Diwan and injustice—sprang from an assertion of the traditional inalienable rights of the tribals on the land and their natural resources.

Two decades after the Naxalbari peasant uprising, described by cultural historian Sumanta Banerji as the movement that for the first time since Independence 'asserted the demands of the poor and landless in the atrophied political scene', the Maoists entered the forests of Bastar. Having suffered reverses in Andhra, the squads in the 1980s began to expand their activities in a region where there was hardly any presence of the State. Adivasis turned to them in the fight against repression by forest officials and the exploitation at the hands of contractors and traders in the beedi business who sought the valued tendu leaf. The Dandakaranya Adivasi Kissan Mazdoor, a zonal committee of the Maoists, mobilized against forest officials who demanded illegal payments from the Adivasis for collection of minor forest produce or those who cut trees to build houses. They also took up the issues of *pattas* or land titles for lands brought under cultivation and all those who were threatened with eviction. The issue of fixing the price for the tendu leaf was another very important step and one that had far-reaching effects.

In the early days, as engagement with people's issues began, the Maoist cadres took up individual cases of exploitation like non-payment of dues and demand for bribes. But, as Sundar notes in her book, *The Burning Forest, India's War in Bastar*, even when 'the exploitative nature of the state had receded', people saw that 'the Maoists had the power to fight against the rangers and local police' and 'they began to come to them with all sorts of problems, including marital disputes'.[12]

The next important initiative by the Maoists was the setting up of sanghams or village level committees to replace the traditional feudal structures. These sanghams helped settle disputes in a more democratic manner and were the platform where people could raise concerns. Discussions on inequality in land ownership and subsequent redistribution of larger holdings controlled largely by a few families began to take place. This action would pit sangham members against the local village headmen, the sarpanches, landlords and certain hierarchies of Adivasis.[13]

A 'vision of governance' was then set forth with various measures in the development agenda of the Janatan Sarkar. According to literature brought out by Maoists these included running many night schools, rudimentary health services, distribution of seedlings and seed banks being set up and small irrigation projects like ponds. A push was made for social change within the Adivasi community such as an end to bigamy.

As the District Collector of Dantewada admitted, the 'Maoist strength lies in their village-level units which comprise the illiterate common man who like others takes care of his family through earning daily wages.'[14]

But these systems of governance contested the writ of the Union of India and the state of Chhattisgarh which had its own blueprint of development. Naturally, the power of the Indian State sought to destroy this alternative system of government and governance. This was precipitated by the entry of multinationals and corporations eyeing Chhattisgarh's rich mineral wealth. The resources conflict was ratcheted up by the desire to tap the earth as well as the forest for capital and both the Centre and the state of Chhattisgarh were complicit. There are many contributory factors for the new counter-insurgency operations and the birth of the Salwa Judum (the name translates as Purification Hunt). But, significantly, it was near contiguous with the slew of Memoranda of Understanding (MOUs) on mining that were signed. The first Salwa Judum meeting occurred in June 2005, days after the state of Chhattisgarh had signed MOUs with Essar and Tata, the giant corporations who were given captive iron ore mines on the Bailadila Hills.

'Tiger of Bastar' and Birth of Salwa Judum

According to official figures, Chhattisgarh possesses 16 per cent of the total value of minerals in India and is rich in reserves of twenty-eight major minerals like coal, iron ore, bauxite, limestone and diamonds. The Adivasi literally sits atop such wealth but is then condemned to dispossession when prospectors arrive.

Adivasi dispossession by mining was accelerated in Bastar in 2005 by the Raman Singh government's strategy of fuelling anti-Maoist sentiments and creating conditions that could enable the dismantling of the support base Maoists had created in the villages and isolating them by moving the population into official relief camps. The agenda for this new form of colonization was clearly articulated in an official government document entitled 'The Work Proposal for the People's Movement Against Naxalites'. It spelt out the modalities for the formation of a special force and assigned various tasks, called for setting up village defence committees and spelled out the police's role to identify 'friendly villages'. This would morph into the Salwa Judum.

An official narrative on this strategic relocation exercise was amplified by mainstream media. We heard this version when we visited the Collector's office on the day after we arrived in Dantewada. Making our way up the steps to the foyer, Suchitra exclaimed, 'Oh, oh ...Gandhi. I didn't expect to meet you here!' The large portrait of the Mahatma on the wall and an oil lamp burning in a niche seemed particularly incongruous as Gandhian activist Himanshu Kumar's Vanvasi Chetna Ashram had been razed by the state in 2008 and he had been forced to flee, fearing imprisonment. Although he had worked in Dantewada for years, even partnering with the government in some schemes, Himanshu Kumar began to be targeted after he took up cases of Adivasis who complained of rape and violence perpetrated by the Judum.[15]

We patiently sat through two of Gandhi's bhajans relayed on the loudspeaker at the office premises before Collector Rina Kangale appeared accompanied by a gun-toting bodyguard. In her office, Kangale explained the relocation as the Chhattisgarh government's response to increased Maoist violence. Some 30–35 per cent of villages in the district were beyond the reach of the government, she said. So it was decided to move the administrative machinery out and resettle villagers in camps. They were provided with free housing, electricity and initially given free food grains.

She rattled off the measures. 'Currently, they get rice for two rupees per kilo. They are getting employment under the

NREGA (National Rural Employment Guarantee Act), schools have been established and they are protected by the CRPF.' She admitted that there had been some resistance on the part of villagers to leave their homes and be 'resettled'. But, she said, the administration had no choice given the levels of Maoist violence and Adivasis living in great fear of the Maoists.

The manner in which the term 'relief camps' became interchangeable with 'Salwa Judum camps' is not just an oxymoron, but also emblematic of the way the state feigned benevolence even as it carried out its massive dispersal and displacement exercise to insidiously advance corporate interests.

A similar disingenuous official narrative was spun around the origins of the Salwa Judum as a 'spontaneous, self-initiated and peaceful' uprising against the Maoists, precipitated by anger against the ban they had imposed on tendu leaf collection in a bid to leverage the price.

The movement remained elusive in the official records and audits even though it was clearly backed by the state. Pitting Bastar's tribals against each other, on a scale unparalleled in their history, the state cynically deployed local youths into this counter-insurgency movement and used their insider knowledge to form an unofficial and unaccountable force. It is reminiscent of tactics used in Kashmir with the Ikhwans or renegade rebels.

Aiding the Judum were Adivasi youths recruited by the state as SPOs. Lured by the promise of employment and seduced by machismo and power, Adivasi youths enrolled by the hundreds. The police were not overly concerned about the ages of who they were recruiting. Many who joined were minors who were hoping to be inducted into the regular police force at a later stage. Some had not even begun sprouting facial hair and could well be labelled child soldiers.

Pillai explained to us why brute violence was an intrinsic

part of the Judum's matrix. 'Some Adivasis who had learnt the language of might under the Maoists began challenging them and flexing muscle. It was also an opportune time for most wanted men to become leaders in this shadowy force. Men who had been wanted by the police with criminal cases against them could now move freely and fearlessly along with the police.'

Presiding over this rogue militia was the towering figure of Mahendra Karma, labelled the Tiger of Bastar. A controversial figure, he began his political career under the CPI but, nursing huge ambitions of power and pelf, he switched over to the Congress party when he was denied a ticket. The son of a landowner or Majhi, his politics were the antithesis of those of the Maoists. In 1996, he opposed an agitation that was demanding implementation of the Sixth Schedule, which protects tribal populations and enables autonomous development councils to frame laws. In 1999, his name figured in the Lokayukta report for the Malik Makbuja scam whereby in connivance with revenue and forest officials he manipulated the right of an Adivasi to cut trees on his land. He was thus able to transfer land and fell and sell thousands of trees. His dealings with big businessmen and traders helped him straddle the divide between the Congress and the Bharatiya Janata Party (BJP)-led Raman Singh government and is illustrative of the complex interplay of politics that blurred the lines.

Mahendra Karma was a powerful, fearless Adivasi leader who, nevertheless displayed utter disdain for his people's displacement and lives even as he sought to legitimize the Judum by drawing on the legacy of Adivasi revolt. He compared the Judum to the Bhumkal uprising of February 1910 when people rose up against the influx of officials, policemen and foresters that resulted in displacement and rising land taxes. The Maoists too claimed that they drew inspiration from the legacy of the Bhumkal uprising.[16]

Karma's end was as gory as the carnage he had unleashed. He was ambushed by the People's Liberation Guerrilla Army, the armed faction of the Communist Party of India (Maoists), at Jeeram Ghati in 2013, along with other Congress leaders. His body bore seventy-eight stab wounds, inflicted, it is said, largely by women cadres, besides gunshot injuries.

The Salwa Judum itself, over which he presided, had been declared unconstitutional by the Supreme Court in 2011 in response to two writ petitions filed in 2007.

One writ petition, which was civil, was filed by Nandini Sundar, historian Ramachandra Guha and retired Indian Administrative Service (IAS) officer E.A.S. Sarma against the state of Chhattisgarh, calling for an end to the practice of arming civilians, state support to vigilantism, inducting minors into the SPOs and for a ban on the Salwa Judum.

Another writ petition, criminal, which was argued together with the civil, was based on testimonies of victims from 110 villages, who were targeted by the Salwa Judum. It was filed by three CPI activists of Bastar—Kartam Joga, Dudhi Joga and Manish Kunjum, also the leader of the Adivasi Mahasabha. Besides the plea for disbanding of the Salwa Judum and SPOs, this petition also sought an independent inquiry into the rapes, arson and killing, directing the state to rehabilitate and compensate victims and to prosecute all those responsible for human rights violations.

In their judgement of 5 July 2011, Justices Reddy and Nijjar held that the use of poorly trained, low-paid SPOs in counter-insurgency, violated the right to equality and directed the state to disband and disarm all SPOs. The order also directed the state of Chhattisgarh to prevent the operation of any group, including but not limited to the Salwa Judum, to take the law into private hands, to act unconstitutionally or otherwise violate the human rights of any person, and to investigate and prosecute all human rights violations.

Hailed widely in liberal circles, the judgement could not be effectively implemented in spirit. The 'legal death' of the Judum, was thus craftily rendered ineffective by both the Centre and Chhattisgarh. The Chhattisgarh government passed the Chhattisgarh Auxiliary Armed Police Force Ordinance, which regularized all youths appointed as SPOs and even enhanced salaries.[17]

The vigilante tactics resurfaced in many avatars such as the Samajik Ekta Manch, the Naxali Peedith Sangh and others which continue intimidatory tactics against dissent and any opposition to commercial interests by targeting Adivasi leaders, lawyers, rights activists and journalists.

Many camps shut down but the deep fissures created by them have remained.

Cherpal: Adivasis Left in Limbo

The highway that took our bus from Konta to Sukma in 2010 has been widely touted by the Raman Singh government as a shining example of development. Its real purpose was different; the roads were a crucial cog for the militarization of Chhattisgarh and to enable penetration into the inner zones with the setting up of paramilitary and Salwa Judum camps. It is the chief reason why road building continues to be a fraught exercise with Maoists attacking contractors and workers.

Our bus was jam-packed with CRPF personnel and Adivasis. Craning my neck, I struggled to peer at the roadside settlements or strategic hamletting camps, colloquially known as Salwa Judum camps, when they came into view. Injaram, Errabor and Dornapal—these were camps where hundreds of Adivasis had been corralled. Their history and their geographic location along the highway corresponded with the spread of the Judum from Bijapur after 2005 and its tentacles of growing repression stretching up to the frontier town of Konta. Villagers had been brought here by force or had then fled the villages.

We could not get much more than a very brief impression of these roadside settlements but what was unmistakable was the warscape—the twists of ugly barbed wires, sandbags and the presence of CRPF personnel and SPOs—indicators of how the conflict had come out of the forest and onto the highways.

For the Adivasi inhabitants, the camps did not translate into 'relief' or safety. Injaram was attacked by Maoists on 16 May 2006 with four SPOs losing their lives; Errabor was attacked in July of that year. Around forty Adivasis were killed and even small children were not spared on that day of terrible bloodshed. The attacks were part of the Maoists' counter-action for the violence unleashed by the Judum and the Adivasis who had been forcibly taken along on the raids. Near the entrance to the Konta camp, before we were driven away by the Town Inspector, Suchitra and I had seen many 'martyr memorials' or statues of young SPOs with guns, who had died in these battles. Many such statues dotted the Bastar landscape and were a stark reminder of how they were deployed as cannon fodder in a cynically conceived fratricide.

After being denied entry into a camp by the Town Inspector in Konta, we were offered the opportunity of visiting one after our visit to the Collector. We demurred, knowing such stage-managed visits would be futile. A tip-off eventually helped us to decide which of the Salwa Judum camps we should visit. We left Dantewada for a day trip to Bijapur, driving through forests where the spindly outlines of the trees stood like sentinels against the skyline. It was March, the blazing heat had begun and the leaves were falling. The approach of summer with temperatures soaring into the 40s, would make the ongoing conflict, even more relentless. The lack of forest cover would be a handicap for Maoists; on the other hand, the intense heat would make it gruelling for the heavily armed large contingents of the CRPF as they set out on their patrols and combing operations.

We saw no one in the forests: just a flag on the ground was an indicator of who inhabited these territories. I was reminded of what a journalist had told me just before we set out. 'You go expecting to see all the action of a conflict zone. But, in effect, it is an invisible war. Deep in the forests, scenes of violence are unfolding but it is difficult terrain to access, not just geographically but also because of the barriers put up by the state. Adivasis too are extremely hesitant to meet with outsiders. It is difficult to hear their stories.'

I heard how Adivasis tend to run away when they hear the sounds of a car. In some places, as we witnessed many years later, the sound of shots from a hunting gun or bursting of firecrackers is used to inform those in the hamlets of the approach of strangers.

In Bijapur, we came upon Alex Paul Menon, the enthusiastic young Deputy Collector, who acknowledged the initial mistakes of the state, but waxed eloquent about what he described as the model of an ideal village. He was referring to one of the more recently built Salwa Judum camps. Holding forth on the need for a hands-on approach and his bid to interact with as many villagers as possible, he told us how he often ventured right into the interiors on his motorcycle. We wondered at his zeal. Two years later, I read his bodyguard had been shot and he himself had been abducted for ten days by the Maoists. He was set free after mediation by activists Professor Hargopal and Swami Agnivesh.

We also tried to talk with Sai Reddy, one of Chhattisgarh's

journalists who had been arrested under the Special Public Security Act for alleged links with Naxalites. We went to his home which had been recently ransacked and damaged by unknown people. He said he was busy and would meet us later in the marketplace but when he did not turn up, another local journalist, said '*Woh hichkicha raha hai.*' (He is hesitant.)

Three years later, in 2013, I opened a newspaper and learnt Reddy had been stabbed to death by assailants at the weekly market in Basaguda. The Maoists claimed responsibility, saying he had played an active role in the Salwa Judum. Reddy covered issues of health, education and corruption and criticized both the state and the non-state actors; his killing was a very grim reflection on how dangerous it was to report out of Chhattisgarh with integrity.

At the Bijapur market, we met one of the persons whose name was given to us by a contact. He too had been one of Chhattisgarh's poorly paid journalists who write for regional papers and must supplement their income by doing other jobs.

Meeting us outside a chemist shop in Bijapur, he spoke in a low tone. He had given up reporting after being threatened with dire physical violence and even death for an exposé he had done of Chhattisgarh's public distribution system. His wariness about being seen in public with two noticeable outsiders, was a stark reminder of how fear lurked in seemingly sleepy small towns, for those who dared to question the status quo.

He suggested we visit Cherpal Camp, where, he told us somewhat enigmatically, we would get 'a story with a twist'. Accompanied by two young journalists, we set off in the afternoon, down a deeply rutted road, a far cry from the highway.

Cherpal stood cheek-by-jowl with a CRPF camp. Sections of the settlement of huts and rooms appeared deserted. In one of them, a sewing machine stood abandoned. A small crowd clustered around us and spoke of the people going back, dissatisfied with these spaces, which were in such direct contrast to their own homes with expanses of sky and earth and natural light, and where most dwellings had their own courtyards fenced in with bamboo.

Moreover, they were now disillusioned, running on empty. The promises of jobs had dried up. There was not enough work under the Work for Food or the NREGA schemes and no land or forest that could provide livelihood through the MFPs. Vocational training classes for weaving and sewing were never completed and people found these skills did not generate any sustainable income.

The villagers had been going into the forest by day to gather tendu leaves and returned to Cherpal only at night since a register had been kept by the state which they were forced to sign. Word had come to them that it would be 'safe' for them to return and many had abandoned government 'relief' for the spaces back in the forest. Though the term 'Naxalites' or 'Maoist' was not used in the conversations, it was evident the people were referring to the Maoist change in policy that was encouraging them to return.

One youth chatted incessantly, his volubility in sharp contrast to the reticence that had been the norm elsewhere. He explained he was a schoolmaster and spoke earnestly of heading back and teaching the children. Buoyed by the hope that his worth had been recognized by the Maoists, he was confident of his safety.

The role of a schoolteacher had become something of a tussle ever since the government in 2005 had ordered teachers to work only in the camps and the CRPF had occupied the schools elsewhere.

Our tour was abruptly interrupted by a person who had approached us when we first arrived with a request that we drop off some sick children at the clinic run by Médécins Sans Frontières/Doctors Without Borders, on our return trip. He strode across and in frantic tones demanded to know how much longer we intended staying. A child's condition had deteriorated, he said. Somewhat alarmed, we scrambled into the vehicle. Two women got in, one clutching to her chest an infant covered in sores whilst the other cradled a semi-conscious four-year-old boy. She sat in silence throughout the trip to the clinic, tears pouring down her face and we tried ineffectively to offer words of comfort.

The gates were locked but urgent knocking saw a young woman come running up and she ushered the mothers and children inside.

MSF, which won the 1999 Nobel Peace Prize for providing health care in disaster- and conflict-affected areas, has been operating in Chhattisgarh and Kashmir but during the Judum years was forced to keep a low profile. In 2007, a miffed K.R. Pisda, then District Collector of Dantewada, declared he would consider a ban on the organization because its staff had been operating in areas without police permission. He accused their doctors of treating Maoist insurgents injured in encounters. International humanitarian laws, however, say medical personnel should not refuse treatment. MSF, which continued to operate, had a feeding centre at the Dornapal camp. The newsletter spoke of maladies like skin diseases, malaria and respiratory problems and how malnutrition cases were often seen. This is ironic given that Raman Singh was given the epithet 'Chawal Baba' by the mainstream media for his scheme of cheap rice at Rs 2 per kilo.

The binary of those in the forests and those in the camps, echoed by Cherpal inmates, acquired more ominous overtones when we visited the Superintendent of Police (SP), Amresh

Mishra, on our penultimate day. We met him in his office which was surprisingly unguarded, where like the Konta town inspector, he appeared in civvies of a half-sleeved shirt and pants.

'An upside-down, inside-out town where police wear plain clothes and rebels wear uniforms. The jail superintendent is in jail. The prisoners are free (three hundred of them escaped from the old town jail two years ago).' Arundhati Roy's ironic description of the state of affairs in Chhattisgarh resonated as we walked into his room. Ironically, scribbled on a flexi-board with a marker pen was the title of her essay 'Walking with the Comrades' which contained her phrases and which had appeared in *Outlook* magazine just weeks ago.[18]

We asked him about 'Operation Greenhunt', a term that began floating in the media from September 2009 onwards after intensive search-and-comb operations from July that year and a massive three-day joint operation in September. Home Minister P. Chidambaram, claimed it was a figment of the media's imagination and Mishra echoed him, saying there was no such official operation.

What is clear now is that the Centre, ruled then by the United Progressive Alliance (UPA) and the BJP Raman Singh government in Chhattisgarh, were both in agreement for the intensified deployment of troops. These included forces from the CRPF, the Indo-Tibetan Border Police (ITBP), the Border Security Force (BSF) and the Sashastra Seema Bal (SSB) (which began primarily as a border patrolling force). Bastar is believed to be one of the most militarized zones with an estimated 0.1 million 'boots on the ground' for a population of 3.09 million.)[19]

What was significant about our conversation with Mishra was the official delineation of who was a Maoist. Any Adivasi, who chose to stay on in the forest and not shift to the camps, was deemed an enemy of the state. 'I will consider anyone there as a Naxalite or Naxalite sympathizer. He has no business to be there. He is helping them or is part of their camp.'

Continuing to expand on the state's official policy, he added that only those who want to take on the state's forces headlong would choose to stay on. A teacher, recently apprehended near Dantewada, he added, was carrying corrugated sheets. This, to his mind, clearly marked him out as a sympathizer, a Maoist carrier.

In his conversation, Mishra also made some startling remarks on Adivasi society that revealed the extent to which they had been dehumanized in the official psyche. Almost as if imparting revelatory information, he told us about an incident in Supermoda village where four villagers had been killed. 'You know something, their family bonds are not strong. Someone has died and the parents were not even crying.'

His musings on whether the Naxalites were on the backfoot because of the recent intensive operations or his wondering whether it was just the lull before the storm, proved to be prophetic. A week later, seventy-two CRPF personnel lost their lives near the Chintalnar forests in Dantewada district after Maoists ambushed a convoy and set off an IED blast.

The state's definitions of loyalty ripped apart Adivasi communities and left many lives in tattered remnants.

Whilst many families from the Cherpal Camp did make their way back to their villages, some hundreds were forced to stay on in the miserable and makeshift conditions. They dared not go back to Paddeda village, fearing Maoist reprisals. Today they are a demographic blip. Although they have been given official status as citizens, courtesy Voter ID cards, they remain largely ignored, even by those seeking votes. One inmate told a press reporter that campaigners did not even venture past the main road. '*Road pe halla kar ke chale jaate*' (They make a noise only on the main road.)[20]

The Dornapal camp too has many former Salwa Judum members who know they cannot return to the village they once called home. By joining such a force they had crossed the Rubicon.

Some villagers like those of Sarkegudda who fled during the Salwa Judum's reign of terror, were persuaded to return and given help to resettle. Kamla Kaka, a young woman in her thirties, now working as a nurse, recalls the flight and the return.

'Many hamlets surrounding our village like Basaguda and Lingagiri emptied out but we continued to stay on even when the police burnt two or three huts and forcibly took away the villagers. When the terror did not lessen we were forced to leave. I stayed with my sister from 2006 to 2009.'

Rita, another young woman from Sarkegudda, who fled to Andhra, worked and stayed in the chilli farms till 2009. It was Gandhian activist Himanshu Kumar who then persuaded them to return and resettle, giving grains, farming implements, seedlings and so on to help them.

The actions of the government meant that more than 650 villages were emptied out and 60,000 to over one lakh suffered displacement. Many who chose not to go to the camps and live in the forests were outlawed by the state's construct of those in the forest and those in the camps, which meant a total withdrawal of health services, public distribution of food and other entitlements. The complete disruption of a way of life was amplified in the way even weekly markets or *haats* were forcibly shut down.

We had made our journey in 2010 in the naïve hope that we would be able to interact with as many Adivasis as we could and learn more about the latest intrusions into their spaces and ways of living, but the forest itself remained just a shadowy presence. Access was difficult, hearing stories was challenging.

Silences would have to be interpreted with that understanding. As Suchitra remarked by the end of the trip we too were talking in hushed tones.

More than ten years later, Adivasi land displacement and repression continues. Over many subsequent trips I find the lines from Mahasweta Devi's book resonate still: '*...our lives will also be spent wanderin' this way*'.

2

Body

Dornapal. The Salwa Judum had been banned but the camp, set up during their reign of terror, still existed. Eight years after I had first seen the Dornapal Camp, it popped up again as I journeyed towards Konta on the National Highway. I was with a fact-finding team that included Akash Poyam, founder of the website Adivasi Resurgence, Tameshwar Sinha, a local journalist from Kanker, the second largest city of Bastar and headquarters of a district with the same name, and Kritika A., a practising criminal lawyer.

We were accompanying Soni Sori and her nephew Lingaram Kodopi, who along with activist Ram Baghel were proceeding to the village of Nulkatong in the Gompad forest where an encounter had taken place. Soni and Linga had emerged as strong human rights defenders for the Adivasis of Bastar, after being arrested and waging their own personal battles for justice. On this trip, they were trying to get more details for civil rights activists, on the directions of the Supreme Court for what had been described as the biggest anti-Maoist operation. News of this operation had been splashed in the mainstream media, three days before Adivasi Diwas, celebrated on 9 August 2018, as part of International Day of the World's Indigenous People.

D.M. Awasthi, Chhattisgarh's Special Director General of Police, claimed credit for the security forces' 'killings of fifteen Maoists and the arrest of a leading Maoist figure, Madkam Deva, who had a bounty of five lakh rupees on his head. A clarification soon followed. It was a different Deva but he too was labelled Maoist.[1]

In a country, where more than 91 per cent of news coverage on the Maoist conflict in Chhattisgarh is state driven, particularly with regard to the English media, there were few to contest the air of triumphalism over dead Adivasi bodies.

The shooting had taken place deep inside the Gompad forests, considered to be a Maoist liberated zone or the territory where the local communities are now in near-complete control of the rebels. These were spaces into which few journalists would venture, entailing an arduous walk through the forest for at least 15 km.

So, who would tell the stories of the fifteen dead bodies, wrapped in black tarpaulin, bound with nylon and put on public display? Did anyone care that some of these were minors?

Alerted by a distressed phone call, Soni cancelled plans of going to Bilaspur for the Adivasi Diwas function. She rushed to Sukma where she found the grieving families, who had run behind the tractor carrying their dead.

'Waiting for the bodies after post-mortem, they were numbed with grief. Some hadn't eaten for a day, since customarily cooked food isn't eaten till after the death rituals. I ran to procure some snacks. When I returned the family was gone. They had been hustled away, invisibilized just like their stories,' Soni told me as she opened her cupboard in her Geedham home to show me the supplies still stacked up.

Along with local journalists, she and Lingaram (popularly

known as Linga), trekked into the interiors. Lawyer, writer and rights activist Bela Bhatia also visited the villages with a separate team. Both teams concluded the fifteen dead were unarmed villagers, who had been attacked in the early hours of the morning of 6 August 2018 by security forces.[2]

Who would amplify these anguished cries of the victims' families, including a blind father, contesting the official narratives?

The Civil Liberties Committee of Andhra Pradesh and Telangana urged the Supreme Court for a special probe and since the court asked for more details, a group of activists and lawyers led by N. Narayan Rao, the State General Secretary of the Committee, set out for the affected village, entering from the Telangana border, even though the rivers were in spate.

Our team, aiming to converge with them in the forests, set out from Geedham on a rainy August morning. Amidst the lush foliage of the Sukma forests, we saw wraiths of smoke coiling upwards which, on approach, turned out to be two charred buses. They had been set on fire by Maoists the night before, as an act of protest against the killings. Such burning of buses, generally after the passengers are ordered to dismount, is a common practice to signal area dominance and send messages to the state.

Buses have also been targeted by explosive devices, especially those used to transport people seen to be part of the security forces; in 2010, there were twenty-four civilians among thirty-five killed when one bus carrying Special Police Officers (SPOs) was blown up at Chingavram near Dantewada.[3]

Whilst the Maoists said they do not target medical services, an ambulance carrying sick children was attacked in April 2012. The children escaped unhurt. The Maoists said they were targeting security personnel. The incident was a grisly indication of how the body gets entangled in contests of power.[4]

Our mission was urgent. This was a violation of human rights and it had to be presented to the court but it was disrupted a number of times by the police, Central Reserve Police Force (CRPF) and the District Reserve Guards (DRG), stopping the vehicle and demanding to know who we were, asking for our Aadhaar cards and noting our cell numbers. For Soni, Linga, Baghel and the Bastar journalists such surveillance is routine, as Tameshwar who was accompanying us, explained. Often, journalists and activists are detained for hours on end. Or, simply denied permission to move forward. Besides these interruptions, time was lost because traffic had piled up on the rutted bits of the highway. At one halt, Soni pointed out the DRG personnel patrolling alongside the highway. This specially created force largely comprises surrendered Maoists, who are at the vanguard of operations, exposed to maximum risk. Strategically deployed to handle Adivasi populations better, as Deputy Inspector General (DIG) Kalluri stated, their knowledge of the terrain, of the political dynamics of each village is used to leverage maximum advantage.

In a perceptive essay, Akash Poyam observed how the dead on both sides in an insurgency can be from marginalised groups. The DRG are easily identified by Bastar's villagers, not just because they are from the same community, but also because they come from surrounding villages and yet they perpetuate the violence. He charges the government of turning Adivasis into mercenaries.

'Today, Adivasis have been dehumanised to such an extent that many of them do not see their own people as humans. Rampant poverty has created conditions in which unimaginable violence for a little bit of money is quite normal. Those who grow up around violence become desensitised to it. The government gives out bounties for every dead body, creating people who are conduits for state brutality. The DRG men often tell villagers, "We have come for hunting, we won't leave without killing someone." An Adivasi can earn lakhs of rupees as bounty, and promotion, for "hunting" another Adivasi. Eventually this turns into a sport.'[5]

As Bastar natives, members of the DRG can also use their newfound power to settle personal scores. Their brutality is condoned by higher officials.

In 2011, a judgement from the Supreme Court noted the deep fracturing of the Adivasi community; the court criticized the way in which feelings of hate and rage were being used to direct Adivasis into counter-insurgency activities which put them in grave danger. Saying that it runs contrary to the norms of a nurturing society, the court noted that it ought to be a matter of the gravest constitutional concern and deserving of the severest constitutional opprobrium that 'misguided policymakers strenuously advocate this as an opportunity to use such dehumanised sensibilities in the fight against Maoists.'[6]

Activists also argue that the state labels Maoists as lawless and guilty of heinous crimes, but is willing to overlook their violent background if they join the DRG.

Awasthi, current chief of anti-Naxal activities, however, defended the induction on the grounds that DRG cadres were the moral opponents of Maoists. Allegations of their extreme cruelty against civilians are unfounded and part of the strategy to defame them, he said to a group of us press persons.

Watching the DRG patrolling the highway was a sombre reminder of how the ghost of the Salwa Judum walks the land; of how easily violence splinters into various fratricidal forms.

Our long wait was broken by news that the authorities were not allowing vehicles to proceed. A car had broken down, blocking access to a crucial bridge. Vehicles were ordered to return. Soni and Linga were certain it was a ploy to prevent us from going ahead, but a determined Soni was already working out another route to enter the forests so that we might keep our tryst with the civil liberties team.

Since it entailed walking long distances at high speed over slippery forest trails, I decided to drop out and go back to Geedham with Linga who was not feeling too well. He continues to suffer from painful ailments as a consequence of the brutal torture inflicted on him when he was put in prison, a little before Soni's own arrest.[7] (The stories are told in more detail in Chapter Four.)

Trained as a journalist and videographer in Delhi, Linga has been hounded by the police. Undaunted, he continues to document the atrocities being perpetrated on his people and has emerged as a fine videographer. The next day he showed me the video he made during the initial fact-finding to Gompad. The first revelation was the site of the killing. It was a *ladhi* or makeshift shelter in the fields used to store agricultural produce and for Adivasis to stand guard against marauding animals late at night.

Trees on only on one side of the *ladhi* bore bullet marks, casting doubts on the official narrative that there had been a long exchange of fire at a Maoist hideout. A number of men from various hamlets had taken shelter there at night, Linga explained, because news had spread of the presence of security forces for combing operations. In Bastar's forests, the mere entry of the forces triggers fears of arrest and the men flee.

Since there is no mobile connectivity inside the forests, Linga and I spent two anxious days in Geedham, before the team returned. It is through their generously shared accounts that I was able piece together an understanding of what happened in this remote part of India, where some of our most marginalized communities live.[8]

Anyone Can Get Shot: Even Minors; No One Cares

Abhishek Meena, Superintendent of Police (SP), had stated that 160 personnel conducted a search operation on the night of 31 July, after learning that Maoist leaders were holding recruitment meetings for the Jan militia. The Jan militia are the support base for villages, under the Maoist Janatan Sarkar governance model. Functioning as village defence committees, they provide help in logistics but are, in general, not heavily armed. The security forces said they missed this recruitment meeting, but returned to the forest on 4 August and on the morning of 6 August they 'chanced upon the Maoists'.[9]

Villagers and eyewitnesses to the shooting told the fact-finding team an altogether different story. They said those villagers sheltering in the *ladhi* were quietly conversing among themselves. Some had gone for a wash when the security forces arrived and surrounded them. Even though the villagers put their hands up to show they were unarmed, they were assaulted. First came beatings, then the firing.

Among the first to be killed was Soyam Chandra. His head was then bludgeoned with a shovel. He had shouted out aloud that he was the ward watch for the panchayat or village council, but it made no difference. His family members later produced his Aadhaar card to disprove the security forces' claim that those killed were Maoists. Printed below the 'Mera Aadhaar Mera Pehchan' (in Devanagari script) insignia is his address shown as Gompad, Mehta. Ration cards were also produced by the women to show that many killed were minors. Chandra was among the first in the village to be documented under Aadhaar.[10]

In Kashmir, the burden of proof of identity falls on the local inhabitants, who must, at all times, have their crucial identity cards with them or risk being imprisoned or even shot. In Chhattisgarh, politics of identification is even more arbitrary.

When questioned by press persons why unarmed villagers who had Aadhaar cards could be shot as Maoists, the spokesperson for the security forces claimed that even Maoists are known to have acquired Aadhaar cards. The cynical retort is an example of how the Indian State chooses to recognize identity and determine who or who is not a citizen entitled to rights under the Constitution. It is a chilling enactment of its power.

One of the survivors, Karti Sukka, said when the shooting began he started running, his twelve-year-old son Karti Aayta, following behind. Sukka jumped into a flowing rivulet when a bullet hit his leg since he feared the blood would leave a visible trail. Choosing to hide in the forest, he learnt of his young son's death only when he returned home. There were no considerations of age even when firing at a running boy.

Sukka's son used to attend a Porta Cabin school in Konta, one of the bamboo and prefabricated creations set up as a state initiative to make education accessible in zones where schools had been destroyed by Maoists. Aayta was forced to drop out because of the sheer distance. His schoolbag, as a poignant testimony to his school days and aspirations for education, was draped across his grave.

Another minor, seventeen-year-old Muchaki Hidma, used to help look after his blind father, Muchaki Lakhma. When the team met the father he was being guided around the village by a younger son and wept inconsolably as he recalled the shooting. According to the villagers Muchaki did not die immediately; he was in grievous pain and begging for water before he succumbed.

Hearing the gunshots, the women had come running to the spot and security forces began to viciously beat them. Among them was a pregnant woman. Four villagers were taken away, including a woman named Budhri. Two men were released but Deva and Budhri remain incarcerated. Deva, who was initially mistaken for another Maoist leader with the same name, is now accused of being a member of the party.

The villagers were also ordered to vacate their homes for a few days after this incident, on the pretext that fresh combing operations would begin and intense cross-firing with Maoists could pose a risk to them. When the Civil Liberties Committee's fact-finding team arrived in Gompad, it came upon many villagers returning to their homes from Durma.

Padmaja Shaw, who was part of this team, told me the sheer physical separation from the world as we know it and the spaces that these Adivasis occupy, made a profound impression on her.

'There was no access road. We used a tractor for part of the distance on the slippery paths. There was no electricity. No kerosene lamps. No proper drinking water supply. People were placing pots on thatched roofs to catch the rainwater. They had to walk miles to procure a matchbox.'

Nothing of such precariousness is reflected in the media discourse. She found it horrifying that wild allegations were made that these marginalized villagers were Maoists hellbent on blowing up atomic plants or such like.[11]

The saddest part, she felt, was they were not demanding any entitlements from the state. They were subsisting in their own way. It is the state that so violently intrudes into their lives, she added.

Akash Poyam told me, 'This is a place where anyone can get shot at any time and no one will know. No one outside cares. It is numbing to think of the powers of the State even when there is no functioning. Most of these people have not voted in seventy-one years.'

For Soni the trip held painful memories of the unrelenting history of fake encounters and of her *tiranga* rally. A bid she had made to explore the connotations of the flag and citizenship, emotively and radically different from the one deployed in the politics of nationalism. The saddest moment, she said, came when Lakshmi, Madkam Hidme's mother, returned the Indian flag she had given her some years ago, when her daughter became a victim of gunfiring.

'Lakshmi told me that this flag cannot bring justice for Adivasis. "*Le lo waapas* (Take it back)" she said.'

A Tale of Two Images: Mutilated Corpse; Crisp Ironed Maoist Uniform

In 2016, Soni undertook a *padayatra* from Dantewada, beginning on 9 August and culminating at Gompad on 15 August with a flag-hoisting. The story behind the hoisting of the national flag, for the first time, in this '*door naxal prabhavit kshetr*' (Maoist-affected zone), as Gompad is described in officialese, is deeply moving.[12]

The impetus for the *padayatra* was the brutal killing of twenty-three-year-old Madkam Hidme of Gompad and the manner in which the official narrative was played out, branding her a Maoist. According to her village members, many of whom were witnesses, Madkam Hidme was threshing paddy when she was dragged away from her home on the morning of 13 June 2016 by CRPF forces from the Gorkha camp.

An official statement the next day claimed that, following a fierce gun battle, a dead Maoist, identified as Madkam Hidme, a member of Platoon No. 8 Kistaram Area, had been found in the jungles between Gompad and the Gorkha camp.

The deeply distressed mother, Lakshmi, had trekked with the villagers to the CRPF camp to inquire after the whereabouts of her daughter. But when the news of the dead body came in she had no energy or spirit to proceed to Sukma. She waited whilst the others went to claim the body and bring it back in an autorickshaw. Wrapped in the familiar black tarpaulin used by security forces to ferry corpses, Lakshmi identified the toes peeping out. When the tarpaulin was unwrapped she saw the stark nude body of her daughter, mutilated with a long cut across the abdomen, cuts on the nose, ears and chest; the left hand appeared broken at the wrist. It is possible that the post-mortem may have been the cause for some of the mutilations but no explanations were given for the rest.[13]

It is as if the state agencies believe the Adivasi body is not even deserving of the basic standards of dignity in death. Post-mortems are performed in the crudest manner possible. One of the most gut-wrenching comments on this indignity comes in an affidavit filed by a grieving woman, whose husband and son had both been killed in the gunning down of eight civilians during the Edesmeta encounter. Post-mortems had been carried out in the police station and bodies were handed back to the relatives in a horribly mutilated state.

Karam Sukki stated, 'The bodies had been ripped from the chest to the abdomen. I asked, how can I take them back in this condition? I had brought thread for them to be sutured up but all they did was to tie them in *gamchas* and return them to us.'[14]

In the case of Madkam Hidme, there were also startling differences in the way the visual images played out. Whilst Lakshmi got a mutilated and nude body wrapped in tarpaulin, the image released to newspapers, shows a body splayed on the ground, wearing a crisp ironed Maoist uniform and outsized pants, neatly rolled up near the ankle.

There were no holes in the clothing even though the body bore the marks of ten bullet injuries. It does not suggest a fierce fight before the Naxalites managed to disappear into the forests.[15]

The writ petition filed by the Human Rights Law Network states that Madkam Hidme is seen wearing bangles and sporting nail polish. Hardly combat gear of a platoon member.[16]

The killing forced the anguished parents to step out of their isolated hamlet and to venture all the way to the Bilaspur High Court demanding a probe into her killing and possible rape. They also addressed a press conference in Raipur.

It was Lakshmi's continual cry for justice that impelled Soni to start her *tiranga* yatra. 'I saw it as a test. The state was insisting Madkam Hidme was a Maoist and her village was a Maoist zone, whilst her mother wanted justice and said she was an unarmed civilian. If I took a *tiranga* into the village would the villagers respect it? I also wanted this to be a test for a nation and its notions of citizenship and equality.

'Lakshmi asked me what the flag meant. I said the *jhanda* was a symbol of *azadi* achieved after the huge struggle against the British and the identity of a new nation. Bharat. We were slaves and then we became free. The villagers then asked, if they were citizens of the country, why was there no *aam azadi* (freedom for the ordinary person?) They told me they would respect the flag since they belong to India but wondered why the state never accepted them.'

The high court's order for an exhumation and second post-mortem had given Lakshmi hope. When Soni arrived with the flag on 15 August 2016, she accepted it as an affirmation of Constitutional rights for an Adivasi citizen and hoped that justice was in the realms of the imaginable.

But the magisterial inquiry which followed brushed aside the claims of the villagers and hastily concluded Madkam Hidme was a part of a Naxalite organization. Then came the Nulkatong encounters which brought dark feelings of déjà vu. As mentioned earlier, an angry Lakshmi told Soni, '*Waapas le jao* [Take it back] …This *jhanda* cannot bring me justice for my daughter. We are not seen as citizens of this country.'

'It was an education of sorts for me too,' Soni said. 'Can

the state not understand that a woman waving a *tiranga* in a Maoist zone is not waging war on the nation? I was in tears when she returned the flag.'

The inability of Adivasis to even legally contest official claims and secure acknowledgement of injustice, is a stark reflection on notions of citizenship in democratic India. Adivasis are exhorted to participate in electoral politics but how is this citizenship embodied and honoured?

Anatomy of Human Destructiveness: Life and Death of Young Arjun

Even as Soni was offering the tricolour to Lakshmi, a particularly brutal extrajudicial killing was taking place around the same time in another part of Bastar. The killing of young Arjun would be a horrifying example of the way the State flaunts its ability to intimidate, imprison and finally murder an Adivasi youth with impunity. It would also serve as an example of how the State manufactures dominating narratives that muffle the truths of suffering people and communities in resistance.

The German philosopher and writer, Friedrich Nietzsche, wrote, 'State is the name of the coldest of all cold monsters. Coldly, it tells lies, too; and this lie grows out of its mouth: "I, the State, am the people".'

Legal luminary Upendra Baxi uses this quote to illustrate how the politics of dominance thrives because the government continues to nurture a monopoly on determining what is the public interest and the common good.[17]

Increasingly too, there are many attempts to do politics over human rights and discredit those who champion it. One such manipulation by the government, to insinuate what is 'good' for the people, came in November 2021. The National Human Rights Commission (NHRC) held a debate at an official function in November 2021 with the subject: 'Are human rights a stumbling block in fighting evils like terrorism and Naxalism?' The NHRC Chairman, Justice Arun Mishra, a former Chief Justice of India, was present at the function.[18]

Human rights activists and civil society have to constantly find ways of articulation against this singular voice of authority. In Chhattisgarh it was trade union worker, lawyer and human rights activist Sudha Bharadwaj (jailed in the Bhima Koregaon case), who has contested official narratives.[19]

Bharadwaj, who took up the cause of workers and Adivasis who were being branded and killed under the pretext of tackling Naxalism, wrote: 'I could only grasp the enormity of the information blackout—the silence, half-truths and sheer lies—call it the "wall of silence" that exists between Bastar and the rest of Chhattisgarh, when as an active member of the Chhattisgarh PUCL [Peoples Union of Civil Liberties] I joined several fact-finding teams to investigate fake encounters.'

In the Golapalli incident, the *shiksha karmis* and students killed allegedly in 'Naxali cross-firing' had actually been murdered by the police and security forces even after they repeatedly asserted their identity. In Narayanpur the 'dreaded Naxalites' turned out to be Adivasis who had returned to their ancestral villages in search of work.

Bharadwaj observes how in the media, one saw repeatedly 'a total silence about ordinary people on the one hand and cymbal-clashing war cries against Maoists, always pictured as AK-47-toting, with sinisterly covered faces, on the other.

'Each time we uncovered the truth, which, mind you, was absolutely self-evident to the local people and tried to cross the wall, it was buried again under a heap of papers, false statements, half-hearted enquiries, politically loaded commentaries and the inevitable conclusions justifying the atrocities.'[20]

I remembered these words as I read up the file and timeline on Arjun Kashyap's case. Time and time again, various levels of falsehoods were being peddled as official truths, with absolutely no regard for the law. I had first learnt of this minor Adivasi's detention in jail and then his transfer to a juvenile home by another journalist. She had gone to Bastar and reported on the efforts of a legal aid team to get bail. She called me in utter shock some months later, to tell me she had learnt he had been killed in a patently fake encounter.[21]

It was through this journalist that I came to learn more about the legal team who were defending Arjun, before he was picked up and mercilessly shot. Known as the JagLAG (Jagdalpur Legal Aid Group), it comprised a group of lawyers who offered free legal services for the Adivasis of Bastar and was set up in 2013.

Shalini Gera, who has remained in Chhattisgarh since the inception of JagLAG, told me how the impetus to work out of Jagdalpur in Bastar came after Soni's arrest and the custodial violence meted out to her had made national and international news.

Gera had been working as a consultant in the pharmaceutical industry in the Bay Area in California and had lived in the USA for twenty years. She holds a PhD in neuroscience besides an MSc in mathematics. But as she laughingly told me, 'None of this is relevant to my current work.' Her LLB from Delhi University is all that matters, she added.

Explaining her decision to explore avenues in social justice and her radical switch in career, lifestyle and change of country, she said she was increasingly restless in the USA. 'Call me a *bhatakti atma*', that 'wandering soul', was how she put it.

She said she kept visiting India from 2006 onwards and acquainting herself with various people's struggles. It was during a visit to Chhattisgarh and her meeting with Sudha Bharadwaj that sealed the decision regarding the area of her work. Bharadwaj urged her to look at how the conflict had overshadowed the human rights abuses being perpetrated on the Adivasis.

For this Gera would need to gain an understanding of the justice-seeking mechanisms. There was a compelling need for good lawyers and Bharadwaj told her to study law, '*Ek aur degree leh loh,*' she said.

In a striking parallel, Bharadwaj, who had a degree from the IIT Kanpur, had taken up law whilst in her forties, at the request of labourers, who felt she would then be their best representative in understanding and arguing their cases.

So Gera, in her early forties, enrolled at Delhi University in 2010 and there met Isha Khandelwal, who had also switched from computer programming to studying human rights and law.

It was around this time too that Soni had been brought to Delhi and Gera became associated with the case, like many other of Delhi's lawyers and civil society members. Soni's incarceration and sexual abuse in custody illustrated the broken justice system, which so affected the lives of thousands of Adivasis of Bastar. Concerned civil society members and legal activists felt that whilst there were people working in Delhi, a dedicated team should work among these marginalized communities at the ground level. Gera, along with Khandelwal, was joined by Parijata Bharadwaj (no relative of Sudha Bharadwaj) who had a degree from the Tata Institute of Social Sciences and a law degree, and Roopesh Kumar, also from TISS. It was this founding team that went to Jagdalpur to live and work out of shared quarters and office spaces, from where they hoped to attempt some new interventions.

Initially the emphasis was on collecting and accessing data

through Right to Information and documentation. They began getting familiar with the way the state conflated Adivasis with Naxalites and the way hundreds were being locked away under false charges. People came to them for legal help.

One case was that of Arjun.

The news of his killing and of being branded as a Naxalite was couched in the standard language of the police statement: 'Notorious Maoist Arjun dead on Chhattisgarh–Odisha border.'

S.S. Kalluri gave out more details and the media was putting out stories with epithets like 'hardcore Naxal', a 'dreaded Jan militia commander' of Chandameta and 'member of the Machhkot Local Organization Squad'. The forests, close to the Odisha border, where he was said to have been shot, was described as 'a Naxal den'.

Arjun, according to the police, was allegedly involved in three crimes: blowing up an ambulance during the 2014 Lok Sabha poll in which seven people died, killing a sarpanch in Koleng and committing the murder of another villager from Kadanar.[22]

What mainstream media persons were not told and what emerged later was that this 'absconding Naxal,' aged seventeen, had appeared in a juvenile justice court in Jagdalpur on 27 July, just a few weeks before his killing, and that he was already battling these false charges against him. As a lawyer remarked, it is beyond comprehension that a Maoist would have been attending hearings.

A petition was later filed by Arjun's father, Sulo Kashyap, through JagLAG, demanding an independent judicial inquiry into the killing and the various acts of lawlessness perpetrated by the security forces on him and his family.

Nikita Agarwal, who had by then joined JagLAG, provided me with a detailed deconstruction of the encounter, elaborating the processes by which the law in Bastar failed the Adivasi youth at every juncture and, in the process, failed the Constitution.

Arjun was the only son among six sisters and his father Sulo wanted to give him an education, she explained. He was enrolled in the Koleng school where he was attempting to clear Class Ten. On 16 May 2015, as he was returning from the Tokapal market where he had gone to sell a goat, he was abducted by the police and kept in illegal detention.

When he failed to return home, his father went in search of him and then filed a missing persons complaint. Fearing that his son might be tortured as is customary, he approached the Additional District Judge in Jagdalpur, informing him his son had not been produced before any magistrate in accordance with the law. Almost as if in response, the Durba police then presented the boy as one Arjun, son of Kordi, aged thirty, an accused in an ongoing case of blowing up an ambulance.

The discrepancies in the age and name of his father, should have revealed it was a clear case of mistaken identity since, at the time of the alleged incidents, he was a minor boy studying in the local school. But, as Agarwal points out, this arrest of a minor, shown to be adult, was just the beginning of a 'collapsing legal system.'

In contravention of the law that demands he should be produced before a magistrate within twenty-four hours, he was held for two days and taken to a school for interrogation. Agarwal explained how the rights of detainees in Bastar are totally ignored. 'The police and CRPF detain villagers on a regular basis in CRPF camps, in schools, colleges and even toilets. Schools, in fact, were used as detention centres widely during the Salwa Judum days by the Special Police Officers and the police for the purpose of interrogation, detention and torture.'

Arjun was sent to jail without regard for his age and

remained there for four months with adult convicts even after an order to transfer him to the only juvenile home for boys in Jagdalpur. The order followed scrutiny of his school documents and the testimony of his school's principal which showed he was a juvenile.

It is a stark reflection on the juvenile justice system that Arjun's case dragged on for a year instead of the stipulated four months and he was first refused bail on the grounds that he came from a Naxalite area. The magistrate for the Juvenile Justice Board maintained he would be 'safer in judicial remand' claiming, 'it is not established that on returning to his village he will be safe from moral, physical or psychological dangers.' This is such a telling reflection of how mindsets of those in authority reflect the colonial idea of the White Man's Burden. Adivasis are perceived as being without agency or intellect; those who must be civilised and 'saved' from the Naxalites. Tragically, as events played out, Arjun needed to have been saved from the clutches of the security forces.

Eventually, Arjun was given bail by the Juvenile Justice Board on 30 December 2015. He attended the Board's hearings regularly except on one occasion when he was unwell. The date for his next hearing was slated for 31 August 2016. State intervention cut that out.

In one of the most brazen acts of lawlessness, police and security forces entered Arjun's home at the midnight of 16 August along with two Naxalites who had surrendered. His mother Sanki, father Sulo, wife Payko holding his infant son Karsan, sisters Jhunki and Pando are all witnesses to the way Arjun's hands were tied to his back and he was dragged away despite their anguished cries.

His father, who went in search of him the next day, was told by Koleng villagers that they had seen the police with a body wrapped in the familiar tarpaulin. Late at night, Arjun's body with visible gunshot marks as well as injuries indicative of torture, was returned to his family, who had waited all day at the Durba police station.

On 22 August, Sulo relocated his family to Palenar because of the continuing intimidation by police. A week later, Sulo's daughter, Jhunki was declared to be a 'surrendered Naxalite', forcibly taken away and detained at the Livelihood College in Dantewada. Accompanied by an NDTV journalist, Soni visited the young woman who categorically denied the police story and said she wanted to go home. She was set free only after three months on 7 November and her father, Sulo Kashyap, was subjected to beatings and more threats the next day. This assault was followed by offers of land and a job if he kept his mouth shut.

Fears for his family kept him away from filing an official complaint all through 2017. Only on 2 January 2018 was he emboldened to file a petition demanding a full inquiry.

In a heartening order on 23 January 2018, the judge gave interim orders for Sulo's protection and asked the state of Chhattisgarh to respond to the question of compensation. There has been no reply. The case is stuck; the application for urgent hearing has been declined on the grounds that it is not of an urgent nature.

The family relocated once again back to Durba but have no lands. Sulo has no ration card for this village and is dependent on others to procure rice and other supplies. Soni told me how he visits her a couple of times asking what has come of the case. '*Mera kasoor kya tha?*' (What was my fault?) he asks plaintively.

Why was Arjun singled out? His father told the legal team how he had tried so hard to keep Arjun safe in the risky spaces of a Naxalite zone by giving him an education. But, did these very aspirations turn dangerous?

Soni told me that Arjun came under the scanner because '*woh padha likha tha.... Gaon ke logon ko pakkad keh le jate toh sawal karta...*' (He could read and write...he had begun questioning police, when they tried to pick up people).

'Arjun was unafraid,' she added. 'That was enough for him to be branded as Naxalwadi or for police to see him as potential Naxalwadi.' There is a huge emphasis placed on the need for education but an educated Adivasi, one who uses his powers to critique, is singled out, often by both state and non-state agencies.

Whilst reading Anna Burn's award winning novel *Milkman,* based on Ireland's troubles, I was struck by her use of the term 'investment of hostility' to define the police's relations with the local community. She writes: 'According to the police, of course our community was a rogue community. It was we who were the enemy, we who were the terrorists, the civilian terrorists, the associates of terrorists or simply individuals suspected of being but not yet discovered to be terrorists.'[23]

Is there a similar investment of hostility in the way Adivasis are perceived by law-enforcing agencies and is this then embedded in the national consciousness through official narratives?

Hidma Karram, one of the villagers who gave testimony before the Juvenile Justice Board in Arjun's hearings, spoke to journalist Malini Subramaniam about the predicament of the Chandameta villagers. The nearest roadhead, Koleng, he said, is a few hours away. Every villager was a suspect in the eyes of the police as there is a hill known as Tulsi Dongar in the vicinity which is frequented by Maoists transiting between Odisha and Chhattisgarh. Even walking to the weekly *haat* or market in Darba became a high-risk activity as Arjun's case showed.[24]

Such weekly markets, a crucial connection with the outside

world for Adivasis with a forest-based economy, have become spaces that today pose grave risks, even for women. Villagers who come to buy or sell mahua, tamarind and other forest-based products have been victimized as 'Naxalis'.

Oyam Tulsi, thirteen, was killed on the way to a weekly market in January 2016 and her killing was shown to be a Naxalite encounter. Podiyami Lakmee, sixteen, was picked up whilst buying clothes at the Avapalli bazaar and after two days' detention, she was sent to the Jagdalpur jail.[25]

Chandameta, which originally numbered about a hundred families, gradually emptied out because of such relentless persecution. Besides the continuous unsettledness, routine activities like selling a goat or collecting firewood become a life-and-death proposition.

Living Under the Shadow of Death

The full gravity of such danger was exemplified during my visit to Godelgudda where three women were shot at on 2 February 2019, whilst out to gather firewood. One of them died. The official account of a 'Naxali encounter' was successfully challenged only because Kawasi Lakhma, an Adivasi minister in the newly formed Bhupesh Baghel Congress government, raised an alarm and demanded compensation for this extrajudicial killing.

About a month after the incident, I accompanied some journalists along the newly constructed road, slated to go all the way to Jagargunda. We passed Gorgunda, Polampalli, Kankerlanka and Puswada. These were the *thanas* or police cum CRPF camps, which veered up every five kilometres or so, as road building is accompanied by its corollary of camps.

The state's focus on rapid construction of roads cutting through the thickly forested Maoist region and the subsequent mushrooming of camps has become a major friction point.

Maoists oppose it vehemently and mark out contractors for abduction, targeting both the road equipment and the workers.

Awasthi, the police chief in charge of anti-Naxal operations, who we met at the end of this trip, said road building has enabled greater access to medical facilities and fostered a parallel economy, like the stretch from Cherla to Kistaram, where autorickshaws ply and small kirana shops have sprouted. That is undoubtedly true but then why were there so many demonstrative acts of dissent against this 'development' agenda? Why did as many as twelve protests take place against the building of roads and the corollary of camps from October 2020 to June 2021? Adivasis, I learned through my field trips, suffered great feelings of insecurity because they associated *thanas*/camps as spaces of incarceration, sometimes torture, forced labour and repression.

Their interaction with police was one of fear. They approached *thanas* largely to inquire after someone went missing or they had been witness to the person being picked up by security forces. Road building was, therefore, viewed with suspicion as it only brought yet another *thana*/camp.

In October 2020, the villagers of Kakwadi of Dantewada district came together to dig up a portion of a road under construction saying they did not want a security camp but wanted, instead, a hospital, a school and an Anganwadi (rural child care centre). Tameshwar Sinha, in his report, noted that the sarpanch was among those present in the protest and that the villagers told him they feared such camps which incarcerate them, under the guise of being 'Naxali'.[26]

The setting up of a camp near Silger village in Sukma district on the road to Jagargunda, became the flashpoint in May 2021, drawing angry protests from over 5,000 Adivasis who staged a sit-in for four days. The Silger camp, sited just three kilometres away from the Tarem camp, came up without prior approval of the Adivasis whose land it occupies. The acquisition was done without holding a Gram Sabha. According to the provisions of the Panchayats (Extension to Scheduled Areas) Act, which ensures some degree of self-governance for people living in the Scheduled Areas, the Gram Sabha must approve the acquisition through a resolution.

During the Silger protests, three villagers died on 17 May when security forces opened fire. The security forces claimed they were forced to retaliate because Naxalite cadres, under the guise of protesting villagers, had provoked an attack. It was, in fact, a telling reflection on why the villagers really do associate camps with violence.

The Bastar police in an official note states fourteen new security camps were established to provide security cover for road construction but most of these camps remain even after the road project is complete. For the villagers, these camps are sites of continuing oppression and surveillance.

For journalists too, camps are the checkpoints where the state chooses to exercise its powers of surveillance and control. One can be stopped and questioned or made to wait for hours.

Fortunately, our fact-finding team was not detained and after the mandatory checking we were allowed to go ahead. We reached Godelgudda hamlet consisting of some sixty households, around mid-day. Most of the able-bodied inhabitants were out collecting mahua flowers as it was the month of March.

With us was Pushpa Rokde, the Adivasi woman journalist, whose work must negotiate the complex path of writing truth in a deeply conflicted land. She often files reports on violence perpetrated by both sides and has intervened to help secure the release of villagers rounded up by police during an exercise. But in February 2021, Pushpa was threatened by Maoists, not for her writings, but for having taken up work as a supervisor of road construction projects. Her income as a freelance journalist had dwindled because of the lockdown and she had to resort to one of the chief forms of livelihood in Chhattisgarh—taking up contracts. A *parcha* or handwritten note, frequently used by Maoists to issue condemnations against individuals they consider enemies of the people, was found pinned on a tree. It said that any person, including journalists, would be killed if they took up road construction work as it involves the felling of trees. Another *parcha* was delivered to her home. A massive protest by local journalists had its effect: the zonal committee of the Maoists then retracted and issued a statement saying the journalists were not under threat and could roam freely and report.[27]

Pushpa, who speaks Gondi and Halbi, and is the only woman journalist in Bastar, began to converse with one of the young girls in the hamlet and then brought back in her arms a four-month-old baby, who had been crying. This, she informed us, was the dead woman Podiyam Sukhi's youngest son. She was mother to three other children. Her husband Podiyam Deva was not in the village on the day of the incident. Like many other Adivasis he had gone to earn a livelihood for his family at a chilli farm in Pattigude, Andhra.

When the villagers returned from the mahua picking, Podiyam's mother, an imposing figure, was told to narrate the incident. Speaking in the local dialect which was translated for us, she interspersed her story with gestures and dramatic enactment.

She was sweeping the house around 8 a.m., she said, when the sound of three gunshots rang out.

Knowing Sukhi was out with other women to collect the firewood, she ran towards the sounds.

In Bastar, it is the women who run towards an encounter site and the men who flee deeper into the forests, for they know they will certainly be picked up and arrested. It is the women also who venture long distances for forest produce or to fetch water.

Near the large expanse of water fringing the hamlets, she came upon Kalmu Deve who, though writhing in pain with a bullet injury to the groin, urged her not to stop but to press ahead where Sukhi lay grievously injured.

'Sukhi was still alive, begging for water. But the security forces had already begun pushing her into those plastic wraps used as body bags. They began carrying her to a vehicle that was on the main road near Kankerlanka camp. I begged to be able to accompany her but they refused.'

Frantic phone calls were made to her son who rushed back from Andhra. At the Dornapal police station, he learnt his wife was dead and brought her dead body home accompanied by the police party. Even her last rites were performed under the scrutiny of the police.

Kalmu Deve, who had recovered from her injury by then, told us that she, Sukhi and another woman named Somri, had seen several boot imprints on the ground as they came out of the hamlet and were discussing this when a posse of security men came towards them.

'We shouted out we were not Naxali, we were unarmed. They paid no heed, opened fire and Sukhi was hit in the chest and I in the groin. The third bullet flew over Somri's head and she fled to the village.'

The SP of Sukma, who was transferred for reasons unconnected with this incident, claimed the firing was in self-defence and that Sukhi died in cross-firing. The villagers were adamant: there was no encounter.

Compensation of five lakh rupees was paid to Sukhi's husband Deva and he was promised a job. The villagers said that the Dornapal police station had begun sending tins of powdered milk for Sukhi's baby. Kalmu was given one lakh rupees.

What were Deva's own expectations of justice? Would he pursue a case, demand an inquiry?

He shrugged off questions with '*Kya report...jo ho gaya soh ho gaya*' (What report... what's done is done).

His response is indicative of a deep distrust of the judicial system, and reflects the villagers' hesitancy to deal with the police. Their *pada* or hamlet had been branded as 'Naxali.' Six men were already being held in the Dantewada and Sukma jails under the charges of being Maoist or having links with Maoists. Two villagers, Podiyam Rama and Madkam Unge, were detained on the day of firing and released later.

The visit to Godelgudda helped us to glean some understanding of the moral complexities faced by people residing in a zone where all roles are reversed. In a perceptive essay, entitled 'Mimetic Sovereignties, Precarious Citizenship: State Effects in a Looking Glass World', Sundar writes, 'Even as Maoist guerrillas "wage war" against the government, as Section 121 of the Indian Penal Code that is routinely applied to insurgents defines it (Government of India 1860), the government, in turn wages war against its own citizens, the police protect the land against the people, seeing them as security threats to the unfettered exploitation of minerals by corporates. The Maoists, in turn, mimic a state laying sovereign claims to territory and practices of governmentality.'[28]

At Godelgudda which came under the Karrar panchayat, there were some trappings of state governance: an Anganwadi worker comes to inoculate newborn infants, rations are picked up from Polampalli; but there is no electricity and the people have never participated in elections. One house had a solar panel, the usage of which would probably have needed permission by the Maoists, since it is a hand-out by the state.

In this seemingly idyllic landscape of trees and a large waterbody, two structures bore witness to the violence it had witnessed. The first was the shell of a concrete school building, roof caved in, that must have been blasted by Maoists during the days of the Salwa Judum when many such school buildings were used to house security troops. The second was a small red tier-shaped memorial to a woman, surmounted by a sickle. Besides her name and date of death painted on the surface, there was a framed photo and her few personal belongings in the form of a comb and small tin box. These are the memorials put up by Maoists to commemorate those killed in fighting.

It is the practice of Adivasis, especially Gonds, to put up a stone or two to mark the passing away of a member of the family in open spaces near their hamlets, coloured with pigments from trees. Increasingly, these plaques are amalgamating traditional Gond art with modern symbols to document encounter killings.

One such memorial plaque to villager Hedma Ram in Sulenga village, Bijapur district, photographed and documented by writer-journalist Kamal Shukla, depicts three panels. The first panel shows a man resting whilst cattle graze. The second shows him surrounded with men with guns. In the third he is seen dead with animals, including a crocodile, as witness to his encounter.

I thought of the statues to the SPOs along the highways and realized how each side is now using memorials to mark and chart territories in a conflicted terrain.

Blown to Smithereens for a Parcha

As we drove through the forest towards Godelgudda we saw the white pamphlets or handwritten notes by Maoists, called *parchas*, fluttering from the branches of trees. We wondered what messages they contained and wanted to take a closer look, but were warned against getting down from the vehicle because of the danger of an exploding device. One such landmine had taken the life of a villager, just weeks before.

Powerful improvised explosive devices (IEDs) are increasingly being used by Maoists in warfare and claim several lives. More policemen in Chhattisgarh have lost their lives in blasts and landmines than those killed in direct combat. In 2019, an IED was responsible not just for killing many security personnel but also took the life of civilian Bheema Mandavi, the BJP Member of the Legislative Assembly (MLA). It naturally made headline news.

However, the death of twenty-one-year-old Sodi Deva of Bodhrajpadar, who had died earlier in the same year, scarcely made a ripple. An explosion had blown his head away from his body when he picked up one such leaflet. The morning after our Godelgudda trip, we set forth for the dead man's village to try and understand why he, a local Adivasi, felt compelled to pick up the leaflet, weighed down under a heavy stone, when he was aware of the dangers of IEDs.

Passing many camps, we came into the village. A charpoy was brought out and the villagers, including children, clustered around us, as we sat under a canopy of trees. It was not just a story about the Maoists' planting of the device which killed Sodi Deva but one that involved the entire community and was inextricably bound up with the many forms of oppression. School teacher Anil Indo, who speaks Hindi, translated for us and Sodi Dula, the father of the youth who was killed sat next to him. The villagers began telling us about the sufferings they faced after the Elarmadgu camp, housing the CRPF and DRG, came up about a kilometre or so away from the village.

On 20 January, one of the villagers, Kawasi Lakhma (not to be mistaken for the Congress MLA with the same name) was rudely awoken and picked up by security forces at 4 a.m. and taken to this camp. On 7 February, Sodi Dula and two others were also picked up and kept in the camp for days before being sent onto to the Bheji Thana or police station which is seven kilometres away.

They were made to do forced labour like chopping wood, sweeping and cutting vegetables and were assured they would be released after the elections if they agreed to be shown as surrendered Naxalites.

This phenomenon has gained currency in Bastar with security forces offering cash and other incentives for those who show themselves as 'surrendered' irrespective of whether they are Maoists or not. Many Maoists have indeed surrendered and been inducted into the DRG but, like encounters, many surrenders are fake and shrouded in controversy.

The law demanding that people who are picked up must be produced before the magistrate after twenty-four hours can be circumvented by taking recourse to the pretext that the person is a surrendered Naxalite, since there is no such requirement for harbouring those who have surrendered. Police use this ploy for custodial detentions to claim people are voluntarily living in *thanas* or camps. Many are then coerced to join the DRG.[29]

Of the men held from the village, Dula had not been asked to surrender, but he was interrogated and accused of hiding because he had chosen to sleep in his uncle's house that day. His explanation was simple. He had drunk too much toddy.

Family members would frequently visit the *thana* to ask for the release of their members. On 5 March, when villagers were returning from the weekly market or *haat*, police sent word they would release the men provided all the villagers presented themselves before the *thana*. Accordingly, some thirty-five people riding on a tractor, a common mode of mass transport, proceeded towards Bheji. They passed the IED booby trap, providentially from the other side. Sodi Deva who had gotten down, noticed the leaflets weighed down by a stone and with the patel, Podiyam Ganga, informed two policemen who were in a small grocery or kirana. They abused him and ordered him to go and pick up the *parchas* adding that his father would not be released, should he refuse.

It is part of police tactics to order villagers to tear up and take down these *parchas* that Maoists leave behind in their propaganda war. This was what compelled Deva to put his life at risk. He crossed the road, reached for the *parcha* and the IED was triggered.

Ganga, who was a little distance away on his cycle, saw the young man's decapitated body flung to the top of the trees on the other side of the road.

Newly appointed SP of Sukma, D.S. Merawi, told us he had taken swift action by transferring the police but did not want to demoralize the forces since, he said, they had not knowingly put the man's life in danger. He himself been seriously injured in an IED attack some years ago; and added that had the tractor been travelling on the other side of the road, casualties would have been much higher. Compensation was paid to Dula for his son and a First information Report (FIR) filed against Maoists; the FIR also stated that Deva picked up the papers of his own choice.

Is 'choice' the appropriate word in this deeply layered conflict in which the Adivasi body seems expendable?

Serious crimes are nonchalantly brushed aside with little or no agreement on the rights and dignity of unarmed civilians by both state and non-state players.

The leaflet that took Deva's life was distributed on 8 March, the very day that Maoists were calling for celebrations as International Women's Day. After the incident, the police ordered Adivasis to lead the way to the site, regardless of whether there were more explosives, a charge that in some nations could be viewed as tantamount to using citizens as human shields.

Trauma of Rape, Intimidation: Why 'Gudiya' Took Her Own Life

In the early hours of 19 December 2018, the body of a seventeen-year-old Adivasi girl was found hanging from a tree in her courtyard in Pandu Padda, Sameli. I read the post on social media with despair, since I had been following her story and fight for justice on the timelines of Chhattisgarh's media.

Through reports I learnt young N (name withheld) had some months earlier, gone missing whilst out gathering firewood near her home. She was found two days later in an unconscious state near a nullah. She alleged sexual violence by security forces.

A fortnight after her suicide I visited her home and her uncle, Jayant Netam, who speaks Hindi, tried to give me an account of what had happened to their 'Gudiya' (a term of endearment for young women in Chhattisgarh).

Netam told me he had personally visited the CRPF camp at Palnar when she went missing but is not aware of whether any formal complaint was filed. She was found in an unconscious state near the rivulet or nullah and taken to Dantewada District Hospital. The police restricted access, maintaining a register, even for family members but curiously Devti Karma, local politician and daughter of slain Salwa Judum leader, Mahendra Karma, was allowed to remain in the room along with a woman Deputy Superintendent of Police (DSP), Dineshwari Nande.

The uncle says that even as N was regaining consciousness

around 9 p.m., she was subjected to a volley of questions by Karma and the DSP and asked whether she had been attacked by cattle herders (*gai charane walle*) or had come in contact with a live wire and suffered an electric shock since this is commonly used against marauding pigs. Police later claimed '*usko current laga*'.

The next day, the girl told her mother she had no recollection of making any such statement to the police and stuck to her account of being accosted by men who blindfolded her, carried her across the rivulet and subjected her to sexual violence.

Later in the day, she made her statement to the DSP, with her mother present and also her uncle, since he is the only family member who speaks Hindi, which is the official language used. Some parts of the statement were rewritten to accommodate omissions and clarifications.

In accordance with procedure, she also made a full statement before the magistrate, during which she was accompanied by a nurse.

A woman of few words, N was forced to narrate her personal agony over and over again. Her uncle said she reiterated each time that the men who accosted her were in *chitkabra* (khaki) or uniform. And that acts of sexual violence had been perpetrated on her body. ('*Kuch kiya gaya.*') She confirmed men had been on top of her.

The Mahila Adhikari Manch, which made efforts to support her, have in their report, voiced concerns about the ways and insensitivity with which hospital authorities and police dealt with the case. They did not follow guidelines and protocols necessary for a victim of sexual violence.

How did the DSP and a local politician's daughter deem it fit to make suggestions and put words in her mouth when she had barely gained consciousness? Was she medically fit for interrogation? Were her clothes preserved for forensic examination?

The medico-legal reports were not given to the family. Nor were any hospital records. The woman's complaint of pain in the lower abdomen and a urinary infection were ignored in the Dantewada hospital. When she later sought treatment in Raipur, she confided to members of the Mahila Adhikari Manch, that she was so distressed by the continuous and intrusive presence of security personnel in the Dantewada hospital and the apathetic attitude of the staff that she just wanted to get out as soon as possible.

Intimidation was used to falsify N's narrative. Police came into three hamlets of Sameli village on 23 September and spread the word that it was at the instigation of her uncle and father that she had contradicted her statement to Devti Karma and the DSP. A local youth, Manglu, was also picked up that day and N's father threatened.

Against this backdrop of threats to the community, the Adivasi Samaj decided to hold a meeting the next day where N was asked to recount her statement in front of 300 people. The Adivasi Samaj and the Mahila Adhikari Sangh, which did its own fact-finding, concluded that there had been no pressure on the woman to give a false statement against the police and she was truthful.

Such pressure of continuing to reiterate her truth and recall private agony, the burden of being weighed down by pressures on her community and family and the trauma she underwent left N in severe emotional distress and anxiety. She continued to suffer physically from her urinary infection. Her uncle said she had confided in friends that she found it difficult to resume her normal duties of stepping out to collect water or firewood. There was no recourse to counselling; Deepika Joshi of the Mahila Adhikari Sangh sees this lack of a supportive environment springing from a patronising view of indigenous communities, especially when the accused is from the security or police personnel and the power equations become problematic.[30]

On the intervening night of 30 and 31 December, young Adivasi Gudiya took her own life, illustrating the systemic and institutionalised violence in Bastar.

Sexual Violence as Strategy

While the history of rape in war is as long as the history of war itself, it has been ignored or just regarded as an 'unfortunate by-product of warring', warranting little if any attention in the 'high politics' of global and national security.

After centuries of silence, there came a marked shift in the dominant understanding of perceiving sexual violence in war, in the wake of international recognition of the mass rapes during the armed conflicts in both Rwanda (1994) and Bosnia-Herzegovina (1992–95). Rape in war was no longer perceived as a regrettable but inevitable aspect of warring. It was now viewed as a strategy, weapon or tactic of war and the appointment of a Special Representative on Sexual Violence in Combat, demonstrated the UN Commitment to combating conflict-related sexual violence.

This recent understanding of sexual violence as a weapon of war has permeated the works and thinking of feminists and activists in India, who have begun documenting this form of violence. Deployed in conflict zones as a means to crush tribal movements and to suppress Dalits in class wars, women's bodies are here treated as territories to be conquered, claimed or marked.

In Chhattisgarh, during the years of the Salwa Judum, sexual brutality was used systematically along with beating, burning of homes and killings as a means of enforcing submission. Many fact-finding teams heard searing accounts although the ground situation and complicity of the state in the crimes made it almost impossible for organizations like the Committee Against Violence on Women (CAVOW) to personally verify each complaint. Major fieldwork and investigations were also not possible because people were constantly being dispersed from villages and homes.

In 2007, the CPI leader Manish Kunjam, crossed the border into Andhra to collect petitions from people that included women making complaints of rapes. Some of these testimonies, especially on rapes by the SPOs, became part of the writ petition filed by him, Kartam Joga and Dudhi Joga along with another writ petition filed by Nandini Sundar, Ramachandra Guha and E.A.S. Sarma seeking an independent inquiry into the Judum's activities.

The repercussions of an inadequate justice delivery system were felt when four women of Samsetti village in Dantewada, who had made a complaint in 2009 of rape by SPOs in 2006, dropped out of the judicial proceedings. No judge had been appointed to hear the rape case for many months and the arrest of Kopa Kunjum, the man who had helped them file the case, added to their discomfiture and fears.

For Adivasi women, who see the *thana* as a place where the gravest human rights violations can take place, the challenge of actually reporting sexual violence and seeking justice is still fraught with huge risks.

But in the period spanning the last three months of 2015 and the beginning of 2016, a remarkable precedent was set up. Groups of Adivasi women came forward with testimonies that became the basis of FIRs against security forces. The cases were filed after three separate incidents of mass sexual assault, physical assault and looting occurred after combing operations. These were in Peddagellur of Bijapur district between 19 and 24 October 2015 and in Kunna of Sukma district almost simultaneously. Then between 11 and 14 January 2016, cases of rape and molestation took place in Nendra of Bijapur district.

Among the testimonies recorded was that of a young girl around thirteen years old, who was pursued, blindfolded and raped by at least three persons whilst out with the cattle. In another case, a woman's breasts were squeezed to see if she was lactating or not. This is an obnoxious form of sexual violence, used by troops on the pretext of determining if a woman has borne children or not, as according to popular belief Naxalites opt not to have children.

In Kunna, a woman who was not lactating was mocked with ugly slurs by security men who said they would help her conceive. At one home a woman's undergarments were burnt, nailed to the wall and a phone number scrawled underneath the taunt that it was a helpline that women could call. A woman who protested 'Why are you catching and stealing my hens?' was physically assaulted, blindfolded and then raped.[31]

It was to record these incidents of systemic violence that the women set out from their remote hamlets where there is little or no network coverage. They trekked several miles, some accompanied by small children. Breaking the silence, coming forward to name the perpetrators in alien and often hostile environments and exploring the possibility of justice was a political act of immense courage. What would be the outcome of these explorations? What happens when Adivasis go to court?

3

Court

On 1 November 2015, history of sorts was made; women from a remote forest outpost, Peddagellur, with the nearest roadhead, Kothaguda, more than 17 km away, successfully filed a case against security forces. Subsequently, two other cases were filed respectively by the women of Nendra and Kunna.

The filing of the FIRs, citing violence under the amended rape laws and one under Protection of Children Against Sexual Offences (POCSO) was made possible as civil society, women's groups, lawyers, Adivasi leaders and intrepid journalists came together to coordinate efforts.[1]

In the Peddagellur case, it was initiated when the Women Against Sexual Violence and State Repression (WSS), received a tip-off from local journalists about some incidents and contacted the administration, who asked for the women's statements and the community's go-ahead. The remote locations were a challenge but the WSS members knew that weekly markets or *haats* are spaces of information-gathering and points of contact. It was at the Basaguda *haat* that the women's team met with those from the affected villages and confirmation of rape and violence was video-taped and shown to the Collector. At his suggestion, the WSS members went on motorcycles to the remote hamlets to record testimonies. He also gave the impetus for a follow-up to more villages, enabling two more women to make their statements.

It was on 1 November—the month that marks the anniversary of the day Chhattisgarh attained statehood—that official testimonies were recorded in a long-drawn-out affair, before various bureaucrats: first the Collector, then the Superintendent of Police (a woman), the Assistant Superintendent of Police and Sub-divisional Magistrate (SDM), all testimonies requiring the help of a translator.

For Nendra and Kunna villagers, filing complaints was even more challenging. Thirteen women of Nendra, who tried to file in Bijapur, were told by the Superintendent of Police that although their statements were recorded, the FIR could be filed only after *jaanch* (investigations), a pretext, which is in violation of the amended section of the law that makes it mandatory to file on receipt of information of offences like rape, disrobing and molestation.

Excuses were trotted out like needing to consult with higher officials. It was only after a press conference took place that the police eventually filed an FIR on 23 January.

The delays proved physically and emotionally exhausting for the women, some of whom had small children accompanying them. They had made the 65-kilometre-long journey from home and camped in Bijapur for five days, in biting cold weather. The procedure of making statements, one after the other, before the various administrative officials became more stressful after the police ordered another round of *bayaans* (statements) when they suddenly realized these should be recorded after the FIRs and not before.

Isha Khandelwal of JagLAG (Jagdalpur Legal Aid Group)

told me how the Adivasi women, already in alien surroundings, found directions like 'Lift up your head' or 'Speak out, loud and clear', whilst recounting their most traumatic experiences, to be emotionally exhausting. Humiliated and tired out, one Adivasi woman, sitting on the floor of the Bijapur Collectorate, said, 'It would have been easier to forget what we have gone through. What we have had to face here is almost worse.'

The militarised milieu and police obduracy posed a stiff challenge for the women of Kuna, who sent an appeal to Soni, after the troops left the village. Seven women, who wished to testify, were wary of running into the same forces that had terrorized them. A cordon had been thrown around their area. Paramilitary forces and police patrolled the road to the Sukma police station.

Personnel at the Dantewada police station did not allow the complaint to be made, saying it did not fall under their jurisdiction, even though there are provisions in the Criminal Code that cognizable crimes can be filed at any police station. The seven women, accompanied by Soni, had to detour all the way to Jagdalpur, to appeal to the administration. Hearing out the women's complaints, the Deputy Divisional Commissioner accepted the written application and forwarded it to various authorities, including top police officials like the Inspector General of Police (IGP) of the Bastar range. But still the police authorities and the district administration made no attempt to contact the women and failed to register the complaint. It was only after a massive protest of thousands of Adivasis was staged by the Adivasi Mahasabha on 23 January that the FIR was registered on 27 January. However, sections did not specifically mention rape, limiting the offences to 'outraging modesty' and 'disrobing'.

Korcholi and its surrounding villages have a long history

of violence, sexual assaults, loot and plunder by security forces but the attempts to file an FIR came to naught. On 7 May 2016, hundreds of villagers set out at dawn for Bijapur where they gave their testimonies before a three-member team comprising of E.N. Rammohan, former Director General (DG) of the Border Security Force (BSF), Dr Virginius Xaxa, Director of the Tata Institute of Social Sciences (TISS) in Guwahati and Sunil Kuksal of Human Rights Defenders. They then testified at the Kotwali *thana* but, despite assurances and repeated efforts, including another visit to the Gangalur police station by women who had experienced sexual violence in July, no FIR was ever filed.

Besides this major hurdle in filing an FIR, there is another challenge at this stage—that of language—which crucially affects the quality of testimonies recorded. Official translators tend to echo biases that Adivasis are Maoist supporters and this colours the statements. For this reason, the WSS arranged for another translator besides the one provided by the magistrate.

Even before investigations could begin, police officials began claiming the complainants had levelled false complaints at the instigation of Maoists to slander the forces and demoralise them.

During the Nendra proceedings, Indira Kalyan Elesela, then the ASP for Naxal operations, remarked sarcastically, that allegations of rape will keep coming. 'Does it mean we will lodge an FIR every time?' he retorted.[2]

A week after the Nendra complaint, a group that calls itself the Naxal Peedith Sangharsh Samiti (Committee of Naxal Victims), led by Madhukar Rao, a former Salwa Judum leader, staged a rally in Bijapur, shouting slogans and targeting individuals of the fact-finding team. Slogans were raised against Arundhati Roy who had nothing to do with the filing of the complaint!

Such tactics are reflective of the constrictions on the free flow of information in Chhattisgarh. Narratives are tightly controlled by the police and compliant media barons, who because of their business interests in mining, align with the state's policies. Journalists, the majority of whom are freelancers, are often threatened with arrests. Bastar's stories remain in the shadows.

However, a brief window of visibility was made possible with the filing of these FIRs, followed by reports in national mainstream media. The National Human Rights Commission, which has often failed to react, took cognizance of reports in the newspapers and set up its own inquiry. A press statement stated it had found prima facie evidence of rape, sexual and physical assault by the state police personnel and that the state government is vicariously liable. It recommended interim monetary relief.[3]

It was at the next level—the investigation of the crimes—that the limitations of the justice delivery system became painfully evident. When investigations actually began, the women complainants were not very forthcoming because of fear. In the Peddagellur case, the DSP, a woman, went into the affected villages with a huge posse of security troops. Although she was in civilian attire, alarmed villagers ran away. In this conflict zone they associate security forces with the violence inflicted on them. It was also evident that pressure from the top had begun to be put on these villagers.

Besides, the process of identifying individual perpetrators was a risky exercise since a good section of the police force comprises surrendered Maoists from the same region, many of whom used to visit the affected villages.

This raises the pivotal question of whether justice can be done if the perpetrators—the same police and security forces—are part of the inquiry.

Observing the unsatisfactory progress of police investigations, a team of officials from the National Commission of Scheduled Tribes, who visited in April of that year, made a strong demand for an independent inquiry.

Supreme Court lawyer Vrinda Grover argued that given the powers and status differences between the complainant and the accused, and that the complainant might have little knowledge about the investigation procedures or their rights in law, the state needed to take immediate steps. She suggested it work with civil society and appoint independent and credible oversight for the investigation.[4]

Far from doing any of this, the state chose a confrontationist approach, targeting those who had enabled the silence to be breached. It can be no coincidence that award-winning journalist Malini Subramaniam and the JagLAG began facing attacks almost simultaneously. Subramaniam was forced to leave as were the lawyers. No sooner had the lawyers gone than a vicious physical attack took place on Soni Sori. The message was clear.

No Place for Truth-tellers

In February 2016, I went to Jagdalpur, hoping to follow up stories on the struggle for justice. Instead, I got embroiled in events and became a witness to the hounding out of the JagLAG lawyers and an outstanding brave journalist. They were grim indications of how perilous spaces are for truth-tellers in Bastar.

Two days before I left home, I started getting news that Subramaniam was being attacked. A journalist based in Jagdalpur, she had written a series on atrocities against Adivasis over the past year for *Scroll*, a national news website. She had lived in Bastar for years, as the head of the office of the International Committee of the Red Cross, overseeing water and hygiene projects. After completion of the projects she chose to stay on and do journalism because she wanted her daughter to finish her schooling.

It was only after she switched to reporting, that Subramaniam acquired the 'outsider' tag by police and organizations like the Samajik Ekta Manch, who started accusing her of tarnishing the image of Bastar and its police.

A vigilante group, led by former Salwa Judum members, and backed by small-time politicians, contractors and traders, the Samajik Ekta Manch, had sprung up ostensibly as a mass movement against Maoism. But its rallies targeted all those who spoke up against gross human rights violations.

On 10 January, members of this group visited Subramaniam's home and warned her against her reporting. The police, obviously working in tandem, visited hours later and claimed they needed to investigate complaints against her. The editor of her news portal took up the issue with the Chief Minister but Subramaniam was still summoned twice to the *thana* to provide information about herself, her family and her landlord.

On 7 February, after she had returned from a field trip to gather details on an alleged fake encounter, Subramaniam was confronted yet again by members of this vigilante group near her home. Raising slogans they exhorted her neighbours to throw her out, branding her 'Naxal *samarthak*' (supporter). Later that night she received texts and images on her phone from a prominent member of the group, of a programme they organized in which effigies of Naxal supporters were burnt. Around 2 a.m., a motorcycle went past and stones were hurled at the house, shattering the windshield of her car.

Having failed to lodge an FIR, she and members of JagLAG, along with Bela Bhatia met with the Collector, who said he had tried to dissuade Samajik Ekta Manch members from taking the law in their own hands.

Eventually an FIR was lodged against unknown persons for trespass and damage, without mention of the three she specifically mentioned. The IGP of Bastar, S.R.P. Kalluri, also visited her at home along with SP, R.N. Dash, to 'understand the situation' and assure fair investigations. In a telling comment on the collusion between the police and the Samajik Ekta Manch group, he defended them as civilized and decent, adding, 'You wish to stay on in Jagdalpur, right, then they are in a majority while you all (he meant Subramaniam, the legal aid lawyers and Bela Bhatia) are in a minority,' leaving Subramaniam to wonder if this was a veiled threat.

On 13 February, Subramaniam received a call from her landlord who resided in Raipur that he was being summoned by the Jagdalpur police to record a statement.

A few days later her domestic help, who had signed as witness to the car's shattered glass, was also summoned to the police and asked questions on who visited the home, how much she was paid and why she did 'undignified' housework. Hours after she was sent back home, she was summoned again to the police station at 8 p.m. In reply to a call made to the SP, Subramaniam was informed that investigations indicated it was the domestic worker who was behind the hurling of stones and shattered glass. Released at midnight, the woman was distraught and in huge anxiety about her family, since the police had made inquiries about her brother.

The next morning at 8 a.m. on 18 February, the police were back at the domestic worker's doors saying she was needed for more interrogation. Subramaniam's landlord was also feeling the heat with policemen making incessant calls, demanding he come immediately to Jagdalpur.

This intervening night of 17 and 18 February saw a similar pattern unfolding at the premises of JagLAG. It began with the ominous midnight knock. The landlord, who lived in the adjoining house and has a taxi service, was summoned to the police station and his car impounded late at night. He was allowed to go home in the early morning and told Khandelwal and Gera that the police had issued an ultimatum. They must leave or he would face the consequences.

That afternoon, whilst at the JagLAG office cum residential premises, I saw a man on a motorbike whizzing up and down the narrow lane. Their domestic worker clutched my hand in terror and said she recognized him as a policeman from the nearby *thana*, even though he was in mufti. A group of the Samajik Ekta Manch went past the main road, raising slogans against the lawyers. The police made a trip later in the day at the landlord's house and warned him. Eviction must take place within a day or two and not a week. In public, they claimed eviction is a private matter between landlords and tenants. But the acceleration of intimidation on all those who had any associations with the lawyers made it evident the state was on a mission to hound them out.

This pressure had been building up over the past year because the nature of the work of JagLAG was increasingly bringing them up against the police.

As the conflict intensified, more and more cases of extrajudicial killings and police atrocities came under the spotlight. 'Local lawyers whose families lived in Bastar were extremely vulnerable and so increasingly people were turning to us as counsel for cases of extrajudicial killings,' said Gera.

Police statements charging them with being 'Maoist lawyers' began to circulate. The first hint of trouble came when the local Bar Association issued a resolution prohibiting local lawyers from joining them. They claimed rules to that effect in Chhattisgarh, but this resolution was successfully challenged.

Then, a note was privately circulated, claiming 'Shalini Gera and Isha Khandelwal are fake'. The women lawyers made a statement before the police when called to do so but the repercussions were significant. The Bar turned hostile even though the charge was patently absurd. It forbade local members to associate with the two women.

The clamour of 'outsiders' rang stridently through the town. Threats of arrests and pressure on all those who had any dealings with them, created such a vicious climate that Subramaniam, Khandelwal and Gera had little choice but to pack their belongings hurriedly and prepare to leave Bastar.

Rumours circulated that a young member, who had joined the legal aid group just a few weeks ago, could be picked up for interrogation. Soni came by to bid a tearful farewell to the lawyers. She told me she too was receiving veiled threats. I saw her heading off into the dark night, riding pillion on a motorcycle driven by Rinky, a young associate, before I boarded the same overnight bus as some of the team. In the early morning when the bus halted, I was given the news of the attack on Soni. A little before Geedham, the duo were forced to stop. Three men caught hold of them and smeared a chemical substance, believed to be dye used to brand animals, on Soni's face, causing severe burns. I almost retched as I saw images of her blackened swollen face, the eyes barely visible, being circulated on social media.

Some years later as we drove past the scene of the attack, Soni said she first thought the intent was to physically darken her face, but after a while she began experiencing such intense burning that she realized it was a much more lethal one. It is a measure of her resilience, one that has been handed down to her children, that they have started referring to the spot as Mummy's make-up room!

Overpacked Jails and 'Naxali' Offenders

Whilst in Jagdalpur, I accompanied Khandelwal to the court premises briefly. I sat in the corridor, whilst she went into the office of a lawyer. A few minutes later, I saw an undertrial being brought in, escorted by armed police. Dressed in a simple, blue-checked lungi, a well-worn shirt and bare feet, he seemed visibly poor. He was what is colloquially termed as a 'Naxali' offender. In effect, there is no such offence listed in law. Yet, hundreds of Adivasis incarcerated in South Bastar's packed jails were charged with being Naxalites or having associations with them. Old men, aged women, juveniles were being labelled 'dreaded' Maoist commanders and spent years in jails before their acquittal.

JagLAG's questioning of who is perceived as a Naxali offender, like the man I saw being brought in, and of the processes that were sending them into Bastar's jails, as well as the way courts functioned, was what irked the police. The group's documentation of the criminal justice system was revelatory. Official data by the Prison Statistics of India, under the Home Ministry in 2015, said that twenty-eight prisons in Chhattisgarh with a capacity of 7,552 inmates had a population of 17,662 inmates, making the occupancy rate at 235.5 per cent, the highest in the country.[5]

Ajai Mandavi, who runs carpentry classes for jail inmates in the Kanker jail, told me of a time when the inmates slept in shifts since it was not possible to accommodate all of them lying down. That was the time when Santosh Yadav, the intrepid journalist, had also been jailed. Interestingly, latest figures show Uttar Pradesh has overtaken Chhattisgarh in occupancy rates. Possibly not because Chhattisgarh has lessened its number of prisoners, but simply because Chhattisgarh has begun building more jails.

The study undertaken by JagLAG between 2005 to 2012 showed that despite the high occupancy, the conviction rate was very low: 4.3 per cent. Information obtained through the Right to Information (RTI) at the Dantewada District and Session Court during the period revealed that 95.7 per cent of all the Session Court trials end in complete acquittal of all accused on all charges.

It was Sudha Bharadwaj who voiced concerns as a lawyer about these injustices within the justice system. She questioned the manner in which Adivasis, with little access to legal services, were being picked up to spend lengthy periods in jail, for what was no crime at all, as is evident from the rate of acquittals.

Villagers, she said, complained of being routinely picked up during search operations and accused of being Naxalites or having connections with Naxalites.

They are brought before a court that adopts a security-centric approach, and even though there was very little evidence against them which merits a trial, their cases stand little chance of being dismissed. The cases go on trial because magistrates do not exercise their own discretion and rely solely on police versions. Adivasis are further disadvantaged because the court conducts business in formal Hindi and there is a dearth of Halbi or Gondi interpreters.

A pattern of picking up Adivasis after any incident of Maoist violence like an explosion or landmine blast had emerged. The FIR that is filed simply states 'unknown persons' are behind the act and then those picked up are fitted into the case. Charges can range from having weapons, explosive materials or simply of being Naxalites. The connotation of 'Naxali' triggers a hardening of attitude on the part of the court and bail is hardly ever given. Lawyers in Dantewada, I was told, scarcely even bother to press for it. They continued with arguments until the acquittal, which is almost inevitable, given that there is very little evidence brought against them.

By laying emphasis on the so-called menacing nature of the crime rather than evidence, the police enables large swathes of the Adivasi population to be routinely and remorselessly put into incarceration. The greater leeway to prosecution agencies means there is little or no accountability for eventual failure of the prosecution.

Then there is the Chhattisgarh Special Public Security Act, enacted in 2005 with its broad and vague definitions of what is unlawful. In Section 2(e) of the Act, the words 'tendency' or 'encourage', used in conjunction with various definitions of unlawful activities, lends huge scope for misuse. Just about any pretext is excuse enough for arrests. In one of the more bizarre of cases, two traders of Bilaspur were picked up for the crime of selling olive-green material.

What becomes clear is that the whole trial process itself becomes the punishment, with people spending years in jail before acquittal. Since charges fall under the grievous category, security concerns are cited and, as in the Burkapal case, the accused are often not brought to court for months and years on end on the pretext that there are not enough personnel to escort them. Trials drag on and on.[6]

Legal aid lawyers, when allocated by the state, seldom visit the prisoners because there is fear about representing a 'Naxali' offender. A jail rule on compulsorily photographing every visitor is a further deterrent and the only opportunity to discuss the case comes on the date of hearing. With no briefings, undertrials are ill prepared for their experiences in court.

Advocate and legal researcher Shikha Pandey who was with JagLAG and worked in Bastar for a few years, has written a paper in which she examines the National Investigation Agency

(NIA) Act, enacted in 2008 for a Central Government agency that is responsible for investigation and prosecution of offences related to national security.

The paper examines the judicial precedents and demonstrates how vagueness and ambiguity in Section 22 of the Act has been used by the state of Chhattisgarh to create an unintelligible classification of offences related to left-wing extremism. This classification violates the procedural rights of Adivasis. As an example, she points out how the absence of a pleader of choice at the remand stage means that 'the accused is unable to bring complaints regarding custodial violence, forced confession or medical illnesses to the notice of the court at the first instance.'[7]

Legal luminary and human rights activist Vrinda Grover sums up the plight of the Adivasi in her study on Bastar's undertrials. 'Crippled by ignorance of law, unversed with legal procedures, unaware of the evidence and witnesses marshalled against them by the prosecution and unfamiliar with the language of the proceeding, the Adivasi undertrial stands at a distance—no more than a mute spectator.'[8]

I gained some awareness of the plight of a 'mute spectator' and Bastar's broken justice system through the story of Madkam Hadma, an Adivasi who, in his solitary, quiet desperation, had attempted suicide.

Loneliness of an Adivasi Undertrial

Ratna Madkam, from Sarkeguda, had stopped by at the JagLAG office before going on to the Dantewada jail where her cousin Madkam Hadma was lodged. When I asked her about the case, she was a little hesitant but she did, however, recount the bare outlines of how this cousin, from Chinnegellur, a village that lies deep in the forest and in the Maoist belt, found himself in jail.

He had come to stay in their village to help in the building of a house, a practice of voluntary community labour that is prevalent among Adivasis. Then on 27 March 2015, there was a minor IED blast near the Basaguda camp and the next day, CRPF troops from the camp swooped down into Sarkeguda. The forces pounced on Hadma, who was sleeping in a corner of a home, and hauled him away although villagers swore he was with them during the time of the incident and could not be held responsible for the blast.

The village of Sarkeguda had been in the spotlight because a commission was inquiring into the killings of seventeen people by CRPF personnel. Villagers alleged that ever since the hearings began, the CRPF, acting in reprisal, was continually harassing the villagers with arrests and illegal detentions.

After Hadma was picked up by the security forces, the villagers followed them till they reached the Basaguda camp. They made phone calls to the lawyers in Jagdalpur, who in turn phoned the personnel in Basaguda camp. They were informed no civilian was being detained. There was no further news and the lawyers lost contact with the villagers since the network in Sarkeguda was patchy.

It was only after a prisoner from Dantewada was freed that news of Hadma came in. He was in the same jail, held under grave charges.

Visiting him in jail, Gera of JagLAG learned how he had been badly tortured inside the CRPF camp at Basaguda almost as soon as he was taken there. He was made to lie down with his hands splayed out whilst troops stomped on his palms. Blades were used to slash the soles of his feet open. He was then hurriedly shifted to the police station as camps are not authorised to hold civilians. It is surmised this was done after the lawyers' calls started coming.

At the police station, the torture continued and Hadma was informed he was arrested for having caused the explosion. He told Gera that in sheer fright he tried to end his life. Possessing next to nothing, he started stuffing his lungi into his mouth in a bid to gag himself.

Rushed to the hospital in an unconscious state, he was hastily produced in court after he was revived. The court was not informed that he was being produced from a hospital and that he was going back to it, in total violation of the criminal procedures, which stipulate that once a man has been produced in court, he is in its jurisdiction. If he is to be taken elsewhere, the police must duly inform the court.

When Gera met him in jail, his body still bore visible signs of torture. But the attempt to establish it was stymied since the Bijapur court judge was on leave and did not take up the application for several days. His order for a medical examination took eight days to reach the Dantewada authorities. The hospital authorities too did not act speedily. Twenty days were lost and so was the medical evidence as the injuries had healed.

The charge sheet arrived three months later but the judge had been transferred and no hearings took place for nine months. In the charge sheet the police claimed that on 28 March, the Naxalites had been firing at the police, one of whom they said was Hadma but that he ran away. On 29 March, during the search in the jungle they happened to come upon him and picked him up. The police produced two SPOs as witnesses, who apparently recognized him. They claimed they could hear the Naxalites calling out to each other by their names and Hadma's name was uttered.

Eleven months later, the two eyewitnesses contradicted themselves. They said they were a kilometre away from the firing and therefore could not have recognized him. Nor could they have heard anything other than gunfire coming from behind them. Hadma was eventually acquitted.

The significant takeaway from the case was that no Adivasi in Bastar was safe, especially an Adivasi from a village deep in the forests where everyone is viewed as a 'Naxali.' He could be thrown into the maws of the carceral system, no matter how ludicrous the evidence. The fact that the villagers of Sarkeguda were witness to Hadma being picked up from the village and not the forest, that he was in the village on the day of the explosions and so could not be held responsible, and finally, that the women presented themselves in front of the Collector and SP to give their version and signed an affidavit, had no effect.

'The case would have collapsed on its own accord,' said Gera, 'we were keen, however, on establishing the torture he underwent at the camp and in the police station. But we could not do so.'[9]

Hadma spent more than a year, for no crime at all, in grim isolation. His impoverished family could make the journey to the Dantewada jail only a couple of times because of the distances and inadequate public transport system. Ratna Madkam, his cousin, too had her own compulsions and could not visit as often as she would have liked. Gera recalls how in desperation he requested help to procure the most basic toiletries like soap for a bath.

Less than Equal: The Court Is 'Theirs'

'I am a black man in a white man's court. This should not be.'

Nelson Mandela's words uttered in court, exposing the injustices under apartheid, when he was being tried for incitement in November 1962, could well apply to Adivasis with regard to fair trials in Indian courts.

In Chhattisgarh, the perception of being less than equal

citizens with an inequitable justice system, was exacerbated with the setting up of two designated Special Courts in 2015—one in Bilaspur and another in Jagdalpur in 2015, under the NIA Act.

The Jagdalpur Special Court has jurisdiction over the trial of all Naxalite-related cases registered in the seven conflict-affected districts of Bastar. It presides over all Scheduled Offences, irrespective of whether the NIA is involved in the investigation or not.[10]

Pandey's legal research paper on the NIA Act, analyses how indiscriminate use of the law against the Adivasi population coupled with the enforcement of the Special Courts, led to a peculiar situation. Most of the Naxalite-related cases, spread over the entire conflict region of Bastar, were transferred to one NIA Special Judge who presides in Jagdalpur. Cases that were to be tried under the ordinary criminal procedure went instead to the Special Court. The Special Court, whose purpose was to expedite trial, instead denuded the existing trial courts of jurisdiction. Some 500 cases registered under the Scheduled Offences instituted and tried under special criminal procedures, meant there was derogation of essential procedural safeguards against arbitrary prosecutions, denial of access to justice, and the denial of a right to a free and fair trial.[11]

The overwhelming load and the lack of infrastructure compounded delays which further impacted on prisoners' rights and access to legal representation.

One of the most startling cases of this judicial quagmire cited in the research paper is entitled the 'Kafkaesque case of Raju, son of Pugdu'.

Raju, aged sixty, had been arrested from his village in Kilam, Narayanpur, accused of being a Naxalite and the case was registered under the Unlawful Activities Prevention Act (UAPA), along with other serious offences. Developed as an anti-terrorism law, UAPA defines 'unlawful' as those activities which are intended to support secession or any action that disclaims, questions disrupts or is intended to disrupt the sovereignty and territorial integrity of India. Since there are no objective criterion laid down for such categorization, the security forces in Bastar tend to brand any Adivasi as Naxalite.

Raju's defence counsel had raised the question of his arrest as being one of mistaken identity and had pointed out the discrepancy in the name of the father of the accused. Then the case was transferred to the NIA Special Court on 6 December 2016, in accordance with the Chhattisgarh government's notification. But Raju's case records were not transferred despite reminders to the record room in Kondagon.

He remained in jail, not knowing the nature of his alleged crimes or possible options for his defence. Even though the delays in the trial process were due to these administrative lapses, he was twice denied bail by the NIA court. His family was forced to go in appeal at the Bilaspur High Court, situated 500 km away from their home.

His files were traced only after the Chhattisgarh High Court issued a notice to the state government on an appeal. From the records it was learnt that sixteen others, held under the same case, had already been acquitted under the regular criminal court and ordinary criminal procedure court in less than a year. Raju was ultimately given bail. But, he still had to spend considerable time and money in travelling from his village to Jagdalpur on every day of hearing.

'The case study underscores how the inequitable criminal justice machine in a conflict setting is transformed into another tool for the harassment and persecution of marginalized communities,' observes Pandey's paper.

Soni, who gets innumerable requests for help whenever

someone is picked up, described the agonizing days for the family members because of this inequitable justice system. They run to the *thana* in their own *zilla* and when they cannot locate the person they have to fan out in many directions, wondering in which jail he has been lodged. The necessary activities of earning, attending to domestic chores, cooking, sleeping all get completely disrupted. 'I have received so many distress calls asking for help to trace the missing father, or son, or daughter. Earlier they would seek help for the release. Now, the fears are heightened. They ask if the missing member is alive or dead. "*Didi, kuch paper mein aaya?*" they ask.

'Prison is living hell but it holds out hope. One day the person will be released, one can visit loved ones in jail. But being in the possession of the police at the *thana* fills them with chilling dread. When they are told UAPA has been applied because the concerned prisoner is a "Naxalite", they are totally baffled. What does this law even mean? Under what grounds can a person leading the life of a civilian, going about his business, be termed Naxalite? There is the heart-breaking question: '*Uska galti kya hai?*''

A lawyer told me how in 2020 even as the pandemic raged across the world, six persons were picked up after they staged anti-mining protests in Kondegaon district. The families had to run around to find out under which *thana* the arrests had been made and which jail they were lodged in. While four people were traced, two remained 'missing'. It was only after ten days that it was found that the missing two had been charged under the UAPA and, in accordance with the ruling on the NIA Special Court, they were sent all the way to Jagdalpur. For the families this means travelling to what seems like another country, since villages function at a very local level in Bastar. Arranging for legal representation in Jagdalpur was hampered by the fact that it happened during the prolonged first lockdown.

A new order has now been passed by the Chhattisgarh government designating more Sessions Courts as NIA courts and this may ease some of the pressures on the 500-odd cases and a faster turnaround of the cases.

But, there cannot be any fundamental change as long as the bogey of 'national security' continues to be deployed. As Pandey observes in her paper: 'In Bastar malicious prosecutions, illegal detentions, unlawful incarcerations and extrajudicial killings have become a way of life since the escalation of conflict in 2004. The enforcement of anti-terror laws is often perceived as an extension of the counter-insurgency operation in the conflict setting. In the face of insurgency, the concerns regarding national security are invoked as a justification for adopting strategies that thwart the dispensation of justice. Any effort to seek criminal legal reforms must resolve this justification.'[12]

Gera, who believes that anti-terror laws and invocation of national security has led to a broken justice system, said that the only change she has seen over the past years in Bastar, is that now there is open acknowledgement of it and the fact that Adivasis are unfairly incarcerated. She remarked wryly that many parts of India are fast approaching this same Bastar pattern.

'The highlighting of the lawless reign of the Salwa Judum contributed to a certain discourse, injustice to the Adivasis was established to the extent that this present Congress government made it the basis of a poll promise.'

The Justice A.K. Patnaik Commission, set up in 2019, was given a broad mandate for reviewing all cases against Adivasis who are in prison, but activists say it has concentrated more on offences under the Excise Act rather than looking at injustices under UAPA and other security Acts.

'Nothing changed at the ground level. There are still so many complaints of people being picked up, farcical trials are still being conducted. The number of jail inmates is still high.

And the solution to overcrowding seems to be to build more jails,' she said.

The problem, she believes, is that arrests are deployed as a weapon of war. A state is at war; the police need to pick up people as trophies and the court continues to be a rubber stamp. 'It is not as if one can just fix the courts whilst the conflict remains unresolved. It is a given that, if there is this conflict, the state will operate in this manner. If the state, however, continues to believe it can cower people down into submission, it is not going to happen. A political solution is needed.'

Expectations of Justice

What are the Adivasis' own expectations of justice? When and why do they access the courts? Why does Arjun's father, now impoverished, still desperately ask what is happening to his murdered son's case?

I briefly met the women of Nendra, who had filed the complaint of sexual violence when they were returning from Bilaspur. The case they filed more than four years ago, under such challenging conditions, has been stuck because the judicial process demands the individual perpetrators be singled out. But many of the accused cannot be identified. Security personnel often hide their own faces and in some instances, the women were blindfolded.

The justice system in India has no provisions to establish vicarious liability. It does not allow for the chain of command, of culpability of violence.

Ironically, says Gera, it is the Adivasis who have shown greater understanding of this notion of justice. They do not want to mark out any particular individual or have concerns about who actually pulled the trigger in an encounter. What they seek is the state's culpability and accountability.

'The villagers tell us that by justice what they want is for the *gusht* (patrol party) to stop coming into their villages and terrorizing them. They want the killings to stop, the looting of their precious few belongings, the beatings, the vandalizing, carrying off the livestock or poultry...all the violations that come with the *gusht* entering their villages. But the court doesn't see it that way and Indian law does not have the provision to recognize vicarious liability,' she explained.

For many Adivasis the violence inflicted on the body is as grievous as the bid to loot them and deprive them of their wealth. 'In their complaints of beatings they will suddenly talk about the hurt they feel because *murghi aur uske ande bhi leke gaye* (they took a hen as well as the eggs she had laid). Or they will mention that a *bakra*, especially bought for a wedding, was taken away. The judges get irritated because they cannot understand why looting is perceived on the same level as physical assault, but for the Adivasis it is part of the overall repression.'

Adivasis seldom approach the court for settlement of civil matters, preferring to rely on their own Adivasi Samaj to adjudicate on matters of property dispute, theft, marital discord and so on. Of late, Adivasi women from cities have begun going to court and resorting to Indian law to take up cases of divorce, child support and so on if they disagree with the Adivasi Samaj's decisions, believing it has ruled unfairly and in a patriarchal manner. But by and large Adivasis come to court only when cases are foisted on them.

It is only when grievous harm has been inflicted on them as a community that public interest litigation has been sought as the way forward. It was initially spurred by civil society with individuals taking up cases on behalf of Adivasis since they themselves had little access to the court. The most notable were the writ petitions filed against the Salwa Judum in 2007.

It is also a reflection of the warped justice system that those who tried to take recourse to the law had to face retaliation. Kartam Joga, the Adivasi activist of the CPI, who along with two others, petitioned the Supreme Court for action against the Salwa Judum, had to pay a stiff price for his interventions in documenting human rights abuses and violations. He spent twenty-nine months in jail in a case where he was accused of being involved in an attack on CRPF personnel. He was eventually acquitted.[13]

Himanshu Kumar, a Gandhian activist who with his wife Veena, ran the Vanvasi Chetna Ashram at Kawalnar, near Dantewada, was also targeted after he began taking up the causes of aggrieved Adivasis before the Lok Adalats, the police *thanas* and court. He had worked in partnership with the government for several years in sanitation, health and literacy schemes. The change in the nature of work from social welfare to defending human rights violations was what led to him being hounded out. He said, 'If the accused is the state, we become irritants.'

One of the cases that drew the state's ire was when he took up the case of Sodhi Shambo, a woman of Gompad. Shot in the leg in October 2009 by SPOs and security forces conducting a combing operation in her village, Shambo's festering wound would not heal, so she sought refuge in the ashram. Himanshu helped her seek medical care in Delhi. Her statement was recorded from her hospital bed and filed by him in the Supreme Court.

She returned from Delhi and was recuperating at the ashram but when she attempted to go back to Delhi she was forced by police to dismount from the bus. Later, as she tried to leave with Himanshu Kumar by car, the vehicle was stopped at Kanker. She was arrested, police officials saying it was because she had not filed an FIR before moving the Supreme Court. She has since disappeared from the public eye.[14]

Himanshu Kumar became the target, being named, as he said, in some hundred-odd charge sheets. The ashram was bulldozed and brought down. His close friend Kopa Kunjum was arrested, and he himself was forced to flee Chhattisgarh.

Amidst all these dismal stories, one of the more heartening explorations in accessing justice came from the communities of Sarkeguda and Edesmeta, respectively seeking redressal for civilian killings in their village. It was their persistence that pushed the government into setting up one-man commissions for both incidents with Justice V.K. Agarwal being given the task.

The hearings of both commissions, some of which I attended over two years, became a prism through which one glimpsed the way Adivasis perceive justice and how the system treated them, sometimes as caricatures and lesser than equal.

Sab ke Liye Insaaf: Sarkeguda Fights for Collective Justice

On 29 June 2012, many papers and the electronic media quoted the news agency PTI and some official statements to report on a fierce gun battle in the forests of Silger, which resulted in the 'killing of twenty Maoists'. It was hailed as a 'moment of triumph' for the CRPF in the battle of attrition against Maoists; then Home Minister P. Chidambaram claimed the troops were fired upon and responded with great bravery.[15]

Shortly after, the villagers of Sarkeguda disputed this and stated that seventeen unarmed villagers had been killed. A video, shared on social media by Himanshu Kumar, which I saw, articulates their utter outrage and distress. In it an angry young woman is confronting a man, clearly an official, who is on an appeasement mission having brought food and grain supplies. She asks him why the government wants to provide aid to Naxalites and retorts, '*Hamare satra logon ko yahan khada kariye.... Tab hum ration paani lenge* (Produce our people, all seventeen of them, and only then will we receive the rations you brought). She also demands to know whether the young girl in the list of victims was also a Naxalite. '*Aur woh chhoti ladki ...woh toh asli Naxali thi!* (And that young girl. Wasn't she a real Naxalite?)[16]

The woman is Kamla Kaka, a nurse and resident of Sarkeguda, whose nephew Rahul was among those killed when the CRPF and police fired on a group assembled in an open space amidst the paddy fields. The villagers disputed the official version that the incident had occurred in the deep forests. In their narrative, they said that on the night of 28 June, people from Sarkeguda, Kotaguda and Renpenta gathered together to discuss preparations for the ritual Beej Pandum or sowing ceremony that begins with the onset of the rains. A party of the CRPF and police came upon them, surrounded them and began firing without any warning. The firing continued relentlessly even when some members shouted out that they were villagers.

The next morning, another villager, Irpa Ramesh was attacked and killed in cold blood by CRPF personnel who had camped out in the village. Ramesh had stepped out of his home at 5 a.m. to check on the situation when he was shot and then clobbered with a brick as he tried to flee.

The official version, narrated at length during the commission hearings, was that a joint party of the CRPF and CoBRA (Commando Battalion for Resolute Action, a special anti-Naxal unit of the CRPF) had set out for an operation on the night of 28 June, on receipt of an intelligence input of a proposed meeting of Naxalites in Silger. One party left from Basaguda; around 10.30 p.m. they heard some sounds in the forest and were suddenly fired upon. The sound of gunfire and muzzle flashes in the dark gave an indication of where the firing was coming from. After taking 'their respective covers', they fired back. Later, eight para-illuminating bombs were used to light up the area, which enabled them to take stock of the situation, including attending to their own injured personnel. Arrangements were then made for a helicopter which arrived at 6.30 a.m. on the morning of 29 June to pick up their injured.

The killings were initially hailed by both the Central and Chhattisgarh governments as a victory over Maoists in Operation Silger, with then Home Minister P. Chidambaram stating that among the dead was a top Maoist named Rahul. It turned out to be Kamla Kaka's nephew, still a student.

At first this official narrative was touted by the media. One of the English-language newspapers carried a graphic image detailing all the security operations under the title 'The Empire Strikes Back'. Buried in the body of the story, were two sentences of the villagers' version that those killed were 'innocent tribals including women and children'.[17]

It was these official canards that triggered Kamla's lacerating outburst, seen in the video. On the one hand, villagers were branded as Naxalites. On the other hand, the state also tried to co-opt them as *aam janta* (ordinary citizens) entitled to the public food distribution system, with rations. She is particularly incensed because the SDM had refused to meet and listen to the villagers' own account of the incident a week before.

Such random labelling is one of the issues that Yug Choudhry, noted criminal lawyer from Mumbai, who appeared pro bono for the villagers, elaborated upon during his arguments. He wondered at the state's rationale in determining who can be branded as Naxalites. He took the example of Sarke Pullaiya, one of the villagers who ran a ration shop and sustained injuries on that night of firing. Pullaiya was first labelled a Naxalite, but during cross-examination it was suggested that he was injured by Naxalites. How was it possible, Choudhry asked, for a person to be told he is a Naxalite, then also told he is entitled to compensation from the state because he was injured by Naxalites!

I met Kamla, a registered health worker or *mittanin*, some years after the video had been shot. She recounted the horrors of a night that cannot be forgotten.

'I had returned home after a delivery case in Bijapur, 52 km away, had eaten my meal and was listening to music on my mobile when the sound of gunshots pierced the stillness of the night. Why have the forces entered our village? I wondered. The firing went on and on. Some people rushed to the site. Flare bombs were later used to illuminate the area and then a vehicle came in to pick up the dead bodies. Three of my relatives including my fifteen-year-old nephew, Rahul, died that night. He was so close to my heart.'

The security forces not only shot the villagers but also physically assaulted them with axes. The savage pattern was repeated the next morning with Irpa Ramesh being shot and then bludgeoned to death, when he ventured outside his house. Anguished villagers followed the troops as his body was hauled away to the Basaguda *thana*. It was here that they learnt of the total number of those killed from the three hamlets—seventeen in all, including six minors.

Sarkeguda's villagers have a history of brutal violence against them during the Salwa Judum years. They had been forced to abandon their homes and had only recently resettled with Himanshu Kumar's help. After this firing incident they decided to fight back. Kamla and some others called up the local journalists and the Tehsildar of Bijapur.

'The police kept saying we are Naxalites but the local media supported us, saying they knew we were unarmed villagers. We demanded the bodies of our dead. One of them had been buried in the *thana* itself. They told us post-mortems were being performed. We were given back the bodies only after 7 p.m. The funerals took place the next day and by that time the national media too had arrived.'

The role of the doctors, who performed the post-mortem under Dr G.S. Dhruv, came under grave scrutiny during the commission hearings. There were such glaring inconsistencies in time and other details that as Khandelwal, who was part of the legal team for the complainants (villagers) observed, it was clear no proper post-mortem had been conducted at all.

Photographs of the dead bodies also showed blunt, shallow wounds in addition to bullet injuries, which according to the journalists, bore out the accounts of brute physical assault with axes.

The national media, through their reports, provided a human face and poignant details of the villagers' lives and hopes. The 'dreaded' Maoist named by Chidambaram as Rahul, was actually Kamla's nephew, a fifteen-year-old boy, studying and living in a hostel very close to the Basaguda camp. He had come home for the vacations along with schoolmate Ramvilas who also lost his life. Ramvilas' aunt was Ratna Madkam. She showed press persons Ramvilas' study book in Sanskrit, with a small note in his handwriting, 'Thee Thou Thine', and explanations on how these were not used in English except in references to the divine. It is a moving testimony to a schoolboy's dreams of education.[18]

Questions about this 'fake' encounter were first raised by the CPI, under its Adivasi leader, Manish Kunjam, with the demand for an inquiry after conducting its own fact-finding. Kawasi Lakhma, Adivasi leader of the Congress, voiced his discontent and the state Congress too disputed its own Central party's version, since the UPA was then in power.

The momentum for justice was sustained by the villagers with women like Kamla Kaka, Ratna Madkam and Rita Kaka staging protests outside the District Commissioner's office and with visits to the corridors of power in New Delhi and Raipur. The Raman Singh government was compelled to announce the setting up of the commission under retired judge V.K. Agarwal.

For more than a year the commission did not even have an office to function out of whilst the police's repression against the villagers grew. People would be randomly picked up whilst sleeping (see the Madkam Hidma case), there were beatings, there was sexual violence.

'We could not go to schools, into the forest or take cattle into the grazing grounds without dread because of these terror tactics. A woman, who begged a soldier not to detain her in the fields since she had young children at home, was asked to squeeze her breasts to prove she was lactating. It infuriated me. One day in sheer anger I went to Raipur and went inside the Chief Minister's cabin to tell him about the police harassment,' said Kamla.

There was also the problem of how to handle the legal proceedings. The commission put up a notice saying it would accept affidavits by the villagers but no one knew what should be done. They approached advocate Sudha Bharadwaj and she especially made a trip to Bijapur that enabled thirty-five affidavits to be filed. One time she had to make a phone call to the judge when she found the villagers had come all the way to Raipur with the affidavits but without their identity papers. The judge, who understood it was the people's first acquaintance with justice mechanisms, allowed the affidavits to be filed, saying identity cards should be produced at the next date. He assured Bharadwaj that the inquiry commission had been instituted to reveal the truth and not to cover it up.

JagLAG stepped in as the villagers' counsel and lawyer Yug Choudhry offered his services pro bono. Parijata Bharadwaj, part of the legal team, recalls the active community participation. 'We were told we would be lucky if anyone deposed but more than thirty turned up. The judge remarked it would not be necessary to have more statements but they persisted. They did not want anyone to feel left out.

'Some of the older women spoke in detail and at great length in Gondi, including tales of violence during the Salwa Judum reign. Unfazed, even when cut off midway, probably because they did not understand Hindi, they wanted to be able to tell their stories. As counsels we get caught up in legalese but here were people speaking truth in their very individualistic ways.

'One of my strongest memories is that of the petite figure of Laxmi, Irpa Ramesh's wife, who said she could not bring back her husband but wanted to testify as a memorial to one who had been killed in cold blood.'

Kamla, Rita and Ratna, who attended as many hearings of the commission as possible, found cross-examination a bruising experience. Insinuations were made that they were Naxalites or then they were labelled as those whose testimonies could not be relied upon because they had not filed a police complaint before filing the affidavits.

Such arguments are a glaring example of the abysmal lack of acknowledgement of what Adivasis face in access to justice. The Sarkeguda villagers, who had gathered outside the *thana* to receive the bodies, were not even allowed to step inside the premises. How was it possible to file an FIR against those that manned the *thana* and who had perpetrated the atrocities? The villagers' way of seeking justice was to protest vociferously outside the *thana* and continue to tell their stories. Since the state had set up a court of inquiry because of doubts surrounding the encounter, it should have acknowledged that filing an FIR isn't necessarily the only prescribed way of seeking justice, said a lawyer for the villagers.

The villagers' ability to speak in one voice helped in bringing about the commission's historic indictment of the security forces. 'They never lost interest or faith, all through the years,' said Parijata Bharadwaj.

In his finding, Justice Agarwal noted that not only was there unwarranted and unilateral firing upon the people assembled in an open ground, and not in a forest as the claim was made, but that many of the people who had assembled had also been physically assaulted and severely beaten according to the evidence. The injuries to the security forces were sustained because of 'friendly fire' or the exchange of fire between the personnel.

The commission also stated investigations conducted by the police had been dishonest and evidence was manipulated

The findings came after exhaustive and comprehensive arguments by Choudhry and others in the complainants' legal team. It came with detailed questioning of the security forces' statements involving ballistics, forensic and medico-legal findings. Hailing the report as a historic one, Choudhry called it a stupendous effort by an ailing judge.

'The state government tried to delay matters, possibly with a bid to frustrate the progress. Our final arguments were over on 24 March 2017 but in an unbecoming manner, the state and security forces dragged proceedings on for more than a year on some pretext or another and we even had to ask for an opportunity to refresh the judge's memory since so much time had elapsed. It is perhaps a reflection of a guilty mind since it is a guilty mind that usually runs away from the verdict. They attacked not just the villagers but also made personal remarks on us lawyers and on journalists attending the hearings, calling them Maoist sympathizers.

'However, the judge did a most fantastic job and in a most unexpected way upheld the villagers' version of truth against the security forces who are generally held in high esteem.'[19]

Unfortunately, in terms of punitive action nothing has moved beyond the report's findings. The very nature of a judicial inquiry is more a state-mandated fact-finding rather than an attempt to hold anyone guilty. After the findings were made public, it was up to the state to take follow-up action, but the ground reality has not changed even after this indictment. There are still extrajudicial killings almost every week.

From the Adivasi perspective as articulated by Ratna, Rita and Kamla in their conversations with me, justice is defined in collective terms—'*Sab ke liye insaaf.*'

A case is seen as part of the larger struggle in which it becomes incumbent upon the community to stand up. The outrage felt and expressed is not just by a particular family or individual or even village, but for the entire Adivasi community of Bastar. The fight will continue.

We Sell Cattle, Not Our People: Edesmeta Encounter

There was a moment of epiphany in the small room at the Jagdalpur Collectorate. Karam Somli, her diminutive frame barely visible above the railings of the witness box, inclined her head straight upwards in the twelve o'clock position. It was in reply to a question demanding to know when she had put her thumbprint on the affidavit, affirming the loss of her minor son in firing by CRPF forces.

Another such moment happened when Karam Manglu was asked how old his nephew Badru was when he was killed in the same incident at Edesmeta village on 17 May 2013. He raised his hand up to the level of his chest to indicate that Badru was just a boy.

Both of them, in their expressions for chronology and age, were demonstrating how they measure time: without the Gregorian calendar or a clock. But this very difference was used by the counsels for the state and the CRPF to cast doubt on their stories and to suggest they had been tutored. Or, that as Adivasis they lacked the sensibility and agency to seek justice and were acting at the instigation of others.

I had seen six of the villagers arriving that morning of 10 March 2018, to give witness for the encounter that occurred a year after Sarkeguda and was similar in many ways.

They stepped gingerly out of autorickshaws, crossed the road with trepidation, their movements betraying an unfamiliarity with Jagdalpur's urban setting and traffic. A youth, who escorted them and was acting as their interpreter, told me the long journey had begun with a two-hour walk through thick forest and three hillocks to the nearest roadhead of Gangalur. From there a vehicle ride via Bijapur to Jagdalpur, took at least four hours. But, said the youth, they were eager to participate and more would have come had it not been mahua picking time. These people were willingly foregoing three days of income.

Entering the labyrinth of the law with its searching questions and suppositions was an exhausting, nerve-wracking ordeal. One could sense their tension from the way they gulped bottles of water during any recess and wiped the sweat from their brow with their *gamchas*. At many stages they appeared baffled by the proceedings or the way things were being suggested to them by the opposing counsels. But there were no contradictions in their accounts of what happened on a night when celebrations turned to terror.

The villagers' narrative has been pieced together through

their affidavits and accounts told to various activists and through reports of various fact-finding teams.[20]

On a night just before the heavy rain spells, about eighty men and young boys had gathered in a field near a *gamma* or local temple to celebrate the festival of Beej Pandum or sowing during which agricultural implements and seeds are blessed and collective decisions are taken on who can farm on various plots of land. As is customary, the women stayed home.

There was singing and dancing before a bonfire, a chicken had been cut and three men went to a watering hole to clean the chicken when they were accosted by CoBRA forces who tried to capture them. They broke away and began running towards another hamlet. In the light of the bonfire the villagers could see their flight. Then came the gunfire which ended abruptly the singing and dancing. People ran helter-skelter, shrieks rent the air and the women in the village ran towards the ground. Seven persons, including the *pujari* (priest), were killed that night.

Dev Prakash, a CRPF constable, was also found dead on the ground the next morning. According to the villagers he died in the same burst of gunfire. Villagers also spoke of how one villager identified as Karam Joga was heard pleading for water before he died. The constable's body and that of young Karam Massa, one of the dead, were taken away to the Gangalur *thana*, by the forces who also forced three men to accompany them.

The other bodies were taken by their families to their respective homes. Punem Bori, in her affidavit, describes how a bullet had gone through her son's waist and exited through the abdomen.

Before any arrangement for the funerals could take place, another contingent from the CRPF arrived next morning and forcibly took away the dead bodies. Angry villagers followed them all the way to the Gangalur *thana* and demanded the release of the three men in custody. Post-mortems were being carried out and it is through the villagers' testimony that one hears of the appallingly insensitive manner in which these are done. Bodies were cut up in a crude manner, no effort was made to resuture the parts—bits of flesh and the body were just bundled up in cloth and handed back to the villagers. Enraged, they staged a protest and threw stones at the police station.

The official version was that the killings occurred on the night of 17 May when 150 personnel drawn from CoBRA, the CRPF and the police were en route to Peediyah for combing operations. Suddenly Naxalites opened fire on them; they returned the fire. In the cross-firing some villagers died. Later, the Additional Director General of Police claimed villagers had died because Naxalites had used them as human shields.

Under attack, the Raman Singh government announced the one-man commission inquiry, by the same judge for the Sarkeguda hearings. Advocate Prasad Chouhan filed a writ in September of that year asking for a special investigation team (SIT) to probe the killings of the villagers by the combined forces. Six years later the Supreme Court in May 2019, announced that the Central Bureau of Investigation (CBI) would take over since it was unsatisfied with the pace of Chhattisgarh state's inquiry. The apex court also directed that the investigation should be conducted by officers who were not from Chhattisgarh.

The CBI's inquiry is awaited but the Agarwal commission, in its report tabled in the assembly, has noted that none of those killed were Maoist and the security personnel might have opened fire in panic. '*Galat dhaarna, ghabrahat ki prakriya*' (False impressions, nervous responses) is what the report states. It also criticizes the lack of proper defence equipment and intelligence inputs that hampers security personnel.

I attended some of the commission's hearings and it provided an opportunity to reflect on prevailing mindsets and attitudes. How does the state and its judicial systems perceive the Adivasis? How do security forces make a distinction between armed Naxalites and unarmed civilians? And in turn, how do Adivasis see the proceedings? How do they navigate the challenges of an alien system? How do they respond when arguments and suggestions proffered have less to do with natural principles of justice and more at lowering their dignity?

During the cross-examination of the villagers, it was repeatedly suggested by counsels for the state, police and CRPF that the Beej Pandum is a night of revelry. One in which everyone would be 'mast' (in a state of happy intoxication). This was clearly an innuendo meant to suggest that all the participants were in such a state of revelry that they could not be reliable witnesses. They would not clearly remember the events of the night when their kin were killed. This drew a rebuke from the judge. He asked that the counsels desist from using the word.

One of the witnesses was asked if he could identify his thumbprint. This drew criticism from the judge who pointed out that he too would be unable to do so. A large part of the cross-examination was spent in suggesting that vested parties had organized the villagers at a meeting in Mataner and facilitated the filing of affidavits by the villagers. In fact, this line of argument was a sad reflection on the state's own lack of sensitivity to justice and its inability to reach out to the villagers and help them testify. Instead, the task fell on legal activists who were then discredited.

At one point it was suggested that the agricultural implements taken to be blessed during the puja were in fact *hathiyars* or weapons! When the CRPF produced its witnesses, one of them insisted that in the light of the bonfire he could clearly see that the people who had congregated were Naxalites because they had guns! But pressed further, he could not say whether the light of the bonfire showed whether there were women or children present.

Other significant points that emerged from the cross-examination of the security personnel was the huge lack of knowledge of the people in whose terrain security operations are carried out. The personnel did not know any of the languages Adivasis speak, they did not know what Beej Pandum was, they were unaware of whether any protocols had been laid down after the Sarkeguda killings. And finally, the troops did not possess night-vision equipment or satellite phones. But they all had guns.

One of the most powerful assertions of dignity came when the issue of compensation was taken up. Counsels for the defendants, suggested that the state's offer of Rs 8 lakhs for each dead person was refused because of threats given by the Naxalites.

In the witness box, Karam Dangal stated simply that they had already sold their goats. He explained, '*Aadmi ko beche jaisa lagega. Iss karan hum logon ne yeh rakam nahi liya* (We sell goats at around the same price. It would seem as if we are selling our people. That is why we did not accept the monetary compensation).

It was reiterated that the only compensation that was taken was Rs 20,000 given by the Collector's office to those injured towards their hospital and medical expenses. The balance of Rs 80,000 was refused by them as was the Rs 8 lakhs offered to families of the dead.

Here were simple Adivasis upholding the sanctity of human life. They did not want money. They wanted the justice system to offer them something beyond that. They wanted to be treated with respect, to have some semblance of dignity restored and an acknowledgement of the gross killings.

What happened in Edesmeta is in indicator of how Adivasis occupy so little space in the Indian collective conscience.

Forgotten by All: The Blindness of the Judicial System

Whilst many Adivasis are now seeing the process of petitions and filing FIRs against state violence as a movement of outrage on behalf of a community, there are also cases where the experience has been so excoriating that they simply want no engagement at all with the state's judicial mechanisms. 'We must give them that space and understanding,' said Gera as she recounted a particularly gross miscarriage of justice.

It was at the request of Linga, the activist whose case was being fought by Gera, that the plight of Irpa Narayan, also lodged in the Dantewada jail, was brought to light. He had not had any court hearing for six long years. It seemed beyond belief, but when the file was studied, it was found that not only had no witnesses been examined but that two others—Midiyam Lachu and Punem Bhima—had been named as co-accused in the same case and were also in the jail. The men lodged together were unaware they had all been arraigned for the same case.

The Investigating Officer's report set out the standard story. That of Naxalites opening fire on a party of security personnel. Couched in standard language was the sentence '*Force ko bharti parta dekh bhaag gaye*' (Seeing the forces in high numbers they ran away).

It added that Irpa Narayan with a bow and arrow was arrested on the spot. Although the police claimed there was heavy firing they could not recover any shells of the bullets. In the charge sheet there was no mention of Lachu and Bhima who were mysteriously arrested two weeks later on separate days. But somehow they had been accommodated into this case.

When an application for bail was put forward, the judge

sent for the file and expressed anger that the defence lawyer had not checked it for such grave discrepancies all the six long years. But the defence lawyer commented the judge too had not carefully looked into the charges and noticed such a gross miscarriage of justice.

Bail was requested for all three but granted only to Lachu and Bhima, the two men whose names hadn't figured in the charge sheet. It took an additional five months before they could walk out. This was because there had been massive displacement in their home village of Surnar in Bijapur district. It was one among others that had been burnt down during the years of the Salwa Judum. The villagers had dispersed to various places and there was no one to stand surety for their bail, since no one had *pattas* or land records anymore. The mother of one of them, who used to try and keep tabs on the proceedings, had died and Lachu and Bhima were consequently forgotten people. Eventually when one prisoner from the jail was released, he was able to make contact with someone who could vouch that Lachu and Bhima were inhabitants of Surnar and they got bail.

Appearing in court whilst on bail was another ordeal as it took at least a day for them to travel to Dantewada. They would stay overnight at the bus stand before they could return as they had very little money. On one occasion, during the monsoons, they were delayed and did not appear in court at the appointed time. The judge threatened imprisonment. When they arrived eventually, they explained that the streams were in spate and difficult to ford. With no cell phones, it was not possible to make contact.

What was amazing, said Gera, was that the judge was insistent on sticking to the letter of the law and threatening them, whilst being totally blind to the lawless process by which they had been imprisoned in the first place for so many years.

Eventually Irpa Narayan, Lachu and Bhima were acquitted, as is part of the standard story. When it was suggested to them that they could perhaps sue for malicious prosecution, they refused. Forgotten by the prosecution, by the judge, by their own village, they wanted nothing more to do with the state, but to fade into oblivion.

4

Jameen

A common refrain in Soni's conversations is that she never chose to be a human rights defender. The decision was foisted upon her by the state. *'Mein toh pehle ek laalchi jeevan jee rahi thee. Maidan mein utri, kyun ki unhone majboor kar diya'* (I was leading a self-centred life but was compelled to enter the arena).

A school teacher and superintendent of the Jabelli ashram school, Soni found herself caught up in Chhattisgarh's complex politics, police conspiracies and business intrigues, showing how vulnerable Adivasis are in south Chhattisgarh. Her father, a Congressman, was the village sarpanch of Bade Bedma village and had laid great importance on her education, encouraging her to study. In October 2011, when in his seventies, he was attacked by Maoists, reportedly because they suspected him of being an informer. His home was ransacked and he was shot in the leg. But, in a strange twist, Soni began to be targeted by the police as someone who had links with Maoists. In her public statements she charged the police with having made wrongful arrests in connection with the attack on her father. She said the Chhattisgarh government (then under Raman

Singh), inducted Budru, the man who had shot her father, into the police services, hailing him as a 'surrendered Maoist' and rewarding him with a house.

Budru, she alleged, was told to shadow and track her. It is a reflection of the murky politics of Chhattisgarh that a man can be a Maoist and shoot someone, be rewarded and then, as a policeman, harass the man's daughter.[1]

Soni's nephew Linga was also being targeted by the police. An outspoken young man, he had spurned offers in 2009 to join them as a Special Police Officer (SPO) and also refused to help identify Maoist *sangham* members in his native village of Sameli. Detained for forty days until a habeas corpus pleas was filed, he left for Delhi after his release, where he pursued a course in mass media, honing his skills as a fine documenter and videographer, as mentioned earlier in Chapter Two. He also became a vocal critic of the state's policies against Adivasis and spoke against the tribal welfare projects, which inevitably sparked adverse reactions.

In 2010, the Senior Superintendent of Police (SSP), S.R.P. Kalluri, made the startling announcement that Linga was second-in-command in the senior Communist Party of India (Maoist), after the killing of its spokesperson Azad on 2 July. Linga was also named prime suspect behind the attack on the house of Congress worker and civil contractor Avdesh Singh Gautam. Kalluri linked many names, including famed activist of the Narmada Bachao campaign, Medha Patkar, writer Arundhati Roy, journalist Javed Iqbal, professor Nandini Sundar as the brains behind such an attack. A police press release went on to name CPI activist Kartam Joga, Soni and her husband Anil Futane as those behind the attack on Gautam.

The waters were muddied because Gautam, like so many others in Chhattisgarh, derived a major part of his business income through contract work; he built schools and so on and reportedly had a business rivalry with Soni and her husband Futane.

In September of 2011, Linga was arrested on charges of acting as a courier between the Maoists and the Essar company that has many business interests in the state. Essar had built the 267-kilometre-long pipeline carrying iron ore slurry from Kirandul to the port of Visakhapatnam, which had been breached by Maoists in many places.

Soni, who was co-accused in the case, was arrested a month after Linga. In the Dantewada police station, where she was held under police custody, she was stripped, tortured and was subjected to sexual violence with stones being inserted into her vagina, at the behest of police superintendent Ankit Garg, according to her petition. This bold declaration with detailing of torture led to an inquiry initiated by the apex court and the medical examination in Kolkata confirmed the allegation. Eventually given bail, she was acquitted in all eight cases. On 22 March 2022, she was found not guilty in the last case filed by the Dantewda police in 2011. 'Can they give the twelve years back to me?' was her statement to the press. Anil Futane was also arrested on charges of being a Maoist. Acquitted in 2013, he died shortly afterwards, whilst Soni was in jail, of serious neurological complaints, sustained perhaps because of the savage physical assault he underwent in prison.

In her small home in Geedham, Soni recalled her days in jail, not in terms of suffering, as I thought she would, but as spaces of learning. 'The state thought they were imprisoning me but jail became my training ground. I gained valuable lessons; every inmate's story was like the study of a new subject. I realized that the only way to live was for one's people.'

Why did she term her earlier life *lalchi* (greedy)?

'I was self-indulgent. I wanted material comforts, good clothes, a fashionable saree, matching hairpins. I wanted to do up my home. Life revolved around me and my family. I didn't know better...'

Jail brought her, she explained, a much better realization of herself as an Adivasi, a political understanding of her community's suppression and the socio-economic dynamics of the state.

'I knew a little about the Salwa Judum and their fight against Naxalites before going to jail because as a teacher with knowledge of Hindi, I used to be approached when the police picked up civilians. I would intervene with huge trepidation. *Bahut darr tha. Police ko dekhte hi mein bahut darr rahi thi'* (I was very scared. Just seeing the police filled me with huge fear).

Behind bars, she says, she not only lost this fear but realized the real intent behind the confrontation between the Judum and Naxalites. She understood the reasons behind the destruction of the Adivasi way of life, of how rapacious greed for minerals and control over land (*jameen*) is the overriding force that has spelt so much suffering for her people.

'I would brush my teeth in the morning, have a bath and then sit down with my sister inmates for lengthy conversations. That is how I came to understand the pain of my people in Bastar, the creation of the Salwa Judum, the Maoists, the nature of sexual violence used as a weapon against women. The fake encounters, the killings. Had I not been sent to jail I would never have been the kind of person I am today.'

Termed a lone crusader, a *cause célèbre*, Soni shot into the limelight, even in international circles, because of the way she spoke out during her ordeal in prison and after her release. There is criticism that she does not head a movement, that she has not built up an organization and works alone: she says she prefers to be perceived as someone who identifies with her people's suffering. Her ability to articulate these concerns and need for support after incarceration and repeated attacks on her, probably impelled her to join the Aam Aadmi Party (AAP). Although she lost the elections, she continued as a member for some years.

Her decision to leave AAP in 2019, she said, was because Adivasis were increasingly voicing their disenchantment of anyone associated with political parties and rather than be identified as an AAP politician she wanted to be considered a social activist.

Even her critics, political and others, cannot fault her courage and matchless energy. Her phone rings all the time. The demands are many: someone is picked up and the village wants her to locate the person and *thana*; a fake encounter has taken place; savage beatings have occurred and the village would like to record the case even if it means carrying the injured on their backs to Dantewada; people have been granted bail but need sureties. Fielding calls, rushing to affected villages, she is always on the move.

I met her in February 2021, after she was recuperating from a head injury sustained when she fell off a motorcycle; she had also suffered from Covid. Still weak, she was nevertheless back in the thick of action. She showed me a video clipping of a protest in Narayanpur she had attended two days earlier, where song and dance was being used to reinforce the Adivasi battle cries. Some 28,000 people had gathered in January, she told me, to signal their discontent with the lease given to the Jayaswal Neco Company for prospecting in the Amdai Ghati *pahad* (hills), which is sacred to Adivasi beliefs.

'*Jal, jungal, jameen hamara hai...*' (The waterbodies, jungle and the land... belongs to us). Transcending cliches, this Adivasi battle cry makes an assertion for the vibrant, pulsating ecosystem of their communities. In this way of life, the community is vested with stewardship of the water resources, the forest and the land. They own nothing; they hold everything that matters in trust for the future. It is this belief that has shaped the contours of Adivasi culture and now Adivasi resistance.

Drawing from images of the natural world, Soni articulated her own concerns with the paradigms of 'development', modern-day education and the obliteration of Adivasi identity, all of which are interlinked.

What was her vision for her people in this twenty-first century? Harking back to a halcyon childhood, she recalled: 'I walked with my mother till late at night in dense jungles with no fear. We lived in such harmony with all those hundreds and hundreds of trees. Now we live in fear. Everything is at risk—these trees, the waters, our mountains, our stones. Even our *insaniyat* (humanity) is under attack.

'*Shiksha* or education is extremely important but, how does it benefit us when children are taught to embrace alien concepts and models that reject our own knowledge systems and moral values? Adivasi children reside in hostels where discourses revolve around building highways and broad roads to facilitate mining and our displacement. How do Adivasis, as forest-dependent communities, benefit from this model of development? Why do we need such broad roads that spell destruction of our forests?

'Our values and way of life are scorned and demeaned. We are portrayed as people who hunt, as if it is a sin. There is no understanding of why we hunt and how we hunt nor is there any acknowledgement that our vision has an innate respect for all life. Adivasis in the *pahads* (hills) acknowledge the bear has the right to live as much as them, their instincts for survival and loss of fear is developed with the hunts. Present-day schooling is alienating our children from this ecosystem. They no longer want to go into the wilderness.'

She spoke with dismay of children returning home without acquiring the basic skills of agriculture, of how to plough fields, collect firewood. 'I went to school (an ashram school known as Rukmini Adivasi Kanya) but, in our days, we learnt all that. I see educated youths playing with cell phones and lolling around at home while their aged parents work. They tell me that they are studying and don't need to know how to sow seeds or plough and will instead do *naukri* (get a job). As what? As a *chaprassi* (a peon), is the answer.'

Poyam too has voiced the disenchantment and dispossession of his generation, of the manner in which they have lost control over what was once their land. His grandmother's village like so many others was acquired for coal mines without due process and by holding fraudulent Gram Sabhas. The settlers' children get the education, jobs, control of land; Adivasis are left with meagre compensation. They work on their own ancestral lands as labourers or servants, he says.

He narrated the story of his relative, a hard-working youth who cleared the entrance exams for an engineering college but then could not study further. He used to hold coaching classes until, one day, he was arrested by the police for carrying a bag of coal that he had procured from the open-cast mine on land that once belonged to his community.

The tale reminded me of my 2010 visit when villagers of Samalwar spoke about three men imprisoned as dangerous Naxalites for prowling around Kirandul. In truth they were scavenging for bits of metal scrap because of their abject condition.

Also disturbing for many Adivasis, is the obliteration of their culture through appropriation and imposition of culture.

'Children are told to celebrate Diwali, Holi, pay obeisance to Sita Mata, contribute towards a Ram Mandir and made to forget their own gods and goddesses. Even our politics is now subsumed into the Hindutva agenda,' said Soni.

Soni was alluding perhaps to the manner in which the Hindutva ideology has permeated to such an extent that even the Congress-led government of Chhattisgarh has drawn up a Ram Van Gaman project with the construction of some fifty-one temples along the sites of the Hindu deity Ram's path as depicted in the Ramayana. Hundreds of Adivasis and in particular the Gondwana Ganatantra Party, under the late tribal leader Hira Singh Markam's aegis, staged a protest against the move. They blocked the highway on 17 December 2020 saying these projects lay in the vicinity of Adivasi areas and their sacred hills. Adivasi organizations argued that implanting the project through government machinery would violate the secular principles of the Constitution.

Adivasis had accordingly given representation to the Governor and President that the Fifth Schedule of the Constitution, which deals with the administration and control of Scheduled Areas as well as Scheduled Tribes, is governed by its own customary laws and that they have their own distinct cultural identity.

The late Hira Singh Markam, the prominent political voice of the 12-million-strong Gond or Koitur community, the second largest Scheduled Tribe in the country, who headed the movement for the formation of Gondwana, believed tribals were entitled to 50 per cent share in proceeds from mining. He would often point to the findings of the Dileep Singh Bhuria Commission tasked with looking into problems of Adivasis.

In a 2014 interview with Poyam, Hira commented, 'Tribals are being ousted, at best, with the market price of land and at worst, through violence, and ownership rights on minerals in their lands remain a distant dream.[2]

The resistance revolving around 'Jameen' is a layered one—on one level there is the struggle against displacement and destruction of the environment brought about by mining; on another level it is for an assertion of distinctive Adivasi identity, their concept of village development, our *pehchaan* as Soni put it.

In 2019 a bid by Gautam Adani and the National Mineral Development Corporation to begin mining in the Bailadila range saw Adivasis gathering in huge numbers, protesting against the defilement of their rivers and degradation of jungles. Like the Dongria Kondhs of the iconic Niyamgiri struggle in Odisha, they also invoked the question of their beliefs and faith. The Nandraj hill, they said, was sacred to them because their deity resided there. The Baghel-led Congress government was forced to halt mining works and utter words of appeasement.[3]

Typically the story did not end there. Markam Hidme, a woman activist who spearheaded the protests, was literally dragged away by police on International Women's Day on 8 March 2021 and charged as Maoist. Cases under UAPA have been slapped against her.[4]

Legendary Battle Against Bauxite India

> *'His spirit was quite broken. Why does coal or mica appear if he breaks ground?...'*
>
> —*Chhoti Munda and His Arrow*, Mahasweta Devi, translated by Gayatri Chakravorty Spivak

Tribal resistance has a long history and Central India has seen many uprisings, many of which centred around control and access to the land and its resources. One of the people's movements that sprang up in Madhya Pradesh in the 1990s was the Ekta Parishad which demands that local communities get ownership and control over natural resources. The Parishad sought livelihood rights for forest dwellers and assertion of their rights against exploitative systems. It encourages participation by the women and tribal leaders and puts emphasis on struggles for land, helping landless peasants and Adivasis to get titles or *pattas*.

One of the amazing women activists of the Parishad is Indu Netam of the Gond tribe who led a remarkable struggle as a young woman against mining in her native village of Merkatola (now in Kanker, Chhattisgarh) in the early 1990s.

Meeting her at her home in Korer, a village near Kanker, she spoke of the legendary battle against Bauxite India that had used fraudulent means to acquire land which they claimed was for plantation projects.

'It began in 1989 when we found trees being felled in the *nistaar* forest of our village (*nistaar* land allows concessions for villagers to collect forest produce for their domestic use only). We were told the land had been given to the landless. Then we came upon people boring holes and these were for prospecting for sillimanite, one of the best raw materials used in high alumina refractories.'

Inquiries revealed that the *pattas* had been illegally transferred to the names of non-tribals and they had in turn sold the land to Bauxite India which had obtained the licence for prospecting. Netam began organizing the villagers and filing complaints, protesting that decisions on mining had been undertaken without consent of the Gram Sabhas and that the land acquisition was fraudulent. Bauxite India responded by secretly buying over many of the villagers. The movement was split and the Jal, Jungal, Jameen Morcha was formed to begin several morchas.

One day, Netam confronted the forest minister at a public meeting and bombarded him with the facts, raising questions. The police swung into action, rounding up all the activists present and taking them away in their vehicles.

'I saw the police jeeps. In my anger and zeal, I leapt onto the footboard to try and stop them. The vehicle drove on and on, with me clinging for dear life, for quite a distance.'

Netam too was jailed along with others. But, fortunately, an official inquiry was launched and eventually not only were the activists released but fifty-nine people who had been involved in the fraud were jailed.

A significant peoples' victory, but as Netam told us, one that came at a bitter cost. The community had been split and in the intervening years till action was taken against the company, the villagers were routinely harassed. The corporate world has continued in such divisive tactics to displace the Adivasis and the wars have only intensified.

Since those youthful years, Netam has grown in strength, continuing to lead many other struggles against displacement. She is the convenor of the Adivasi Jan Van Adhikar Manch which is a network of Adivasis working on issues of forest rights and who insist that the local community has to be a stakeholder in mining projects and other developmental works.

A keen proponent of Adivasi *asmita* (pride), she fights for her community's self-esteem, for recognition of its indigenous knowledge of health, dietary habits and so on.

The Railway Line of Displacement

A railway line project is currently underway to link Rowghat, containing some of the state's largest iron ore deposits of the Matla reserve forests in Antagarh district of Chhattisgarh, with Dalli-Rajhara, where the Bhilai Steel Plant (BSP) manages its manual ore mines. Much of the ore is depleted at Dalli-Rajhara and the BSP is dependent on the Rowghat mines for continuing operations.

The railway project with multiple townships, envisaged across the Rowghat range spanning the districts of Kanker and Narayanpur, adjoining the Abujhmadh range, will impact community lives in at least forty villages. Moreover, as this region falls under the category of the Left-wing Extremism Division, as categorized by the Ministry of Home Affairs, the work on the railway line is preceded by the setting up of a vast number of security camps to house the CRPF and the Sashastra Seema Bal (SSB). Such construction also spells displacement. Significantly, these security camps are funded by the Steel Authority of India (SAIL), the country's largest steelmaker and is the first such instance of a corporate entity funding state militia to provide protection for the development of its mine.[5]

It raises concerns and is a telling comment when the safety of iron ore is seen to be more important than the safety of the people of the area. The acquisition of lands and sanction for mining on them and the heavily militarized milieu that will follow are sure to have a profound effect on the lives of its inhabitants. All this has raised many crucial questions. Whose land is it anyway? Who has the right to exploit the land's mineral resources? Do the legitimate concerns of the Adivasi matter to the state? What are the processes by which such land may be acquired? Why was due process not followed?

The story of this railway line began with the Centre seeking land to build an Indian Institute of Technology and approaching the BSP for some of its surplus land. A deal was then struck whereby, on exchange for 130.23 hectares in Bhilai, the Chhattisgarh government would give land in and around the Rowghat region to the BSP which was given a lease for its mining operations in Rowghat in 2009.

That very decision of *adla badli* or form of land transfer is problematic, say activists, because it raises the question of how and why the BSP, a government-owned sector, had surplus land in Bhilai in the first place, public land that had not been bought like a corporation would have had to do.

The practice of *adla badli* has been limited in Chhattisgarh thus far to agricultural land within the same or adjoining villages to allow agriculturalists to exchange their land in order to consolidate holdings and not have them fragmented into several places.

This *adla badli* deal thus raises questions on the manner in which industrial land in Bhilai is being equated with lands given by the Collectors in Narayanpur and Kanker, to the BSP in exchange. These are areas that fall under the Scheduled Areas Act. Under the Act, there are several constitutional and legal safeguards to protect the land rights of the Scheduled Tribes and to address issues of land displacement. Gram Sabhas have the power to take decisions to regulate access to community forest rights and stop activities which affect biodiversity, forests and wildlife. The transfer thus goes against the very spirit of the Act.

With little transparency about the acquisitions and the manner in which they were undertaken, many pieces of land have already been transferred by the Collectors to the BSP, especially in Antagarh district.

Some twenty-eight farmers of Kalgaon who decided to put up a challenge collectively against the acquisition of village commons where they had worked since 1980, faced huge difficulties.

Their experiences indicate the alacrity with which all processes were bypassed and Gram Sabhas manipulated. It also displays the way in which bureaucracy stonewalls and thwarts the peoples' efforts to access their *pattas* or titles.

Hriday Ram, one of the petitioners, who has a bundle of papers and records of Gram Sabha resolutions from 1998 stating there are no objections to him getting the *pattas*, has sent applications to the Collector, to the Patwari, the Sub-divisional Officer (SDO) and even the Chief Minister, but received only a deafening silence.

The first inkling of the BSP acquisition came on 2 October 2015 when the SDO brought in security personnel from the camp and told the villagers he needed their assent for the transaction and took some signatures under coercion. Three days later, a complaint was made to the Collector by some villagers that they were not in agreement to lands being taken away.

On 8 October at a larger meeting, 280 villagers told the Collector yet again that they did not want to give their assent. Almost ten months later in August 2017, there was a formal announcement of certain *khasras* (plot numbers) being acquired by the BSP and once again letters were sent to the various officials, to the Collector, the Patwari and the Tehsildar, but no answers were forthcoming.

A Right to Information (RTI) application unravelled the truth. Despite the villagers' objections, the process of acquisition had been proceeding. The village, a large one, had been divided into opposing groups and one group had written in saying they were in favour of the acquisition.

The law mandates that all objections to acquisitions must be heard but the Tehsildar contrived to have a Gram Sabha meeting meant for this purpose, without the knowledge of the dissenting villagers. This was despite the fact that the nays had been categorically put on record multiple times in writing.

Interestingly too, records of this Gram Sabha proceeding on 3 April 2017 signed by the Collector made no mention of the particular *khasras* or plots to be acquired. Instead, villagers were promised a hospital and a school and other entitlements. Some seventy signatures were taken but it was by no means a quorum.

The particular *khasras* that are to be transferred are detailed only in a small note at the end of the records but, significantly, the copy that the villagers received did not contain this crucial information.

The RTI applications also revealed how way back in 2015, lands had already been given to the BSP and the announcement of a meeting to consider objections was just a pretence.

There was another issue, that of whether the lands could be categorised as forest land. According to the Forest Rights Act, just one document giving such evidence is sufficient. The villagers who had given such evidence in 2016, did not hear anything. It was only after the JCBs (excavators) had moved in and prefabricated huts constructed that the court hearings began. Instead of moving with urgency since it was a matter of dispossession of tribals from below poverty line, the matter was moved to a date more than two months later.

Everyone in India knows it is a *fait accompli* once construction begins. No court is going to stop a project, especially one with as high stakes as this one. Land acquisition simply bulldozes all opposition.

The ready compliance of the court to see things only through the perspective of the state's definition of development and the overarching prism of 'national security' has meant that Adivasis get short shrift. Even their environmental rights are dismissed, as one recent judgement revealed.

Mohan Singh Darro and some other villagers raised the question of the environmental clearance given to the BSP, enabling the ore to be dispatched to Keonti by road transport as part of 'interim mining'.

The earlier environmental clearance was given for the excavated iron ore to be dispatched through conveyors and loaded at the Rowghat railway siding but, since the project is yet to be completed, an amendment was sought.

This amendment was not made known to the public and it was only much later that the court was petitioned on the grounds that heavy vehicles carrying ore on the roads would create dust and damage crops as well as pose health hazards.

The petition was dismissed but what was significant was the verdict: 'The submission of the petitioners could have been appreciated when such condition of violence do not exist and the laws of the land can take effect in normal conditions. If the unnatural events of the Naxal movements intervene to resist the laying down of railway line, then the circumstances also warrant the special measures to be taken in the interest of the country.'(sic)

Further down the order notes: 'It appears road to prosperity to all is strewn with sharper thorn.' (sic)

The question is, sharper thorns for whom?

Part Two

WOUNDED VALLEY

Stories from Kashmir

Photo credit: Adil Abbas

5

Siege

'We prepared our ears for both screams and silences.'

—Malik Sajad, artist

On the night of 4 August 2019, Meenu Patigaru, an entrepreneur and owner of Anantnag's first boutique, peered out of her window. A strange scene was unfolding. Two people on the road, presumably on their way to hospital since no one else would be about at that hour, suddenly took cover and hid. Then a whole convoy of vehicles went by, but at very slow speed, almost as if it was to be a hushed exercise.

'What is happening? Is there going to be a war at the borders?' she wondered. Meenu, as a young woman growing up in the 1990s, the decade of armed conflict, was no stranger to turbulence and violence. Gunfights between militants and Indian armed forces had raged around her neighbourhood.

Equally disturbing was the splintering of Kashmiri society and the fear induced by the Ikhwanis or renegade militants, who had begun taking control of the town in the latter half of the

1990s. Also known as *sarkari* (government) militants, Ikhwanis were nursed by the state to outsource killings and to terrorize the dissenting citizens. One morning, as Meenu opened her boutique in 1995, a man warned her that a decree was going to be issued ordering her to shut it down. 'None of the militant groups had issued any such threats before. I learnt it emanated from Seth Gujjar, one of the Ikhwanis,' she recounted.

Meenu was then only in her mid-twenties. But she decided to confront the Ikhwanis and went into their camp at Janglat Mandi, a neighbourhood in her town.

'I was told Gujjar was not present but that I should meet with Liyaqat Ali.' A former militant, Liyaqat switched allegiances to become commander of the Ikhwan-ul-Muslimeen, the chief Ikhwani militia that provided support to the Indian armed forces.

Meenu recalls, 'There were a number of people waiting and I saw a man being slapped repeatedly. I introduced myself to Liyaqat who said he recognized me since he was my senior in school. When Gujjar arrived, he reprimanded him and then said I had nothing more to fear.'

But, after a few days, Liyaqat himself started phoning her and making sexual advances, even telling her, '*Tum aa jao, meri bibi ghar mein nahi hai*' (Come over my wife is not at home). 'I was very scared but I swore and screamed at him. He threatened me, saying he would come over with a gun. For more than a month I didn't dare to go to the boutique.'

Liyaqat, for some reason, did not go further than his threats but Meenu's uncle was not so fortunate. An Ikhwani named Taheer 'Phuffu', a nickname given because he stuttered, shot him dead because he refused to hand over his newly bought van.

Having witnessed such horrendous violence, Meenu was conditioned to various levels of unsettledness and vulnerability, over the decades. But in August 2019, Kashmir was gripped with an eerie air of uncertainty, she said.

The week had been very strange. Additional troops, estimated at over 28,000 personnel had been rushed in to the already heavily militarized Valley.[1]

Next, the federal government ordered all Amarnath *yatris* or pilgrims, tourists, foreigners and migrant labourers to leave the state; resident non-local students of the National Institute of Technology, Srinagar, were taken out by bus late one night. A guest house owner told me how he received police orders around midnight insisting he tell all guests to leave. Jittery residents of Kashmir had begun stockpiling rations and there were long lines for refuelling vehicles at petrol pumps.

Falsehood was officially floated with the Security Advisory issued on 2 August stating that the government of Jammu and Kashmir (J&K) had received intelligence inputs of terror threats with specific targeting of the Amarnath Yatra.[2]

I had texted Meenu on the afternoon of 4 August to put her in contact with an Indian anthropologist who had come in from the USA. She texted back: '*Filhaal afwaah garam hai ki aaj raat ko curfew lagega*' (Rumours are rife that there will be curfew tonight).

That was the last I heard from her till we met in person two and a half months later and she was able to tell me more about the strange convoy of stealth and the silence that was imposed for months.

'My elderly mother and I were completely alone. My brother was in Delhi. I got a hurried call from my sister. She had heard there might be mass arrests and she and her husband were wondering what to do. We went to bed amidst the tension and remained in suspense until the next day, when we heard on television that Amit Shah [Home Minister of India] was going to make a big announcement.'

On 5 August, on the floors of Parliament, Shah announced

the abrogation of Article 370 through a Presidential order and the break-up of J&K into two Union Territories. More than 70 lakh Kashmiris were left in a state of complete shock.

There have been attempts to explain the abrogation of Article 370 as a measure to do away with Kashmir's special status and bridge the unnecessary chasm between Kashmiris and the rest of India. 'One nation, one Constitution,' was how Prime Minister Narendra Modi put it.

The reality, as A.G. Noorani, an advocate and constitutional expert observed, was far more complex. 'Vile passions,' he wrote, 'have triumphed over elementary concern with the law. The Presidential order is patently unconstitutional.'[3]

Article 370, which recognized the special status of J&K and gave it some degree of autonomy, was not a mere provision enacted by the Constituent Assembly of India. There was a reason behind this special status conferred outside the Constitution of India. It followed from the historic event of the signing of the Instrument of Accession in October 1947. The enactment of Article 370 was a solemn pact that came about after protracted negotiations for over five months in 1947, between the Government of India and the government of J&K. Some of the special provisions conferred were that it exempted J&K from certain provisions of the Constitution of India. J&K would have its own Constitution and the Indian Parliament's legislative powers were restricted to subjects of defence, foreign affairs and communications. If other powers were to be extended to the Indian government, prior consent of the state government was required.

These special provisions provided the legal basis for Article 35A which protected the right to property of the people of J&K. Non-permanent citizens of the state were not allowed to own property or be appointed in government services. Over the years, a number of executive Presidential orders had hollowed out much of Article 370. But even so, scrapping or even changing the law through a presidential order, he argues is patently unconstitutional. For any changes to Article 370 the Indian Parliament needs the consent of the state legislature. In a crafty move the Central Government had earlier suspended the state assembly and imposed President's rule. Amit Shah claimed in Parliament that concurrence with the Centre was therefore given by the Governor. However Noorani states categorically that the Centre's appointee cannot give concurrence to the Centre and also has no power to amend the constitution to make Jammu and Kashmir a Union Territory.

With its people robbed of statehood and the reorganization into two Union Territories, Jammu & Kashmir now comes under direct rule from New Delhi. Another devastating repercussion for Kashmiris that has to do with scrapping of Article 35A is the creation of a series of categorizations through which Indians—who had previously been debarred from owning land or access to government jobs—would now be able to claim residency rights in what is still 'disputed territory'. Furthermore it affects the status of Kashmiris who had fled during the years of armed struggle and gone abroad but still had the right to claim residency under the Kashmir Permanent Residency Act. Kashmiris are alarmed with these moves that they see as attempts to alter the demographics of a Muslim-majority disputed region.

Rumours of Article 370 being scrapped had been in the air, along with the revocation of Article 35A but few thought it would be carried out in such secrecy and with the extent of repressive measures that kept Kashmir under massive siege. They included huge restrictions on movement with road blocks and concertina wire barricades, imposition of curfew, the shutdown of the internet, mobile services and landline phones and the massive arrests which included even the leaders of J&K's major political parties.

'We learnt of the scrapping of Article 370 at 11 a.m. My *maamu* (uncle) was literally robbed of speech for a full hour. He could say nothing,' said noted lawyer from Shopian, Habeel Iqbal, with the gallows humour that comes so readily to Kashmiris.

Meenu says her first reaction too was one of complete dark amusement at the fate of those who used to wave the tricolour. '*Mujhe hassi aii ki jinhone sub seh jyada India ka saath diya thah unhi ko arrest kiya ja rah tha*' (I found it amusing that those who had supported India so strongly were the very ones who were picked up).

The absurdist theatre of arresting mainstream politicians, who had continued to believe in the democracy of India, participated in elections and were constitutional representatives of their people, was reiterated by the guest house owner in Srinagar, who told me with mock irony that the Indian State had scripted a brilliant Sufi fable. 'Who would believe it? Mehbooba in jail? And the Abdullahs locked away too. All the politicians in jail. The businessmen in jail and maulvis in jail. The students in jail. The lawyers in jail. The pro-Indian and anti-Indian both in jail! Such equality. Jail for all.'

For H (name withheld), a young student, news of the fate of her homeland came in a dramatic and agonizing manner. She posted on social media: 'Yesterday at the Srinagar airport, a few of us stood huddled around the only working TV near one of the boarding gates that was showing the news. I, a Kashmiri, who had spent the past week panicking, partly paralyzed with fear and uncertainty, not knowing what imminent doom lay in store, scrambled across the waiting area to seek a spot within earshot of the TV. I couldn't see what was going on, but I could hear the address. I knew at that moment that I was going from "not knowing" to "knowing", all the while debating with myself whether I even wanted to know what horror would befall us now, a people who had already been subjected to so many shades of horror before.

'So there I was, listening to the news at a nearby spot as if eavesdropping on the future of my own home and my people—because that's what you do when you live under siege, holed up inside your houses without any communication to the outside world, imagining the worst in your head as the streets that run near your locale like veins inside a human, are populated by armed men who share neither your history nor language.

'And there I was, suddenly hit with all the weight that comes with knowing the sinister designs that will shape the future of Kashmir. But there I also was, knowing my family and my relatives and neighbours and my people were trapped in their home, tense and confused, some probably ill and unable to get to the hospital, curfewed in and worse, still not knowing what had just happened.

'Today, a few days later, there has still been no news from Kashmir, all channels of communication have been cut. And now the curse of not knowing what is happening falls upon us: those outside.'

The curse of not knowing. Or then knowing and not being able to communicate it. For journalists inside Kashmir, who were living the siege, the complete telecommunication shutdown with snapping of internet services, mobiles and even landlines and the physical restrictions on movement made not just reporting impossible, but all aspects of journalism, including the important verification and triangulation with authorities. It was a frustrating and hapless experience.

Quratulain Rehbar, a young independent journalist from the volatile town of Pulwama, living in a hostel in Srinagar, had warned her mother that the phone services might be snapped and she should not worry. 'I had elected to stay on despite the worsening *haalat* (situation) because I wanted to carry on working. On 5 August, despite the warnings of curfew by aunty (the woman in charge in the hostel), I decided to walk to the offices of *The Kashmir Walla* where I once worked. Armed with nothing but my press card I went down streets. Troops were everywhere with their guns.

'Even though we had no access to television we came to learn of the scrapping of 370 and the decimation of the state. Some of us cried in collective grief. I read out Agha Shahid Ali's poems.'

The poet, who died in 2001, is still an iconic figure with Kashmir's youth. His poem 'Postcard from Kashmir' resonates with the pain of losing one's homeland and identity.

> Kashmir shrinks into my mailbox,
> my home a neat four by six inches.
> I always loved neatness. Now I hold
> the half-inch Himalayas in my hand.
> This is home. And this is the closest
> I'll ever be to home...

For Rehbar the personal and political, as with most Kashmiris, intertwined. She worried about her homeland and then her family; in particular about her brother, principal of a school in Shopian, who was routinely harassed by security forces and with whom there was no way of establishing contact.

'We journalists set up a routine over the next few days, that of meeting up to have tea, to stay in touch and also to exchange news.'

A week later, the government set up a media facilitation centre at a hotel. It was later shifted to a single room in the Department of Information and Public Relations in Srinagar. The internet and mobile connections had been suspended, but the Net and computers were made available for a limited time to journalists. Waiting their turn, they scurried to send off emails or then even to make up pages to be uploaded for the news portals. Having to report from government-controlled spaces with limited timings and regulations made a mockery of the concept of journalism. But, despite the restraints, Kashmir's intrepid journalists started assembling facts and documenting, almost out of sheer habit. Sanna Irshad Mattoo, a young Kashmiri photojournalist, said she set out with her video camera from day one, without concerns of when the recording would be used. It was all about bearing witness.

With her experience of conflict reporting, Rehbar made a beeline to the Shri Maharaja Hari Singh (SMHS) Hospital where she spent three days. She had to negotiate a passage through the barricade of razor wires past Baba Demb, the small freshwater lake or lagoon, and Fatah Kadal, one of the seven legendary wooden bridges of Srinagar. They had not spared even the access roads to the hospital.

The ubiquitous concertina wires, so much a part of Srinagar's cityscape, had been rolled out to enclose almost every road, *kadal* (bridge) and even monuments. The famed Ghanta Ghar in Srinagar's Lal Chowk, named after Moscow's Red Square because of Sheikh Abdullah's Marxist leanings, was swathed in concertina wire all the way to the top. It became truly symbolic of the times and a widely used meme.

Inside the SMHS premises, Rehbar found desperate relatives of patients fretting because they had no transport or even money to go back home. A collection was made to take the body of a dead woman to her own district in a private ambulance. Patients were also being brought in with pellet injuries—the tell-tale injuries testimony to the manner in which security forces routinely deal with civilians, who may be on the streets.[4]

At the sprawling Lal Ded Hospital, many doctors could not come in for the first few days because of the curfew. The challenge of contacting them and sending them to various wings and faculties, in the absence of telecommunications, was achieved by setting up a loudspeaker on top of the building.

Present on the morning of 5 August at Lal Ded was Nisar Dharma, a journalist. He was there to admit his wife for her scheduled Caesarian operation when he heard the words *moklovukh* (done away with). His essay for a memory project brilliantly captures the cadences of birth and new life, amidst turbulence, uncertainty and endings.

He writes how standing in a queue for the paperwork, a man approached, saying something in gibberish. 'I can only understand the words "moklovukh" (done away with)...Article 370 has been abrogated. He finally makes sense.'

But even then Dharma clings to disbelief. 'You must have got it wrong.'

The words are repeated as he waited outside the 'clamour' of the labour room along with two Gujjar shepherds in their khan suits, and the omnipresent smell of phenol and blood. His daughter, Nowsheen, is born later that day and Dharma records the entry. 'I recite the Azaan in her ears, thinking about the land and the times she is born in.'[5]

Medical anthropologist Saiba Varma, who was in Srinagar during the clampdown, described how concertina wire had been used to divide the city into manageable martial units, preventing the movement of people, goods and information. Innumerable checkpoints were manned by officers with whistles and guns to 'guide you back from where you came.' Varma described the siege as an 'infrastructural war', quoting Stephen Graham, the geographer.[6]

Graham, whose book *Disrupted Cities* analysed the collapse

of New Orleans during Hurricane Katrina, examines the intersectionality of technology, security and urban life. He notes how we take so much of today's infrastructure for granted until it is disrupted. Circuits of communication can be attacked by terrorists or then exploited for political ends such as the deliberate devastation of the urban structure by the Israeli military in the Gaza sieges.

Varma, who had experienced the turmoil of 2010, said that this time the complete clampdown and suddenness was an exercise, in 'breaking Kashmiris' spirit, by not allowing them to share even the most basic levels of information such as news of illness, or of a death.'[7]

Innumerable stories have been gathered and shared about how a myriad of disruptions of infrastructural flows caused immense suffering to the Kashmiri people and how they severely impacted basic human rights. People were unable to contact loved ones or friends and express concern or worries about their safety and well-being, people were unable to seek medical help, to call for ambulances, women on the verge of delivery had to walk miles, doctors could not get to patients in time, nor were people able to access medical expertise, people were unable to earn or manage a business, children were deprived of the right to education and to play. Not a single aspect of life remained unaffected.

In his beautiful village near the Manasbal Lake, M (name withheld) recollects the uncanny quiet which prevailed with the cessation of daily human activity in the fields and the market corners, as troops patrolled every *galli* (alley). The maulvi was warned not to give any sermons, no *tarana* (political sermon) was allowed in the masjids. Holed up largely indoors, children had to be appeased with a steady diet of television. 'Turkish serials became our favourite viewing but after a few weeks the subscription for Tata Sky ran out and there was no way of renewing it.' *Ertugrul,* based on the rise of the Ottoman empire and described as the Muslim version of *Game of Thrones,* became a favourite in many households of Kashmir.

Inured to interminable days of shutdown, Kashmiris have learnt to store up rice and other essentials by sheer dint of habit. The tradition of women having kitchen gardens or vegetable plots (*wairds*), especially in the rural areas, ensures a small supply of vegetables throughout most of the year. But the severity and extent of this lockdown and patrolling of soldiers made it risky for the women to even come out of homes and walk the short distance to the *wairds.*

A woman living in Srinagar, without access to kitchen gardens, said, 'I lived on rice and chillies and rice with turmeric for oh, so many weeks. The best gift I received was when an associate finally came to Srinagar after a month, bringing with him a few pumpkins and gourds from his fields.'

Venturing to seek medical attention or procure necessities, meant an often humiliating encounter with security personnel at the checkpoints that were set up. Journalist and writer Farah Bashir spoke of her elderly father's plight in Srinagar on social media. He had hurt his hand and needed medical attention immediately but was stopped at three checkpoints on his way to the pharmacy, situated just a kilometre away and lost a lot of blood. She posted later: 'Anyone's a threat. My father is seventy-six…'

Meenu recalled how pharmacies and chemists used to be allowed to function during curfews but this time the sheer bloody-mindedness of the security personnel was noteworthy.

'I received a request from a young man, who desperately needed his medication for his psychiatric problem. He had been stopped a number of times on the street but eventually was allowed to proceed. I walked from the house to our family-owned pharma, which is just a short distance away but a *fauji* (security personnel) stopped me as I bent down to lift the shutters of the pharmacy saying, '*Dawai nahi milega*' (Medicine will not be made available).

'I told him I needed to dispense a certain medication and the pharmacy belonged to our family, whereupon he actually said '*Ab meri ho gayee*' (But now it's mine), waving his gun.

'A Kashmiri policeman stepped in and asked me to go and get a curfew pass but that was when it hit me, this declaration that everything in Kashmir was now theirs because they had the brute power. Since then we hear it routinely but that was my first rude shock.'

Shrieks in the Dark: Return of Night Raids

On the night between 10 and 11 August, about a week after the siege began, shrieks pierced the silent darkness of Heff Shirmal, a village in Kashmir's Shopian district. The screams, according to villagers, came from the Chillipora Rashtriya Rifles camp, where youths had been detained. A loudspeaker placed in the room ensured that the shrieks of tortured persons would serve as a warning message to the surrounding villages.[8]

In the 1990s, the Indian State had responded to the Kashmiri armed struggle with a no-holds-barred policy. Collective punishment and torture of civilians was a crucial component of the army's counter-insurgency operations as human rights organizations recorded.[9]

This phenomenon made a comeback in the first few weeks of August 2019. Operations were carried out against the citizens; night raids, mass arrests and torture were redeployed on a large scale, as part of the state's strategy to pre-empt any protests against the abrogation.

Despite the tightly controlled spaces, news of terror tactics filtered out and intrepid journalists managed to break the news to foreign publications. Pen drives carrying the images, videos and written copy were smuggled out and by September, the cries of the Valley were being heard around the world. The BBC, *Washington Post, New York Times, Al Jazeera, TNT* and others reported on the beatings, use of electric shocks, illegal detentions in army camps or police stations. The Indian army spokesperson dismissed the allegations as 'completely baseless and false,' and asserted that the Indian army values human rights but the foreign media refused to retract and said it had evidence in the form of visuals of injuries and medical records.[10]

In October, I personally visited certain districts and met with people, who narrated how *khauf* (terror) had been unleashed. During the night raids, troops stormed and vandalized homes and took away the men.

In a village in Kulgam district, we met with a man who had been illegally detained for fifteen days. He was distraught because he was released on condition that he turn in his eighteen-year-old son.

The son, he said, was on his way to buy medicines when he and a group of others saw a Rakshak, the specially designed bullet-proof vehicle used by troops. In the confusion of getting away, he dropped his phone.

Confiscating mobile phones is a well-known tool of intimidation and surveillance in Kashmir. They are checked for images and may be confiscated. The owners are told to collect them from a police station or an army camp where interrogations may take place, even though the 'crime', it would appear, is the mere possession of one.

Rehbar told me how the security personnel patrolling the streets had once pounced on her brother and insisted on examining his phone, presumably because he sports a beard. The wallpaper showed him speaking in front of a microphone but the soldier argued it could be the barrel of a gun and kept haranguing him, 'Tell me where you keep this gun.'

The Kulgam boy's father, who was narrating the story of a dropped phone, said he sought the neighbours' help to accompany him to the police station and report the incident that very night. But the neighbours were too scared and the Numbardar (powerful official in the village who used to collect revenue and liaise with police) said it was late and they would do so the next day.

At midnight the Special Task Force (counter-insurgency wing of the J&K police force) and the army arrived at his house with the cell phone and demanded to know the whereabouts of the boy. They then proceeded to vandalize the house, breaking every windowpane and wrecking the refrigerator. The father was a taxi driver; they damaged his vehicle, a Sumo.

He was hauled away first to the Khadwani camp and then the Wanpoh police station, where for fifteen days he was illegally detained. During this time, he was told that if the family would persuade his son to report to the station, his house might be spared the bulldozer.

'My son was terrified. I was in such *zehni* (mental) torture, far worse than any physical pain, but what else could I do. *Hum sub mar jayenge* (We will all be finished), I told him.'

When we met him, his son had already spent three days in the police station and the family was hoping he would be released as assured by the authorities. With no FIR or paperwork, there was no point in approaching a lawyer, they said.

A small grandson sat near his feet, playing sometimes and then breaking off, to gaze at us. This boy had been a witness to the vandalization, had been affected by the teargas shelling that preceded it, had seen his grandfather being hauled away and now knew his uncle was in the police station. How do such traumatic experiences translate for 'children without childhood', to borrow Palestinian poet Mahmoud Darwish's phrase?

Whilst leaving the house, we saw a number painted on the wall. All the other houses in the hamlet also bore numbers. This, I learnt, was the village profiling, unofficially undertaken by the army from 2017 onwards.[11]

People told us the Rashtriya Rifles (the counter-insurgency unit of the Indian army) had done extensive surveys and a census that noted the number of youths in a household, where they studied, who visited, the layout of the house and surroundings and many other private details. The house was then allotted a number which was painted on the wall. A warning was given not to deface or paint over the number. Such detailed information was a ready reckoner for the million-strong troop deployment to carry out night raids systematically and for the mass incarceration of hundreds of youths.

Listening to the accounts of the night raids, it became clear how several forms of terrorizing and rights abuses were taking place. When we entered the home of a family of labourers in Turkawangam of Shopian district, the first person I observed was an elderly woman, painfully hobbling around in a tattered *pheran*. Her husband, Azir, told us she was not in good mental health and was still recovering from the shock of being pulled out of her room where she was fast asleep, a week after Eid was celebrated. She was dragged out, he said, with scant regard of her dignity, by troops from the Special Operations Group (another name for the Special Task Force) and army personnel from the Rashtriya Rifles Chillipora Camp, when she was not wearing a salwar, or a covering over her head.

Earlier in the day, some militants had fired upon the army

personnel and this night raid, along with that on several other houses, was clearly part of the collective punishment.

The targets were the two minor grandsons. Their father, Sameer, was used as a human shield as the troops searched the house to ferret them out. The crime of using civilian people as 'human shields' shot into the limelight when Farooq Ahmed Dar was tied to the bonnet of a vehicle by Major Gogoi. Kashmiris, however, point out this was standard practice since the 1990s. It is common for the security forces to coerce a civilian, very often children, to be part of the cordon-and-search operations (CASO) and to lead the way into rooms or a street cordoned off.

CASOs, which began in the 1990s, enabled by the Disturbed Areas Act, entail the cordoning of villages or a neighbourhood whilst house-to-house searches are carried out.

The terrified grandsons had tried to escape, one of them climbing up a tree, the other seeking shelter in a neighbour's house. Both were caught and held at the Zainapora police station. No charges had been filed against them till the date of our visit, presumably because they are minors.

The grandfather said his grandsons used to help augment the family's income during the apple-picking season and the arrest had worsened their economic plight. The two boys too were in mental agony and often asked about their grandmother, who was still in a dazed condition.

Also arrested on the same night in the district were three others from Ganawapora village. I met with some of the families. Two of them lived amidst Shopian's famed apple orchards, quite a distance away from the main town and relatively isolated.

In one home, amidst the hiss of a pressure cooker in the kitchen, the sister-in-law of tractor driver Aijaz told us that a cordon was laid down after the incident in which the militants opened fire, whilst he was still working in the fields. He was questioned by the army and asked to provide personal details but was not detained. Later that night when the war on the people was waged, he was whisked off to the Chillipora camp along with the two minors and another man.

The anxious family was told he was being held to facilitate the door-to-door searches, a brazen admission that the civilian population is used as human shields. The family hoped he would be released soon, instead he was handed over to the Zainapora police station. It was difficult to visit him, said the relative, because it is at a considerable distance away and no buses were plying because of the civilian strike or *hartal* that prevailed for months after the siege, as a mark of protest by the people.

In the third home, the sister of Nasir told us that when the night raid took place he was at his *nanihal* (mother's parental home). The troops beat up his father and demanded he escort them there. Nasir had chosen to spend the night away from home after he had seen the cordon being placed. The sister added that the DSP was insisting on a community bond from the villagers before Nasir's release. Increasingly deployed during the siege, people were being coerced into signing a bond to guarantee the release of a person held under Section 107/51 of the Jammu and Kashmir Code of Criminal Procedure (CRPC).

We also heard accounts of torture of youths who had been taken to the army camps. The sister of a young boy from Heff Shirmal, whose shrieks had been relayed through a loudspeaker to his father waiting outside the camp, said he could barely walk after he was released. There had been reprisals and more raids after his story was carried in the international media.

One boy had become so mentally disturbed that he did not spend the night at home but chose to hide away in various places. '*Aap ghar ki talaashi le sakte*' (You can search the house),' said a relative when one asked to see him, revealing how the terms of 'search' had been so normalized they were used routinely in speech.

Near the Redwani Bala army camp in Kulgam, youths said they often spent nights roaming the streets as it was too dangerous to risk being caught in the nocturnal swoops. They took us on a guided tour; hardly any house had been spared. We saw shattered glass windows, the torn wire mesh in a bathroom, smashed wooden frames of windows and, in one place, the mark of a bullet on a wall on the main road. A youth said it had occurred when troops had randomly fired, simply to scare the inhabitants of a building in the lane behind.

We heard how B (name withheld) was being regularly summoned to the army camp and had undergone several beatings. Once even admitted to hospital, he told villagers he did not have the right to refusal since he feared for his two young daughters.[12]

The Indian State does not classify the three-decade-long insurgency in Kashmir as a conflict and so evades all protocols of the Geneva Convention. International Humanitarian Law though is very clear that the act of shifting punishment to any individual or group of individuals who have no responsibility over any dissenting act done by others, who happen to be part of the same group, is an offence in humanitarian law.

Collective punishment has historically been used as a defence tool by occupying powers to curb resistance movements.

In Kashmir, the distinction between combatants and non-combatants or civilians was blurred and increasingly, counter-insurgency operations began to be directed against the Kashmir population as well as the militants.

The widespread use of torture on the civilian population during the siege validates the findings of the seminal report on torture brought out by Kashmir's noted human rights group, the Jammu Kashmir Coalition of Civil Society (JKCCS). Torture, says the report, 'emerges as one of the ways of retaliation by the State against the Kashmiri "other", seen as a challenge to its very legitimacy.'[13]

Shopian's citizens bear the brunt of many CASOs and night raids and are brutally targeted because this district has been home to many top militants, including Riyaz Naikoo and Saddam Padder. It is also the region where there was a big people's uprising in 2009, after Nilofer and Asiya, two young women, went missing from the orchards and their bodies were found in ankle-deep waters of the Rambiar river, between two army camps. Forensic examinations stated they had been raped. A community-led stir rocked the town for many months but despite promises of justice, the Central Bureau of Investigation (CBI) probe claimed they had drowned and not been raped or murdered.

Pellet Guns and Other Horrors in Habak

Shanpora in Habak, a locality close to the Hazratbal shrine and straddling the Tailbal Nullah, a canal running off the Dal Lake, is home to labourers and a strong working-class population. It became the target of relentless night raids and pellet firings and its inhabitants say they came under intense scrutiny because of the proximity to the Foreshore Road, through which there is a lot of VIP movement, since it skirts the picturesque Dal Lake. The people of this neighbourhood are also known for their spirited defiance against the actions of the security forces, a fact which probably also invited such brutal reprisals.

Initially, the people whom we met on a visit during a sunny autumnal afternoon, were guarded and reticent. One college boy, who eventually admitted to being a victim of pellet gun firing, said defiantly, '*Maine kaun sa border cross kiya hai* (What border did I cross?)', implying that he was an unarmed civilian, not a militant with a gun.

His remark opens up the ethical issues of how the Indian State and judiciary persists with allowing the Central Reserve Police Force (CRPF) to deploy the pellet gun or, more accurately, the twelve-gauge pumping action shotgun that dispels hundreds of pellets in all directions. Sometimes there is irretrievable damage to the eyes and pellet gun blindings have rocked the international media.

The Shanpora youth claimed he was hit in the eye with pellets on 7 August, trying to cross the road whilst returning from Zakura. Protests had broken out and there was a strong deployment of the CRPF and Seema Sashastra Bal (SSB), who opened fire without warning, saying the people had no business to be outdoors.

Another youth opened his mouth and showed us how a pellet had struck the upper palate. He got injured as he was gasping and running towards his mohalla, even as troops pursued them on the parallel track across the canal, raining down pellets.

The tactic of using the pellet gun as a weapon of intimidation was exemplified when a schoolmaster claimed that during a night raid, he heard the CRPF conferring among themselves to flush out the inhabitants of a particular house by using pellet guns.

Many of Habak's residents named a woman DSP of the CRPF as being especially ruthless during the night raids and claimed she had even destroyed a transformer to keep the locality in darkness.

We also heard accounts of sexual harassment and violence. One woman alleged that there had been a forced entry into the house around 1.30 a.m., her refrigerator was broken, jewellery taken from her locker and a gun was pointed at her throat. There were also reports of a copy of the Koran being desecrated.

The youths also narrated accounts of mass arrests with the police routinely picking up boys, who would be released a week later, if they agreed to provide a list of names of other youths.

These accounts, like those from Shopian and Kulgam, revealed the way Kashmir had turned into one massive carceral system. At one end was the gilded prison of a luxury hotel where politicians were lodged, then there were overcrowded jails, and the local police stations where hundreds were forced to huddle together. In one instance in Shopian, said a lawyer, dogs were deliberately put in the room where the detenues were forced to sleep naked. Many of the detentions at police stations were patently illegal with the police ordering the families to provide food, since they could not cope with the sheer numbers. We also heard of another 'in lieu' arrest whereby the brother-in-law of a youth was picked up by the police when they did not find the person they were seeking at home.

The Lawless Law: PSA and Other Modes of Detention

Thousands of Kashmiris have been put into jail under preventive detention ever since the J&K state deployed the Public Safety Act (PSA), labelled the 'lawless law' by Amnesty International. Introduced in 1978 by Sheikh Abdullah, ostensibly to curb timber smuggling, the PSA allows the state to act against those who may have committed no cognizable offence. It permits detention without trial or charge of individuals for two years, on the pretext of maintenance of public order or security of the state.

An article by lawyer Shrimoyee Nandini Ghosh and legal anthropologist Haley Duschinski, with research specialization in violence, war and power, looks at how laws are the 'paperwork warfare' deployed in Kashmir.[14] It examines how the PSA has become a powerful legal instrument of India's counter-insurgency war and is often deployed as a key component of the State's repertoire of legal and illegal instruments of collective punishment. It has created a 'detention system designed to keep individuals categorized as troublemakers—activists, suspected members, former members or sympathizers of armed rebel groups, lawyers, human rights defenders, journalists and protesters, including children—permanently out of circulation.

The article analyses how this is achieved 'by subverting the evidentiary requirements of criminal law and constitutional safeguards of life and liberty even as it deploys them.'

'In this context preventive detention does not operate as a discreet or extraordinary legal mechanism but rather through a complex grid consisting of fluid and densely interlocking relations among bureaucrats, police, intelligence agents, prison authorities and the judiciary.[15]

This interlocking system and the way bureaucrats, police prison authorities and the judiciary work to create what has been called the 'revolving door detention', was explained to me by Kashmir's noted PSA lawyer, the late Mir Shafqat Hussain.

The orders, he said, must be passed by a magistrate, who is convinced of the grounds of the detention. But, in his career, said Hussain, he came across only two magistrates who carefully scrutinized the orders for preventive detention.

Blatant disregard for even the letter of the law allows the police to get away with extremely shoddy work like repetition, almost word for word, for various orders or showing the same weapons as seized. Absurd, illogical and extremely vague allegations can be made, without any application of mind.

When the PSA is challenged and quashed in court or the period of detention comes to an end, the practice known as revolving door detention takes place. The detainee is not even allowed to leave the gates of jail. The person is instead taken to the Joint Interrogation Centre of the Crime Investigation Department (CID) until a fresh PSA is issued and he is back in jail.[16]

This serial detention has kept pro-freedom political leaders like Masarat Alam Bhat and Shabbir Shah in jail for years and years together.

In 2019, as many as 412 people were held under the PSA. Among them was the former President of the Kashmir High Court Bar Association, Nazir Ahmed Ronga. His dossier claimed that his comment of having the potential to mobilize people to participate in voting even during poll boycotts, was a threat. On his release he was quoted as saying, 'Even if we go by the dossier, instead of being jailed, I should have been rewarded by the government for convincing people to vote.'[17]

Also arrested was the then President of the Kashmir Bar Association, Mian Abdul Qayoom because 'he had emerged as one of the staunchest advocate of secession ideologies.' A lawyer remarked how this meant that anyone could be held merely for holding an opinion or viewpoint. The Law Society of England and Wales, a professional body representing more than 180,000 solicitors, wrote a letter to Indian Prime Minister Narendra Modi expressing grave concern and calling Qayoom's arrest politically motivated and a consequence of his work as a lawyer and representative of persons detained under the PSA.[18]

The members of the 1050-strong Bar Association in Kashmir went on an unofficial strike against the arrest of their office-bearers with a notice asking them to desist from work. On the days that I visited the courts in Srinagar and Shopian in October, there was hardly any legal activity. The Bar Association had, however, designated seven lawyers to take up pending bail and PSA cases, whenever families of those arrested came to court and also to provide advice to those whose kin were arrested during the clampdown.

The fact that there were severe restrictions on mobility during the first few weeks after 5 August and there was virtually no access to legal mechanisms had added to the huge anxiety of the people. Habeel Iqbal, the lawyer from Shopian, recounted how one distraught woman had banged on the doors of his house, desperate because her son had been taken away and she had no access at all to justice.

A lawyer from Handwara said the heavy restrictions on movements for at least twenty days would have made it impossible for people to have stepped out of their homes. He wondered how district magistrates could then have passed the orders for the PSA, if they could not be at their appointed places.

In Srinagar, I met lawyer Shah Faisal who had been assigned six PSA cases after 5 August. One of the detenues from Pampore who owned a pharmacy was accused of selling drugs but there was no FIR filed under the Narcotic Drugs and Psychotropic Substances Act or other sections of the Criminal Code. Instead, a PSA had been slapped against him.

In another case, he told me, a youth from Nowhatta, downtown Srinagar, close to the historic Jamia Masjid, was shown in the dossier as being twenty-six years old. But the detention order intriguingly stated: 'In early nineties you remained affiliated with various subversive activities...(sic).' In the early 1990s, he would have been around ten years old!

Among the PSA detenues was also Qazi Shibli, editor and founder of *Kashmiriyat*, whose case is named in *Time* Magazine's 2019 list of Ten Biggest Threats to Press Freedom.[19]

Shibli was first picked up and taken to the local police station in Anantnag on 27 July with nothing but the T-shirt he was wearing, his pyjamas and a few hundred rupees, to answer questions on his Tweets and a report on additional troop deployments. He was shifted to Central Jail in Srinagar and on 8 August, charges under the PSA were slapped on him. The next day, along with some twenty other detainees, a military aircraft flew him out of the Valley to the Bareilly jail. Next to him was a boy from Kupwara. In Shibli's words, 'We knew we had nothing more to lose, so we started reciting poems. He had a really nice voice. Better than me. We recited "Hum Dekhenge" of Faiz (Ahmed Faiz). There were policemen guarding us and the plane was very loud. We recited louder.'[20]

PSA detenues are often deliberately lodged in jails outside the Valley, like Kot Bhalwal in Jammu, making it difficult for relatives to visit. In 2019 this went one step further. Prisoners were actually flown out to as far away as Uttar Pradesh. Shibli's family was not informed of where he had been imprisoned for nearly forty-five days. His order was quashed after nine months, and upon his release he went back home. But, in a reminder of just how fragile this freedom can be, Shibli was arrested again by the cybercrime police one year later and held under Section 107 of the CRPC for a few weeks.

Interestingly, it is Section 107 that has now gained currency in Kashmir, as I found during my visits to the sessions and district courts.

I set out hoping to meet Mir Urfi, a criminal lawyer who handles several detention cases, especially those of juveniles. It was still a period of the communication shutdown and no mobiles were functioning so I was unable to contact her and fix a time or place. Helpful lawyers at the entrance of the sessions court told me to simply head for a particular sofa in the corridor of the sprawling complex. Urfi, they said, would from time to time, make her appearance there. That was how so many hapless families sought her out.

I sat down on the sofa and whilst waiting, a young woman with a baby came in and sat down next to me. A little later, escorted by policemen, a young man handcuffed and in chains, came up to us. He was clearly one of the detenues being presented in court. The woman hurriedly deposited her baby on the sofa next to me and ran out, presumably to let other members of the family know of his presence. I watched as the baby rattled and played with the man's chain as he smiled in delight.

Children in Kashmir often play 'police' and mimic real-life scenes of frisking and arrests, but this claiming of handcuffs and a chain as a toy was a surreal and poignant first for me.

In the afternoon I saw families who had come to court sitting in the sunlit garden having lunch and a few policemen even allowing the detenues to join in. It could well have been a picnic in a park. Arrests and visits in court are so normalized.

When Urfi appeared, she told me how a new trend in the post-5-August scenario was the use of Section 107, a colonial legacy of preventive detention for 'habitual offenders'. It allows for preventive detention on the grounds of an executive magistrate receiving information that a person is 'likely to commit a breach of the peace or disturb the public tranquillity or to do any wrongful act that may probably occasion a breach of peace or disturb the public tranquillity'.

Proceedings under this section, require the person to be taken before the executive magistrate or concerned Tehsildar who will ask why show cause should not be ordered to execute a bond with or without sureties for keeping the peace for such a period, not exceeding one year, as the magistrate sees fit.

Urfi added that in many cases the procedure requiring the person to be brought before the Tehsildar or magistrate is skipped and the person remains in custody for as long as the police wishes. Families are warned that if they insist on the formalities, the PSA with its more stringent conditions will be applied.

An eleven-member team of advocates and human rights activists, who visited Kashmir in October 2019 and examined all the violations in law, points out in its report, that there is no notion of community bonds in law and that it amounts to collective punishment.[21]

Families with whom we had spoken in Habak and Kulgam and Shopian had complained how such lawlessness by the police was a means of extortion and bribery. One youth in Habak said how every week before Friday, four or five youths would be held and released on payment of Rs 20,000 and on providing the names and contacts of some other youths. Or 'customers' as he sardonically called it.

Lawyers also revealed that the police simply did not produce any paperwork, making it difficult for families and lawyers to access the courts, which were hardly functioning in any case.

The fear level, already high, was heightened by threats of sending the arrested persons to faraway jails with the name of Andaman Islands also being bandied about.

Urfi also told me that in at least four cases, the state was forced to revoke the PSA after the family had made an intervention through the court stating the person arrested was a minor.

The police admitted to having arrested children, one as young as nine years old, but said they were released on the same day itself. Its statement on the release is refuted by many lawyers and parents who said so many of the arrests were illegal.

Iqbal, in a Tweet, remarked that by rampantly using laws like the anti-terrorism law, the Unlawful Activities (Prevention) Amendment Act (UAPA), against minors the Kashmir police was creating a generation of 'Unlawful Children'.

'When our Internet Is Killed, Don't Forget We're Still in Here'#Jammu#Kashmir Tweet

Around the world, governments are increasingly resorting to regional or complete internet blackouts to suppress protests and dissents. One of the most recent examples is the way Myanmar's military junta seized power on 1 February 2021 and blocked access to social media platforms. Then it imposed a near total internet shutdown on 15 February as protests and demonstrations mounted across the country.

Also known as blackout or kill switches, internet shutdowns are defined as an 'intentional disruption of internet or electronic communication rendering them inaccessible or effectively unusable, for a specific population or within a location, often to exert control over the flow of information.'

A shutdown can take the form of blocking certain websites or making apps inaccessible or a full blackout, when all internet-based applications, platforms and pages are made inaccessible.

Access Now, a digital rights group, points out that India leads the world in ordering internet shutdowns, and in terms of frequency and duration, Jammu and Kashmir accounts for more than two-thirds of the Indian shutdowns ordered.[22]

In 2016, the mobile internet was suspended for 133 days in the wake of protests following the killing of the militant, Burhan Wani. In 2019 and well into 2020, the communication shutdown was unprecedented with internet and mobile and telephone services deliberately disrupted. There were 213 days of absolutely no internet and 550 days of partial or no connectivity.

There was no official announcement by the Indian State for the full blackout that began at midnight on 5 August 2019 in Kashmir. NetBlocks, an international organization that maps internet freedom in real time and believes open, secure and reliable connectivity is essential for rights, put out its warning Tweet.

'Urgent: Severe internet disruption registered in #Srinagar, #Kashmir with backbone access largely severed by India from 18:00UTC, information blackout poses immediate risk to safety and rights of individual; incident ongoing. #KeepItOn

'Incident ongoing...' That ongoing incident went on for 550 days before 4G connectivity was restored and cost Kashmir's economy $4.2 billion, according to a tech expert.[23]

Writer Farah Bashir posted: 'Our neighbour had a baby boy in August 2019. Four months ago, he started walking and speaks intelligible phrases at 18 months now. That's how long it took for restoration of 4G.'

Even when 2G internet was restored, the access remained extremely precarious as localized shutdowns of the internet in specific districts or areas, often accompanied by mobile phone disruptions, are commonplace, sometimes lasting for up to a week.

Anuradha Bhasin, executive editor of *Kashmir Times*, challenged the legality of the internet shutdown and movement restrictions in the Supreme Court. It should have merited urgent hearing but it was only in January 2020 that the apex court agreed that suspending internet services indefinitely is impermissible. The judgement abdicated its judicial task of deciding upon the constitutional validity of the internet suspension to a Special Committee composed of members of the executive.[24]

The Indian State argued like many countries, that it had concerns of safety and the need to curb terrorism. But, Access Now says, digital rights and the internet become human rights issues. In addition to limiting the right to freedom of expression, assembly and privacy, disruptions become the cover for state violence and rights abuses. In 2016, the UN adopted a landmark resolution that condemned intentional disruption of internet access by the government. The resolution reaffirmed that 'the same right people have offline must also be protected online.'. What are the costs of such deliberate disruptions?

The 'digital darkness' that Kashmir was plunged into for months and months had a huge impact on the socio-economic well-being of its people. British scholar of cities and urban life, Stephen Graham, has written and given talks on the way cities and urban life today is shaped by increased movement and mobility. Digitalization or the application of digital technology, facilitates these webs of 'invisible infrastructure' that usually become noticeable only when they cease functioning. Disruption is the new form of warfare.[25]

In Kashmir, examples of infrastructure that was severely impacted included all forms of banking; people could not pay bills online, they could not even pay credit card bills nor could they purchase goods or utilities online via their cards.

They could not access information nor could they text or communicate with one another. It was not possible to book rail or plane tickets or make appointments for medical consultations and so on.

Students could not pursue digital online courses or even apply for admission to colleges. Inability to access WhasApp services crippled the practice of telemedicine and consultations; crucial medical records could not be uploaded. WhatsApp groups that helped fix and procure best market prices for saffron or apples and other agro-produce could not function, causing huge losses for traders. All online news portals from Kashmir came to a screeching halt. News could not be disseminated. The media suffered revenue losses, loss of digital access and digital subscribers.

Websites and pages run by support groups on social media,

offering help and counselling to vulnerable persons, were no longer functional and so on.[26]

Severance of the internet caused a crippling economic blow to Kashmir's crucial horticulture, tourism, IT and handicrafts sector. In a report released on 22 July, the Forum for Human Rights stated that economic losses to the tune of a staggering Rs 40,000 crore (USD 5.3 billion) since August 2019 were registered in the region. The data is based on estimates provided by the Kashmir Chamber of Commerce and Industries.

The communication blockade with its bid to disempower and control Kashmir's population had a profound effect on Kashmiri society. Intense feelings of powerlessness and extreme vulnerability imposed by this form of collective punishment on the Kashmiris, can be summed up in a pastiche of some Tweets, posts and bytes, given below.

- 'My son was to start school this year. I tried to tell him why this is not possible. But how do I explain why the State has mandated he can't see the animation videos he liked to watch on YouTube before going to sleep.'—*Young mother to me.*
- 'My aunt (Phoofi) has died in Makkah this morning. She was there to perform Haj. If anybody could convey this message to my father in Rakhi Lajura Pulwama. My uncle ***** is posted in District fire service station Pulwama. Somebody, please give me any suggestion to make this message reach my home.'—*Tweet (sic)*
- 'Anyone from Pulwama district living outside Kashmir, who have any message for family or friends can inbox me that message with address. I'll try my reach [sic] every address'—*Facebook post (name withheld)*
- 'When our internet is killed don't forget we're still in here.'—*Tweet by Sabah Haji, Isolating Smartly*

- 'Most of my calls from home are from a doctor friend. He calls me to check various technical details on "update" a critical App for doctors, for which he has subscription to but cannot access without internet.'—*Post on Facebook by Farah Bashir.*
- 'Certificate of Achievement for Government of India. World's longest ever Internet Shutdown. $2.4 Billion lost. E-commerce destroyed. 50,000 artisan jobs lost, export declined by 62%, tourism declined by 86% and 45% adult population showing symptoms of mental health deterioration.'—*Tweet by Kashmir Reading Room.*
- 'Mr Ambani's words are nice. Mobile telephony arrived in Kashmir in the mid-2000. And since then Access Now has described internet shutdown of 2019–2020 in Kashmir as "world's longest internet shutdown". Lastly imagine Mr Ambani shooting and uploading his video from Kashmir'.—*Tweet by Gowhar Geelani in response to Mukesh Ambani's video entitled 'Make 2 G a part of history as India marks 25 years of telephony.' (sic)*
- Those who could not place orders for fiction due to the world's largest internet shutdown in Kashmir since August 5, 2019, do read posts and tweets of chosen and privileged bureaucrats, cops and docs who wrote during the E-curfew.'—*Tweet by Gowhar Geelani (sic)*
- 'This is so frustrating… Trying to download the guidelines for intensive care management as proposed by doc in England. 24Mbs and over one hour. Still not able to do so.'—*Tweet by Iqbal Saleem (sic)*
- I wish I had 4G, it took me whole night downloading a paper so that I could prepare for an upcoming ER duty, an internet connection especially in a pandemic is like an eye to the emergency physician. Kindly don't blind us in that eye.'—*Tweet by Khawar Khan (sic)*

- 'Karwa Chauth 2019: Soldiers Wives Can't Do Video Call As Mobile Internet Shutdown in Jammu Kashmir.' *—Tweet by Vishal Rangade (sic)*

The last Tweet is indicative of how the suspension was affecting the soldier on the street who would not be able to avail of the privileges of the top ranks. There was also an unexpected repercussion of the total communication shutdown. Information gathering on militants in the hinterlands of Shopian through *mukhbirs* (local Kashmiris who acted as informers) came to a brief halt, providing opportunities for some of them to appear briefly in public places without any fear.

Two youths, names withheld, had told me how in August militants made public appearances in many villages and exhorted the people to stay resolute in resistance and courage.

A number of posters, believed to be from various militant organizations, also sprang up in villages urging people to resort to the age-old practice of *hartal* or shutdown as part of civil disobedience.[27]

The police had announced that some police stations would allow people to make thirty-second calls to their relatives or those who needed to contact someone on an urgent basis. But, besides the huge lines of people waiting, the prospect of having police eavesdropping or then exercising control was a big deterrent, especially for women. The announcement of functioning of landlines brought about huge relief because people and the community could wrest back some control from such policed forms of communication.

People who had landline connections, turned them into mini public call office (PCO) booths. Boards with 'Free PCOs' sprang up. One woman told me how a gentleman in her neighbourhood would not only allow people to make calls but would also answer calls, patiently listening to messages and noting them down on bits of paper which would then be put in a box outside. People could drop by all through the day and check.

Accessing the Net became the next challenge and a new social tribe emerged: digital nomads or those who were forced to make journeys in search of the Net. The train services from Kashmir to Banihal, on the border, were jam-packed with people who made the two-hour trip to use the Net. But in the winter, heavy snow meant trains were cancelled.

Those who could afford it went even further to Jammu or then all the way to Delhi to do business transactions, or simply to obtain study material for Class Ten students since it could not be uploaded. In the case of journalists, it was necessary to adopt this route to file stories, send out images and compile reports.

Even when the internet was restored, it was tightly controlled with cyber policing and covert mass surveillance on social media. A new Media Policy was announced in 2020 empowering authorities to initiate criminal proceedings, under various provisions of the Indian Penal Code and cyber laws. The official line was that it was to thwart the spread of misinformation, fake news, and to be on alert to any attempts to use the media to incite communal passions, preach violence or to propagate any information prejudicial to sovereignty and integrity. Officials of the J&K Department of Information and Public Relations (DIPR) were vested with powers to determine what constituted fake news or anti-national activities. Effectively, this means that the state now exerts control not just spatially and temporally but digitally as well. It can decide what news can be published or disseminated through social media and effectively pre-empt all expressions of dissent or critique.

For Kashmiris this is a Hobson's choice. Can they put out

crucial information and be truth-tellers knowing it can invite the charge of sedition and stiff sentencing?

This uneven balance, which raises questions about digital equality, is compounded by the ease with which many journalists from outside the Valley were able to tour, visit and publish official narratives vetted by the DIPR. As a law student observed, 'It was clear who were stenographers and who were journalists.'

In February 2021, policing the internet went one stage further with the J&K police's decision to recruit cyber volunteers to flag posts with unlawful content, child trafficking, pornography, radicalization and anti-national activities.

Iqbal raised legal and ethical issues, saying there is no statutory backing or legal framework for such a move and voiced concerns on the question of spying and the creation of a panoptic prison. He wondered how one person could be entrusted to determine the definition of 'radicalization' since there cannot be a universal one, thereby offshoring the duties of a judge onto a lay person. He added that the Supreme Court had already ruled on Section 66A which had criminalized online activities, but this scheme now reincarnates it.

All these measures to kill the Net is an open acknowledgement of the way Kashmiris had developed it into a very vibrant and throbbing language of resistance and protest, with a distinctive identity.

It was in 2010 that along with the protests on the ground, 'news' in Kashmir quickly found another way to move—travelling like quicksilver through the newly arrived phenomenon of internet-based social networking sites. Facebook, Twitter and YouTube had emerged as a critical arena of contestation in Kashmir. Instead of only speaking to each other, Kashmiris were 'suddenly speaking to the world,' observed author, activist and film-maker, Sanjay Kak.[28]

Through their virtual personae, pages like Aalaw (the Group) and identities like Kale Kharab (Hot Head), Nanga Mot (Naked Crazy), Aam Nafar (Ordinary Guy) provided rich commentaries on Kashmiri resistance. Uploading of videos, songs, rap music, footage of gun battles shot on cell phones brought a huge vibrancy.

Today, Facebook and Twitter too exercise rigid control. Twitter suspended many accounts and Facebook too withholds many posts. The fear of cyber surveillance hangs in the air and many users deactivated accounts. I personally 'lost' hundreds of friends on social media after the siege. The exuberant Kashmiri spirit that had informed and shared experiences appears to be in a deadly chokehold.

In this 'I can't breathe' stage, one friend posted recently: 'So much scared am I of uttering a word, that I want to silence my silence now.' (sic)

6

Hospital

I watched a video in the quiet of my home that had been sent by a Kashmiri friend, when I asked about the *haalat* (situation). A new practice, indicative of how it is a people's uprising, had sprung up after 2016. Villagers would rush towards the village where a possible gunfight might take place, after seeing the huge convoys of military personnel going by. Concentric cordons thrown around the site would keep people away from the site but confined at the fringes, they would raise slogans, shout and try and create a distraction. Sometimes protests would erupt after the gunfight was over and troops returning would open fire on unarmed civilians. There were many complaints that they targeted civilians they came upon regardless of whether they were protesting or not. The year 2018 was marked with the killings of 160 civilians, making it the bloodiest year in a decade.[1]

In the video dating to a day in 2018, I could see crowds shouting Azadi slogans, calls for liberation. That was nothing out of the ordinary. What struck me as unusual was the setting. In the corridors of a district hospital in Pulwama, one of the most volatile towns of Kashmir, young people were loudly raising the quintessential slogans of freedom as they wheeled out a trolley carrying a dead man. It was that of a civilian, fatally wounded near the site of a gunfight.

The video was apparently shot after seven civilians were shot dead and sixty were injured when protests broke out at Sirnoo, a village in Pulwama district. Many of the injured had been rushed to Pulwama District Hospital or then to Srinagar's government public hospitals where similar scenes of grief and defiance took place.

Another representative image in *The Kashmir Walla,* an online magazine, captured my attention. People in a hospital, holding aloft cameras and cell phones as they gather around the bed of a civilian who has succumbed to his wounds. Among the crowd, trying to capture this death, is a man, holding in his arms a small girl gazing on, the youngest witness to collective grief.

An image shown to me by Sanna Mattoo has no people. Inanimate objects in a hospital tell the story. Discarded bits of clothing, prayer mats rolled and stacked in a corner, blood-spattered floors, these images speak out. Like the photographs of X-rays depicting pellets lodged in people's skulls or chest, such potent images have been turned into memes of resistance.

This visual repository of extraordinary scenes would never be carried by India's mainstream media. They are Kashmir's own poignant, powerful testimony of hospitals as spaces of suffering, mourning, memorialising and resistance.

On a beautiful autumnal day, the first day of my arrival in 2010, I was whisked off, after a pizza, to the Sher-i-Kashmir Institute of Medical Sciences, known to locals as SKIMS, in the suburb of Saura. Gingerly, I followed journalist Dilnaz Boga as she intrepidly stormed her way through the vast swarm of security personnel who were shovelling and pushing back people and relatives of patients in a very rough manner. That is how

I learnt SKIMS not only had its own security but also had an entire building within its large premises, housing the CRPF. Soldiers were living in a hospital, patients and their relatives were being frisked and asked to produce identity cards. That was my introduction to militarized spaces of Kashmir. The CRPF barracks and hospital continued to share spaces till July 2018 when the CRPF vacated it after repeated demands.

What does it mean for patients in places of healing, to be under distressing signs of occupation? The Budgam District Hospital lies smack in the loop of concertina wires that mark military and paramilitary camps. A young journalist told me an apocryphal tale of a certain hospital bed there that was reputed to be haunted. What generated this story? The ambience of fear and the constant presence of the uniforms? The many broken bodies of the tortured who are brought to this hospital? The probability that the hospital was built on a graveyard?

Shortly after the SKIMS visit, I accompanied other journalists to Kreeri in Palhalan district on a day when a curfew of thirty-five successive days had just been lifted. We met youths who had been shot in the legs when they came out for funerals or protests, but in the absence of any official data we could only take recourse to the Kreeri Block Hospital where Dr Khursheed Ali Khan was able to provide figures. He confirmed what we had learnt anecdotally—that many patients were there because of severe physical assaults by security forces. He also confirmed armed forces moved freely in the complex and two persons who accompanied the injured were picked up for interrogation.

The doctor alerted us to a torture case in which a body was brought for post-mortem with visible signs of torture. It was that of student Farrukh Bukhari, whose body was found flung outside the Chaura police station, after he went missing following a students' protest.

Dr Khan's candid admissions reflected the crucial role of hospitals and the doctors. Could they dare to be truth-tellers as witnesses to the atrocities, torture and flagrant violations of international humanitarian laws?

It was during the conflict of the 1990s that hospitals and the medical staff faced a stark challenge. Hospitals became part of the battle arenas. Militants would sometimes seek refuge in the public medical institutions or were brought there injured. Security forces raided hospitals, including paediatric and obstetric ones. Even the staff were not spared in these crackdowns.

In her book, *White Man in Dark,* Dr Rumana Makhdoomi recalls her days as a medical student in the Government Medical College associated with the Shri Maharaja Hari Singh (SMHS) hospital. It was difficult for a young woman to even go to college with curfews and restrictions on movement. Students, like Makhdoomi, who lived in downtown Srinagar were given a pass by security forces to attend classes or exams. Often this was just a scribble on the back of the hand of the student.[2]

During one crackdown, troops pulled out doctors, paramedics and nurses from wards, operation theatres and the Outpatient Departments and made them squat, facing the wall. She wrote that one tall professor, not to be cowered into submission, refused to bow down. A soldier then shouted, 'Face towards the wall and sit down.'

'No way,' the professor replied. 'Go and get a chair for me. I cannot sit like a criminal.'

Enraged, the soldier put the butt of his gun on the professor's chest and a number of men arrived at the scene. The professor refused to bend and yelled, 'Get your officer. He will understand what I say.'

Ultimately, an officer came and defused the crisis. Makhdoomi wrote: 'The tall professor stood "taller among all the dwarfs"!'

Recounted with some humour, the incident is a lighter example of the way the medical fraternity was getting caught up in the conflict. There were far grimmer examples of violence like blatant interference and denial of the right to medical treatment.

A report brought out by Physicians of Human Rights (PHR) as early as March 1993 details a number of incidents whereby security forces prevented medical personnel from transporting the wounded and raided hospitals. Doctors were forced at gunpoint to identify recent trauma patients. Many of them were arrested, in some cases, after being disconnected from intravenous medication and other treatments. Troops entered operating theatres and destroyed or damaged medical supplies, transport and other equipment.

At the Bone and Joint Hospital in Barzulla, doctors said they were raided three or four times by security forces and on several occasions were taken forcibly even from operating theatres.[3]

The report noted that whilst it was true that many of the hospital staff sympathized with the insurgency, the Indian government's startling admission that security forces may have removed bandages when 'terrorists are suspected to feign injuries', was clearly in breach of the International Covenant on Civil and Political Rights.

Many of those seeking medical care in the 1990s, adds the report, were released detainees who had been subjected to torture. Some of the torture methods used in police custody or in army camps include severe beatings, suspension of the person by the feet or hands, burning with heated objects, pressing a roller across the legs, waterboarding, sexual molestation and electric shocks.

Grisly memories of torture surface in conversations with most Kashmiris, but, besides such oral narratives, there are also bits of documentary evidence, painstakingly recorded by various organizations like the Institute of Kashmir Studies, the human rights documentation of the Jamaat-e-Islami. A booklet I accessed, quotes a doctor writing to Amnesty International: 'I yesterday discharged a patient aged eighteen or twenty who had been in this hospital for three months. Twenty per cent or more of his body had suffered deep burns from a hot clothes iron.' The burns were sustained during interrogation by the army at Sopore.

A common method, widely prevalent even today, is to crush the legs of the detainee with a heavy wooden roller. The breakdown of muscle tissue or necrosis releases toxins that can cause acute renal failure or rhabdomyolysis. Doctors got so accustomed to seeing this kind of kidney failure in patients who had undergone torture, that they began using the term 'physical torture nephropathy'. In 1992, six doctors from the Nephrology Department of the Institute of Medical Sciences published a paper describing ten cases of renal failure between July 1990 and August 1991.[4]

Doctors were thus testifying how torture was being routinely deployed as an instrument of control and to break the will of the people in counter-insurgency operations. The report on torture brought out by the noted human rights organization, Jammu and Kashmir Coalition of Civil Society (JKCCS), details a particularly horrific case that was highlighted internationally by a noted Kashmiri doctor and the medical community.[5]

Muzaffar Ahmed Mirza, a teacher, was found unconscious on the road by locals and taken to the Government Medical College Centre in Srinagar. Diagnosed with peritonitis, inflammation of the lining of the abdominal cavity because of rupture of internal organs, Mirza alleged he had been picked up during a crackdown. An iron rod had been pushed up his rectum which then pierced his chest.

He developed fluid in the lungs after an operation, which on analysis, showed the presence of bile, confirming the gruesome fact that the rod had perforated his liver and ruptured his diaphragm before damaging his lungs. This charge of torture, substantiated by the medical evidence given by the doctor who operated on him, attracted worldwide attention. Unfortunately, Mirza died of infection.

Whilst many doctors openly acknowledged torture by presenting records of the patients' medical condition, documenting was not always easy. Some hospitals, under pressure, began removing medical records that showed patients' symptoms. One doctor told a human rights team that, in some cases, those who had suffered injuries resulting from torture, requested physicians to attribute the cause to a road accident, because they feared reprisals. Doctors were also coerced to write autopsy reports as dictated.

One written admission of such coercion was by a doctor to the State Human Rights Commission which was probing the killing of a civilian, Abdul Hamid Ganai of Ganderbal, in 2003 in a staged gunfight. The doctor confessed he did not carry out any post-mortem but that he and his wife were asked by more than thirty policemen to write a report under pressure.[6]

Another example of tampering with crucial medical records is cited in the book *Do you Remember Kunan Poshpora?* Authored by the five women who re-examined and reconstructed the mass rapes of 1991 and filed a plea in the court, there is an account of how a valuable piece of medico-legal evidence, submitted by the Block Medical Officer, went missing from the police files. The Block Medical Officer, Dr Makhdoomi, told the authors he clearly remembers examining some of the women on a particular date before the second and third examination. But this early crucial medical record went missing.[7]

Sarkari Militants Target Medical Community

The process of directly targeting the medical community began in the latter half of the 1990s with the Indian State deploying Ikhwanis, the '*sarkari*' militants, to unleash unparalleled savagery. There was no official recognition of such an outfit; consequently absolutely no accountability. With their insight into Kashmir society, these *sarkari* militants began to kill members of the medical fraternity who, they thought, were being outspoken. The Human Rights Watch Report, 1996, noted: 'They have been given free rein to patrol major hospitals in Srinagar, particularly the Saura Institute, the Shri Maharaja Hari Singh (SMHS) Hospital and the Bone and Joint Hospital. They have murdered, threatened, beaten and detained hospital staff; in some cases these abuses have occurred in full view of security bunkers or in the presence of security force officers. They have also removed patients from hospitals. These abuses constitute clear violations of medical neutrality.'[8]

One of the most chilling accounts, documented in a report brought out by a human rights team from India, is that of Imtiaz Ahmed Wani, a lift operator at the Lal Ded, Kashmir's largest maternity hospital.[9]

Wani, Publicity Secretary of the Medical Employees Association, was active in organizing protests against harassment of medical employees by armed forces during searches. After one such protest on 5 May 1997, he went back to his home. His wife was away but his nine-year-old daughter and young son were with him. Around 9 p.m., men in Kashmiri dress, armed with guns, got down from two white jeeps used by the Jammu and Kashmir Special Task Force, (a special counter-insurgency outfit that was set up by the state as part of a revised strategy to distance the army from day-to-day terror tactics). They took Wani away by force, telling his daughter he would soon be sent back. A neighbour later identified the men as Ikhwanis belonging to the Ikhwan-ul-Muslimeen, a dreaded outfit led by 'Papa Kishtwari'. Wani's colleagues believe they were directed by the state to silence all protests against harassment of medical employees. The day after his abduction, Wani's mother went to all the police stations making anxious inquiries. On 26 May, she approached the State Secretariat where she happened to meet a young man, who was also searching for his missing brother. He told her there was a body in the Nowgaon police station, with a description that might fit with that of her son.

At the police station she was told the body, which turned out to be that of her son, had been found in the waters of a lake, weighed down by a stone.

A booklet, 'Kashmir Under Torture', brought out by the Institute of Kashmir Studies, reports the death of Dr Farooq Ashai, director of the Bones and Joints hospital in Barzulla. He had reported human rights violations to Amnesty International and Asia Watch. On 20 February 1993, he was shot while driving his car over a new bridge near Barzulla. His wife, who was with him, had to ask the daughter to take over the wheel. He died in the same operating theatre where he had saved many lives.

Official sources claimed the doctor was killed in cross-firing between armed forces and militants, but his wife said he was shot in cold blood by the BSF following an argument.

Barely a month later, there was another gruesome murder. Dr Abdul Ahad Guru, noted cardiac surgeon at the Institute of Medical Sciences, Saura, who had been vocal on the plight of torture victims and had met a delegation from Amnesty International, was abducted by two armed gunmen on 31 March 1993. His dead body was found a day later. Police opened fire on the funeral procession, killing his brother-in-law Ashiq Hussain. Despite a public outcry, an inquiry into his abduction and killing revealed nothing.

The government portrayed the killing as one by militants of the Hizbul Mujahideen, since Guru was associated with the Jammu and Kashmir Liberation Front (JKLF) and there was a history of internecine disputes and violence between the two militant factions. But there were many doubts. Many years later, Indian Administrative Service (IAS) officer and first Chief Commissioner of Information, Wajahat Habibullah, claimed in his book, *My Kashmir,* that it was the J&K Police who got a noted 'terrorist', Zulqarnain, to carry out the murder. Like so many killings in Kashmir, the truth will not be conclusively known.[10]

There are instances too of militants who killed members of the medical fraternity. The parents of G.K. Muju, belonging to the Kashmiri Pandit community and lecturer at Srinagar Medical College, were stabbed by unknown assailants on 6 March 1990. The body of Sarla Bhat, a twenty-seven-year-old Kashmiri Pandit nurse, was found on the street in 1990. It is believed she was killed by the JKLF cadres for being an informer, passing on information of those militants who sought hospitals as sanctuaries or had been admitted.[11]

Trauma of the 1990s

Located in the heart of Srinagar and stretching across ten acres, the Shri Maharaja Hari Singh hospital (SMHS) has stood witness to much of Kashmir's history and weathered some extraordinary situations. The Jhelum river raged furiously through its ground floor during the flood of 2014. Armed personnel have entered its premises and burst teargas shells to dispel crowds of mourning protesters. A shoot-out has occurred in its premises with a gun being passed to militant Naveed Jatt, who killed four policemen and made good his escape, whilst being brought in for a check-up. In its car park, is a memorial to thirty-year-old Ghulam Nabi

Bhat, an ambulance driver, killed in July 1992 by a soldier at the army hospital in Badami Bagh. Graphic artist Malik Sajad, who often maps and records Srinagar's landmarks in his works, alerted me about its presence in a Tweet.

Dating back to 1959, this tertiary care centre is also known to many old-timers as 'Hedwun haaspital.' A dispensary known as Hedwun stood on the site in the early part of the twentieth century, founded by an Austrian merchant and philanthropist named C.M. Hadow. (Hedwun became the Kashmiri pronunciation for his name). Hadow, who came to Kashmir to trade in carpets, also founded a school.

SMHS is one of the six associate hospitals of the Government Medical College (GMC) which lies in the same premises. The GMC and SMHS comprise a sprawl of buildings, some of which are new. The older ones are modelled along colonial lines with long corridors and passages flanked by wards, study rooms and doctors' rooms. It is traversed by hundreds and hundreds of patients and their attendants from the city and the districts on any given day.

One morning, I too meandered through the various winding turns and floors on my way to meet Dr Mufti Mahmood Ahmed. Outside the wards, I saw relatives squatting on the grounds, sometimes with lunch boxes. It was an ordinary day but the hospital was buzzing with activity.

Despite the milling crowds, there was an organized infrastructure in place for trauma and emergency patients. A very different picture from that of the 1990s, I was told by Dr Mufti.

Professor of Surgery and Head of the Department of Surgery at the GMC in Srinagar, Dr Mufti was a senior resident at the GMC in the 1990s and witness to the turbulent times. He recalled there was just one operating table available when the armed conflict began and a heavy load of trauma patients began pouring in.

Designed for routine emergencies, the department lacked the infrastructure and staff to cope with the huge volume of patients who came in with gunshot wounds or shrapnel injuries.

'We were not prepared. People would come directly to the operating theatre in such large numbers, day and night, that we could not adhere to any schedule. We found it difficult to organize ourselves and routine operative work would have to be closed because of the magnitude of trauma cases. Other health issues had to take a back seat. Since the district and sub-district hospital and peripheries were even less equipped to handle cases, SMHS and the Bone and Joint Hospital at Barzulla had to bear the brunt.'

The Pandit exodus, because of the situation in the Valley, added to the crisis and severe shortage of manpower. A number of surgeons working in the faculties, left unannounced, scared by threats of violence and killings. There was also a shortage of equipment, of disposables, even dressings.

As Senior Resident at the GMC, Dr Mufti said he would leave home not knowing when he could head back. He recalled spending three continuous days in the hospital. Senior doctors would take catnaps on trolleys, having performed several surgeries in a row. 'Most of us were not certain about our own welfare and safety. We would leave the house not knowing what we would face during the day.'

Despite the lack of resources and the hindrances, Dr Mufti spoke with satisfaction of the way they learnt to cope and adopted new medical protocols. 'I was a post-graduate student and we were able to do a number of valuable studies, that were comparable with those on a global level. We were seeing far more trauma cases than hospitals in other places.'

One unique case in which two lives were saved was when a pregnant woman was brought into the hospital in an autorickshaw. 'She had been caught in cross-firing and was wounded in the abdomen. Since she was nearing full-term we explored the possibility of a Caesarean. We found the bullet had gone through the uterus and nicked the earlobe of the unborn child. After surgery, both child and mother survived and a paper "Gunshot Wounds of the Pregnant Uterus: 'Baby wins the Battle'" was published in 1995.'

The slow build-up of infrastructure and manpower in SMHS, especially with regard to emergency and trauma, has helped it to cope with the rush of patients that still occurs during times of encounters and protests. But an undertow of uncertainty persists. The conflict is always there, says Dr Mufti.

Another associate hospital of the GMC is the Lal Ded Maternity Hospital. It sits on the banks of the Jhelum, close to the old site of the GMC. When the river ran amok in 2014, it caused even more havoc here than at SMHS. The waters gushed into this tertiary maternal care hospital causing flooding up to the first floor and leaving the doctors, medical staff and patients marooned for two days.

Seven months later, I clambered over the debris of huge bricks and construction material strewn over the grounds, to meet Dr Shehnaz Taing, Head of the Gynaecology and Obstetrics Department.

This collapse of infrastructure, recalled Dr Taing, was the second crisis the hospital faced. In the 1990s, she had also been witness to the exodus of doctors, paramedics and staff from the Pandit community who comprised almost 50 per cent of the medical staff.

Since exams could not be held for years, the peripheral health services like primary health centres, district and sub-district hospitals were the worst affected. Many complications of pregnancy were referred to the Lal Ded Hospital that had to function all hours of the day and night.

This situation was made worse by strict imposition of night curfews when even the neutrality of medical transport was not respected by government security forces.

Dr Taing recollected, 'It used to be frightening. In the middle of the night, they would stop the vehicle and make us stand by the road as they searched.'

'The overload was such that sometimes there would be three or four women patients sitting on the same bed. The delays in getting medical treatment were the cause of so many instances of ruptured uteruses among pregnant women. One indicator of the gradual build-up of institutions and medical staff was when the number of ruptured uteruses began coming down,' she said.

The floods of 2014 saw a collapse of another kind, she added. In the half-submerged hospital, doctors continued to perform surgical procedures by candlelight as the electricity snapped. They used dupattas of patients as dressings. When food supplies ran out, Dr Taing recollects, raw rice mixed with dextrose was consumed. Helicopters whizzed overhead but they were ferrying tourists to the airport. There was no rescue for the hospital and its inmates. *'Hum toh Titanic ho gaye,'* was how a young staffer summed up the disaster. A day later, an evacuation plan was carried out. Mothers with their newly born babies tied to their bodies, made their way across the narrow embankment, with the swirling waters around them, towards the safety of a relief camp.

Deceptive Lull and a New Generation

Kashmir is a land where years are calibrated amidst gigantic swells of turmoil and then calmer waters. The gradual restoration of services in Kashmir's hospitals coincided with the de-escalation of armed militancy in 2003. There was a period where deceptive normalcy prevailed. A new generation of doctors were now in the hospital even as their seniors were registrars. Dr Adil Ashraf, of the Resident Doctors' Association (RDA) spoke of the transition, as 'a period when everything seemed dormant, because actually things were never normal.'

In 2008, Kashmir's reconciliation with the status quo was shattered with the decision to transfer 99 acres of forest land to the Amarnath Shrine Board to set up shelters for pilgrims. Fears of a planned demographic shift triggered protests that rocked the Valley. For the first time after the 1990s, a strict curfew was imposed. Defying curfew, thousands of Kashmiris spilled onto the street. In Jammu, Hindu nationalists blocked the key highway to the Valley to deny movement of essential supplies. It is estimated fifty-seven people were killed and at least 1,500 injured (of whom nearly 600 suffered bullet injuries) between 22 June and 12 September of 2008.

Dr Adil Ashraf, whom I met in a room in a busy ward, spooled back memories to that year when he was a medical student.

'The illusion that '*sab theek chal raha hai*' (everything is going well) was destroyed. We had grown up thinking it was the end of an era of bloodshed,' he recollected.

'Suddenly, we saw a new generation going on the streets to protest. We saw a father having to shoulder his own son's coffin. As doctors we had this perspective because we were part of the Kashmiri community. It was impossible not to be affected. When a youth was brought into the casualty with bullet injuries or head split open by a teargas shell canister, I felt it was some part of me. These were our cousins, our neighbours. It was a very emotional time but, as yet, we did not experience direct interference with our work.'

The direct interference and obstruction resurfaced in 2010.

It was the year of the Machil fake encounter, when three young men of Nadihal village were lured to the Line of Control (LoC) with the promise of employment as porters for the army. They were shot dead and it was claimed they were terrorists, who had infiltrated the border. Police investigations concluded it was a blatantly fake encounter, to avail of the cash and gallantry award that is part of the state's incentives. The army tribunal at first court-martialled the guilty personnel but later suspended the sentence.

Anger over these killings was heightened by the murder of Tufail Mattoo, a young boy returning home from tuition classes. His skull was split open by a teargas cannister hurled at him. No one has been arrested as yet for this killing and the report of the Koul Commission that conducted an inquiry was never made public.

The killings sparked off the summer of defiance in the Valley. Youths came out on the streets, whipped off shirts and confronted the troops barechested. It was also the year of *Kani jung* or the war of stones. Young men and even boys hurled stones at security forces and troops fired at them in turn. Escalating violence did not spare even medical ambulances. Systematic attacks on ambulance drivers and deliberate prevention of ensuring medical treatment for civilian populations was a weapon ruthlessly deployed, much like the 1990s.

Malik Sajad's Tweet of a memorial to an ambulance driver brought home the déjà vu of violence. The memorial he mentioned refers to thirty-year-old Ghulam Nabi Bhat, an ambulance driver, who in July 1992, was deputed to pick up serum from the army hospital in Badami Bagh for a patient with gas gangrene. Accompanied by two attendants in an official ambulance clearly marked by a red cross, Bhat approached the hospital but was killed when a soldier fired at him. Hospitals then stopped plying ambulances at night.

In 2010, direct interference resurfaced with the armed forces' refusal to honour curfew passes and attacks on ambulances. This denial of access even to routine medical attention had repercussions. Patients could not come in for chemotherapy sessions or other treatment. Vehicles could not ply, affecting crucial supply of drugs and other essential medical supplies. Those suffering from diabetes, cardiac ailments, hypertension and other chronic conditions faced immense problems in procuring medication.

Dr Syed Amin Tabish, then Superintendent of SKIMS, told me he had to send out the hospital's own vehicles and seek help from the International Red Cross and the Jammu and Kashmir Health Ministry. 'On at least three occasions I had to publicly appeal to both the security forces and the youth (who were protesting on the streets) for safe passage of medical personnel and their vehicles.'

A fact-finding team of lawyers and human rights activists from India documented how security forces took the battle of the streets right inside the Pattan hospital on 30 July 2010. Testimonies from people and staff revealed how CRPF personnel stormed into the hospital. They broke windowpanes and vital medical equipment. A surgeon, who was among those performing urgent life-saving procedures in the casualty ward and the minor operating theatre, was forced to open the door to the theatre. He found three rifle barrels thrust into his chest. Keeping his composure, he managed to return quickly to the theatre. He saw the CRPF men roughing up staff and bystanders. Some doctors were forced to hide in the bathroom. A young boy, aged around twelve, who had been admitted, was killed, but there are conflicting reports on the killing. It is not clear whether he was shot in cold blood or, as a result of firing on what some media reports allege, was an 'unruly mob'.[12]

It was also the year when pellet guns were introduced as crowd control weapons in Kashmir. Seldom deployed elsewhere in India, this so-called 'non-lethal' weapon is the pump action shotgun fired at high velocity, scattering pellets over a large area. Each cartridge contains 500–600 pellets. The 2020 UN guidance on 'less-lethal' weapons in law enforcement says, 'Multiple projectiles fired at the same time are inaccurate and, in general, their use cannot comply with the principles of necessity and proportionality. Metal pellets, such as those fired from shotguns, should never be used.'

Injuries caused by these weapons posed a new medical challenge. Dr Tabish explained, 'There is no visible entry point so one cannot predict its path through the body. One is not sure where the pellets have lodged. Often, the entire body is affected, necessitating a whole team of doctors—some working on the abdomen, some on the head and throat and chest.'

Over the years, the use of pellet guns would grow extensively as a form of 'crowd dispersal.' Pellet guns were used indiscriminately on protesters, people participating in a funeral or then on those who simply happened to be out in public during a spell of unrest. The deliberate targeting of the upper portion of the body resulted in severe injuries to the eyes and the word 'pellet blindings' entered Kashmir's medical lexicon.

2016: An Epidemic of 'Dead Eyes'

On 8 July 2016, as Eid celebrations were winding down, word spread that state forces had gunned down Kashmir's iconic militant leader, twenty-two-year-old Burhan Wani, in an orchard. Spontaneously, hundreds of people began making their way to his parents' home in Tral. Multiple rounds of funeral prayers had to be held to accommodate the vast number of people and in many parts of the Valley, people poured out into the streets to offer funeral prayers in absentia.

Mourning came at a heavy price for the civilian population. Protests and unrest were countered by disproportionate violence and the magnitude of the crisis in hospitals drew comparison with the 1990s.

A report by PHR quotes a trauma surgeon on the sheer scale and volume of injuries and injured people:

'There were just too many patients. It was unbelievable how these young boys, girls, men and women were being wheeled into the operating theatre in threes and fours and sometimes even more. Just when we would feel a little relieved for saving a life, for doing a good job on a badly injured patient, the door would open and we would suddenly be staring at a couple more dying boys.'[13]

Dr Ashraf recalls, 'It is difficult to express what one felt at seeing these young people with such awful injuries. The only time we paused in our work was when the operating theatres had to be disinfected.'

The SMHS Hospital, which received the highest number of referrals from district hospitals, reported to the media that between 8 July and 9 August 2016 it received 933 people injured by pellets including several who died. The hospital also treated sixty-seven bullet injury cases and thirty-five people injured by teargas canisters.[14]

The summer of 2016 would also witness the 'epidemic of dead eyes', a phrase coined by Ellen Barry of the *New York Times*, to describe the horrendous blindings perpetrated by security forces using the erroneously named pellet guns.[15]

Hospitals witnessed heart-rending scenes with these blinding cases, one of them as young as four-year-old Imran, being brought in by ambulances from various districts. Burhan, a young volunteer who was stationed at the SMHS Hospital to help rush them through to the operating theatre, described the mass anguish. 'The patients would be distraught. "Will I be able to see again?" they would keep asking. The attendants and family would be equally disturbed. There would be huge crowds weeping in sympathy. I would try to reassure them.'

For the doctors in the Ophthalmology Department, the question of 'Will I see again?' was a difficult one. The challenges of treating eye injuries caused by pellet guns were numerous as Dr Sajad Khanday, consultant ophthalmologist attached to the SMHS Hospital, explained to me.

'Patients come together in high numbers and managing them simultaneously is the first challenge. Then there is the unpredictability of the visual outcome since the injuries do not follow a defined course. You have patients with injuries to the cornea, to the conjunctiva, the retina, the lens or the optic nerve. It is really a very complex injury. It is not as if you operate on a patient and you know that post-operation s/he will respond in a particular way. Sometimes despite multiple surgeries, patients don't respond well.'

Since these injuries have not been seen on this scale anywhere in the world, there is a paucity of medical literature on the subject and doctors have had to devise new strategies and medical protocols. The Ophthalmology Department has had to treat at least one thousand pellet eye injuries till date.

Besides the medical issues, the blindings presented another challenge—that of keeping hospitals as a 'safe zone' even as police intimidation and obstruction to duty occurred in multiple ways. Besides the routine practice of attacking ambulances, the police roamed in plain clothes through corridors of the SMHS Hospital, seeking information on those brought in so that they could then lodge cases of 'unlawful assembly' against them—a charge which according to the Ranbir Penal Code, then in force in Kashmir, applied to the assembly of five or more people with criminal intent. (The Ranbir Code, similar to the Indian Penal Code was in force till the abrogation of Article 370.)

The PHR report of 2016 notes how patients were terrified, not just that they would be blinded for life, but that they might be arrested later. Doctors said that they would refuse to give their real names or addresses, making it difficult for follow ups. A common name used was Burhan, after the dead militant.

Hospitals then responded by giving pellet gun victims a particular number which they could use instead of the names on their medical records. Said a doctor, 'We had to ensure that our patients could not only get the best possible care in this centre but that we can reassure people to seek medical treatment as urgently as possible without apprehension or fears.'

Whilst plain-clothes personnel roamed the corridors surreptitiously, the presence of security troops was manifested in other more visible ways. On one occasion the security forces used teargas shells on people who had assembled in the corridors of the hospital to offer prayers for a deceased person. The smoke worsened the condition of admitted patients and made it difficult for doctors to work. The RDA was compelled to issue a strong statement.[16]

Four days later, on 10 August, the doctors made an even more powerful symbol of protest with a sit-in during which they had one eye bandaged. It was their way to register a silent but strong statement against the unconscionable way in which the state was deliberately blinding Kashmir's youth.

In 2018, there was an incident in the Shopian sub-district hospital when security forces opened fire inside the casualty block and blood bank after an altercation with a doctor who had asked them to let them function without hindrance. Doctors were compelled to protest with a sit-in.

One of the reasons why it is easy for the Indian State to get away with such gross human rights violations is that it has refused to use the terminology of 'conflict' with regard to Kashmir and application of international humanitarian law.

Kartik Murukutla, a lawyer in international criminal law and human rights, who worked in the Office of the Prosecutor at the United Nations International Criminal Tribunal, Rwanda, and then with the JKCCS, for seven years, explained that international humanitarian law (IHL) through the Geneva Conventions, Additional Protocols and customary international law, recognizes categories of personnel and objects involved in relief and humanitarian activities. It grants them general protection and specific rights (such as use of emblems indicating their role) to carry out their activities.

'This is the case for international and non-international armed conflicts and would cover categories of medical personnel and objects including ambulances and hospitals. Breach of these protections by any of the parties to the conflict could constitute war crimes (as also recognized by the statute of the International Criminal Court). These protections are based on fundamental principles of IHL on who may be attacked in conduct of hostilities with distinction between combatants and civilians and civilian objectives and military objectives and proportionality.

'But in Jammu and Kashmir,' he notes, 'there is absence of state recognition of application of IHL. Parties to the conflict (particularly state forces) are not guided by IHL and the protections for medical personnel and objects.

'The local criminal law protecting body and property does not really capture the gravity of these violations. In any case these violations are almost never investigated or prosecuted.'

'Shared Suffering': Volunteering in Hospitals

Despite these huge challenges, Kashmir's hospitals have been the sites of amazing stories of resilience and fostering of community spirit. The notion of shared suffering can be explored through the informal but highly organized army of volunteers that sprang up in 2016.

It drew from a concept deeply rooted in Kashmir's Islamic society: *Baitulmaal* (an Arabic word meaning house of money). Essentially it involves a pooling in of resources, time, labour and efforts to nurture and care for one another, especially in times of calamity like the catastrophic 2014 floods in the Valley. In 2016, it provided succour in hospitals.

At a small café, I met Burhan, a young businessman in the travel trade, who was a volunteer at the SMHS Hospital.

'I was at home when on the radio I heard an appeal for blood donations. I went to SMHS and saw lots of volunteers and I too decided to pitch in.'

So began an extraordinary life for almost four months when he, and several others, literally camped inside the hospital's sprawling premises, and functioned like a parallel government.

Duties were divided up. Some volunteers took it upon themselves to cook food in makeshift shelters or tents for the patients and their families and distribute these food packets. A network was set up to speedily procure medicines or medical supplies with appeals often going out on social media. Blankets and linen were provided, arrangements made for financial help and so on.

Burhan was entrusted with the task of ensuring that patients, who arrived in the ambulances from the districts, were shepherded through formalities and rushed to the doctors and operating theatres as quickly as possible.

'I saw patients with horrendous pellet injuries, those with bullet wounds, those who had been severely beaten.'

There was fourteen-year-old Insha Mushtaq of Shopian, whose face was peppered with pellet gun injuries. An ugly gaping wound between the eyes left her unconscious for days with an infection near the brain and she lost vision in both eyes.

One of the most horrific of cases, that still haunts Burhan, is of a nine-year-old boy brought in an ambulance after being shot in the head. He was in an army trolley and had probably been brought in after being taken to an army camp.

'I had to rush him to the Intensive Care Unit (ICU). I don't know if he survived. But, when I was washing out the trolley as part of my duties, I saw bits of what must be his brain sticking to it. Trust me, I had to turn my heart to stone to just concentrate and stay focussed on that task and my work that day.'

Another time an ambulance arrived with two young women who wouldn't let him touch the patient. Weeping bitterly they said, 'Don't touch our brother. He is dead. He has already suffered so much. He was tortured.'

'It broke our hearts. We could not sleep that night. Many of us suffered from depressive spells.'

There were times when the human spirit seemed boundless. A woman handed over her family income for the month, a sum of Rs 40,000 to be used for the wounded. Another man, simply dressed in an ordinary kurta pyjama, gave them the keys to his car and asked them to help take away the stack of notes amounting to Rs 4 lakh, cash he had been saving for his daughter's wedding.

Burhan and Dr Ashraf stressed that the food and volunteering were extended, not just to Kashmiris but also to non-Kashmiris who were admitted in the hospital, as when some pilgrims from elsewhere in the country were hospitalised after a bus accident.

'Social media and television news anchors had given them distorted images of Kashmiris as brutal. We demonstrated our work was humanitarian with no differentiation among people.'

Besides the volunteering, there were many quiet acts of heroism. Like Nurse Firdousa Rashid who walked for seven hours from her village near Tanmarg to the hospital on a curfew day because she reasoned that an ICU without staff was of no use.

A number of ambulance drivers like Abdul Aziz Kala and Mukhtar Ahmad continued to ferry patients despite being beaten up by security forces. Ghulam Mohammed Sofi of Ganderbal was fired upon at Safa Kadal by the CRPF and received injuries in the arm. He continued to drive, using one arm, till he got the patients to safety in the hospital.[17]

Sanna Mattoo, also spoke of a heightened sensitivity that has built up even as photographers and others jostle to capture the images. She recounted how she was at the SMHS Hospital on 1 April 2018 where dozens of people were being brought in. Family and friends of the injured were angry and apprehensive and, when she asked a young boy if she could shoot the X-rays he was holding in his hand, he was brusque and dismissive.

'I did not want to victimise anyone further. I went up near the operation theatre and shot the blood-stained floors. I spent nearly three hours there. Next day I was back. I saw the young boy and this time he called out to me, asking if I knew how a certain medicine should be applied. A trust had built up. He was acknowledging my right to be there with my camera, of bearing witness.'

Volunteers, who wore distinctive jackets for easy identification, have been publicly lauded by the doctors for their organized and selfless efforts but they began to be singled out by troops when they left the hospital. They would be detained at police stations although no charges could be brought against them.

In October 2016, the police ordered them to stop work so they worked quietly behind the scene organizing relief networks.

The months Burhan worked in the hospital have left him with indelible memories. 'I worked mechanically. I got used to seeing blood on clothes. It seemed normal to be peering into a patient's eye to see where the injuries were, as part of a day's work.' But at night there were nightmares that still visit him.

And yet despite the memories of pain, he considers his stint as 'an honour' to have served and been part of Kashmir's collective suffering.

7

Home/Homeland

The siege of 2019, severe as it was, was not the first military lockdown as journalist Parvaiz Bukhari reminds his readers. 'A brutal Indian response to Kashmiri political assertion—and an armed insurgency that is more than thirty years old has created a landscape of unmarked and mass graves, disappeared young men, widows, half widows (women whose husbands disappeared without a trace with no means of knowing if they are dead or alive), orphans and a silent epidemic of mental illness caused by violence.'[1]

Many of the articles, opinion pieces in the national media on the implications of the abrogation of Article 370, gloss over the militarization and decades of occupation that Kashmiris faced since the landing of Indian troops on Kashmiri soil in 27 October 1947. Militarization has permeated every cranny, every corner of Kashmir; it has seeped into the pores of and altered the DNA of its society's matrix and well-being. People speak of military occupation as *bala'y,* a creature with a vicious chokehold on their lives.[2]

In many regions, especially North Kashmir near the borders, the army dominates over all civic issues. It controls water supply, entry and vehicular movement of inhabitants from the walled-in towns like Lolab. It is responsible for the holding of sporting events, runs schools and offered livelihood prospects under the Sadhbhavana programme. How do we view these interventions? Is this concern or control? Or then should it be seen as employing humanitarian rhetoric of care with nationalist and militaristic aims?

For Kashmiris, the abrogation of Article 370 is seen as the continuity of the historic injustices that have been meted out over the centuries, beginning with the way Kashmir was 'sold' with the Treaty of Amritsar on 16 March 1846. The treaty formalized arrangements between the British East India Company and Raja Gulab Singh of Jammu after the first Anglo-Sikh war. Gulab Singh acquired all the hilly or mountainous country with its dependencies east of the Indus river and westwards of the Ravi. It marked the beginning of the extremely repressive Dogra rule, and poet Muhammad Iqbal, popularly known as Alama Iqbal, summed up the sense of perennial loss that Kashmir mourns.

Baad-e-Sabah Agar Ba Geneva GuzarKuni
HurfiZw Ma Ba Majlis Aqwaam Baazgo
Dehkaan-o-Kasht-o- Joyo Khayaban Farokhand
Quoomay Farokhando Chi Arzaa Farokhand!
(Zephyr, if you should pass over Geneva,
Convey a word of me to the league of nations
They have sold farmer, and cornfield, river and garden
they have sold a people, and at a price how cheap)

—Allama Iqbal[3]

After the accession by Maharaja Hari Singh in October 1947, the initial years under Sheikh Abdullah's rule and land reforms of the Naya Kashmir manifesto, brought some comfort as Kashmiri Muslims became proud owners of land. But with the Sheikh's arrest and forms of aggression that continued to pile up, Article 370 was whittled away. In 1987, the façade of elections as a hallmark of democracy was ripped apart with the patently rigged elections. The people's choice of the Muslim United Front (a Jamaat-e-Islami-led conglomeration of anti-Congress, anti-National Front and pro-plebiscite parties) was subverted. The Indian State's bid to control even the legislature was seen as a huge loss of honour and the pervading sense of loss was heightened

Syed Mohammad Yusuf Shah, who belonged to the Jamaat-e-Islami, the conservative religious party in Kashmir, was the Muslim United Front candidate for the prestigious Amira Kadal constituency. He was leading with a clear majority, and the opposing candidate had even gone home, when the announcements were made in which he was robbed of his win. People protested and in a subversion of every form of rights, Shah and his political manager, Yasin Malik, were jailed and held without any charge.

Upon his release, Yusuf Shah crossed the border, went over to Pakistan and took on the name of Salahudin, after the legendary Sultan of Egypt who led the campaign against the Crusaders. Shah went on to head the Hizbul Mujahideen (HM), which with its strong social base in the Jamaat-e-Islami party and its social linkages between leaders and local communities, became a powerful militant group. In 1992 he told an Indian interviewer, 'Slaves have no vote in the so-called democratic set-up of India.'[4]

Yusuf Shah's manager, Yasin Malik, became a core member of the Jammu and Kashmir Liberation Front (JKLF), which had begun as a political outfit in the 1960s and turned to armed struggle in the late 1980s. It made its demand for self-determination, with the cry *Kashmir banega khudmuktar* (Kashmir will become sovereign).

Pakistan was deeply involved in the uprising and provided support, giving training and weapons to all the hundreds of youths who crossed the border after the rigged elections. There were many small guerrilla outfits called *tanzeems* but the two most politically and militarily significant outfits were the HM and JKLF. Pakistan switched its early support of the JKLF over to the HM and a new cry sprang up. *Kashmir banega Pakistan* (Kashmir will become Pakistan).

The geopolitical scenario was made more complex with the situation in Afghanistan. Religious radicals or fidayeens joined the struggle for self-determination, giving it a religio-political dimension.

An important fallout of these developments was the widening gulf between the majority Muslim population and the Hindu minority or the Kashmiri Pandits, who did not share these political aspirations and dreams of self-determination. The Pandit exodus, a tragic chapter in Kashmir's history, is marked by controversy. Unfortunately many crucial facts like the numbers who left, the complex reasons for leaving, the state's role especially that of the Governor, Jagmohan, in facilitating the exodus, the numbers killed and other acts of violence are shrouded in obfuscation. It has become increasingly difficult to sift fact from fiction. Something that even film-maker Vivek Agnihotri takes recourse to with his disclaimer wedged in the opening credits of his film, *The Kashmir Files*: 'This film…does not claim accurateness or factuality of historic events (sic).'

What is clear though is that there were targeted killings of Pandits in the early 1990s; the official figure is obscure and hovers around 300. The fears that were generated along with threats of violence caused panic. Large numbers began fleeing to Jammu and then other parts of India. The night of 19 January 1990 is believed to be the triggering point for the exodus when widespread slogans threatening violence rang out in the streets and hastened the departure of several members of the community. Probably those fleeing believed their departure was temporary and they would return.

But the decade of bloodshed in which Kashmiri Muslims too were embroiled and the two massacres of 23 Kashmiri Pandits at Wandhama in 1998 and 24 men, women and children in Nadimarg in 2003, made the prospect of return bleak.

Some 3,000-odd Kashmiri Pandits chose never to leave and have continued to live among the Muslim communities and not in separate neighbourhoods.

The Pandits who left were not listed as refugees or internally displaced persons by the state. They were called migrants and although some camps were made permanent with construction of buildings in Jammu, the Pandits have continued to express their deep sense of loss and displacement. There is still yearning for 'home' and homeland despite settlement in terms of physical spaces.

I have not been able to accommodate any of these narratives of loss and suffering because the dispersal of the Pandits and other constraints made it difficult for me to access them, especially since I began visiting Kashmir only a decade and more after the exodus.

India's reply to the armed struggle was a massive no-holds-barred counter-insurgency operation with enforced disappearances, custodial and extrajudicial killings, torture and sexual violence becoming part of a troubled narrative. This was compounded when Ikhwanis nursed by the Indian State, unleashed untold savagery on civilians, practically setting up parallel states of governance in Kashmir, even while fragmenting communities and creating distrust and suspicion among people. The complete absence of norms and unaccountability defined the bloody years of internecine fighting and counter-fighting.[5]

The years of conflict also took a heavy toll on Kashmiri Muslim civilians. Besides the internecine fighting between various groups of militants and their supporters, there have been killings of *mukhbirs* or those seen to be working against the interest of the uprising.

A phenomenon of unknown gunmen or Namaloom Afraad had sprung up whereby killings were not claimed by any group or individual and nor were the reasons cited. The general air of lawlessness that prevails has made accountability impossible.

Militancy gave way to an unarmed civil disobedience movement in 2008 but the killings of youths in 2010 saw seething anger being transmuted into a new generation of militancy, under the leadership of the HM commander Burhan Wani. Wani's killing in 2016 led to another massive uprising and this time it was not just the youth that poured into the streets. Women, the elderly, lawyers, doctors and civil society all participated actively with sit-ins and raising slogans.

The latest form of repression against Kashmiris' political aspirations in 2019 is viewed as emanating from the Hindu right-wing agenda, of not just laying siege with militarized might but also trying to fold Kashmir into the Indian imaginary and mythology with the abrogation of Article 370 and snatching away of statehood. Arif Ayaz Parrey, a writer, observed, 'Our current masters do not even want to exploit us. They would rather we cease to exist so that they can have an empty land to fill with their fantasies of *swarg*, paradise. Except 10 million people do not go gentle into that good night…'[6]

Narratives in Indian mainstream media have not given space to examine this landscape of memory or what Pamela Ballinger described as 'terrain shaped by historical processes and, in turn, the field in which the production of memory and history occurs.'

Ballinger's work looks at scattered and divided communities in the border zone between Italy, Slovenia and Croatia, at the conclusion of the Second World War when Italy and Yugoslavia partitioned the region. It notes how anthropological accounts of displacement, loss and nostalgia offer superb microstudies of individual houses and neighbourhoods, as sites of remembrance and social architecture.[7]

As a journalist, without any academic focus, I was nevertheless struck by the manner in which Kashmiris themselves continually do this—placing events, even in their personal timelines within the historical perspective, marking memory sites, often harking back to a collective recollection of earlier atrocities, yearnings, scenes of desolation. It is an illustration of how 'the history of the past continues to wound the present', to borrow a phrase from Robert Macfarlane, the noted mapper of the relations of landscape and the human heart.[8]

Bijbehara, Sopore, Gawkadal, Kunan Poshpora, Machil, Pathribal, Gogo, Cargo, Papa 2—these places come loaded with memory and associations for Kashmiris. They relate it to particular incidents of massacres, mass rapes, fake encounters, unmarked graves and interrogation or torture centres.

My journeys to Kashmir from 2010 onwards, showed me the malleability of time, the way the past was continually shaping present memories. So many people, whilst recounting their current stories, delved back into a deeper past. Some memories were hazy, others far more vivid and stark.

Crackdowns, Human Shields and Home Spaces

M (name withheld on request), for instance, whilst speaking of the 2019 siege and the months he could not venture out of his neighbourhood, did a sudden throwback, recalling a similar long spell of clampdown. He recalled the time when he was about five years old (sometime in the early 1990s). His father, he remembers, had to walk from their village of Sadunara to the Hazratbal shrine—a distance of over 45 km—to buy rice.

The 1990s were the time when the Indian State's counter-insurgency forces were attempting to establish territorial dominance over the countryside. They conducted increasingly frequent and brutal operations and indiscriminate reprisals on civilian support bases.

Crackdowns, the local word for the security forces' cordon-and-search operations (CASOs) and cordon-and-destroy operations (CADOs) were enabled under the Disturbed Areas Act. During these crackdowns, the military-policing made no distinction between militants (armed combatants) and civilians (non-armed combatants). Both were subjected to humiliation, torture and the women to the sexual gaze, even sexual violence.

CASOs meant putting an area under cordon and denying entry or exit to the civilian inhabitants. A public announcement would order men to come out of their homes. They would be interrogated outside—in a field or public ground. Generally, the women remained indoors. House-to house searches were carried out. Often *mukhbirs* or informers also known as cats, in hooded gear, would identify the men, 'suspects' who would be taken away. Sometimes interrogation took place in the neighbourhood itself, in a school, a public building. Suspects would be accused of crossing the border for militancy training or aiding militancy and torture of these men was widespread. Some were taken away, never to return. They became part of Kashmir's 8,000 enforced disappearances or 'missing'. It is believed that the unmarked mass graves dotting many of North and South Kashmir's graveyards contain the remains of these disappeared persons.

M remembered the crackdowns, even as we spoke of the

2019 siege. 'I was young so I didn't join the men when they used to be taken for identification. I didn't stay at home either. I would sit near the canal or the Eidgah. Once I heard loud screams coming from the pump house where the men were being tortured. One of the men fell unconscious. Later he became a policeman.

'I remember too going on the "checking exercise". A rifle was placed behind my back and I was taken along and told to peer through a window of a house and report if I saw anyone there. Only later I understood this as a grave human rights violation. That of using a boy as a human shield.'

The practice of involving citizens in searches is almost routine but the Geneva Convention to which India is a signatory forbids the use and the Rome Statute of the International Criminal Court declares the use of human shields as a war crime.

For the majority of youths in Kashmir, the militarized milieu and crackdowns provided what journalist and writer Gowhar Geelani calls an 'education in violence'. He narrates how in 1996, some twenty soldiers entered their home, asked his father about the number of members in the family and then took Gowhar off to meet an officer called, simply, Praveen. Although the officer assured him he would be released next morning, he was forced to spend the night at the station and released only in the afternoon. Gowhar learnt later that they were looking for a militant commander with a similar family structure.[9]

The incongruity of interlocking spaces, of living with the 'enemy', formed the basis of memories for Rehana, a woman in whose house I once stayed as a paying guest. Our conversations did not generally touch on the political but one day, whilst eating lunch, she began reminiscing about life with her family, before marriage.

She lived in a locality, she said, where many army officers

had their accommodation and, in those days cricket was played by all the children in a common ground. Her brother was friendly with the son of one of the army personnel. Then began the armed conflict and days of CASOs. One day she recognized the army official who entered their house with the troops. 'Fortunately they didn't pounce on my brother as they did on many youths. I don't know if he had recognized him as the friend of his son or not. Some days later in another crackdown, the *mukhbirs* came and went on an assaulting spree. They kept smashing *kangris* (pots with burning embers used to keep warm) on my brother's head and that of others. Woosh, it was terrible,' she said, her eyes rolling and face contorted with pain at this recollection.

The 'enemy' who invaded your home, as her narrative showed, could have been anyone. It could be a local Kashmiri turned *mukhbir* or then the soldier, whose son played cricket with your son.

CASOs began fading out in the early 2000s but were redeployed with intensity after militant Burhan Wani's killing in 2016. The practice of using the local youths for 'checking' or more brutally forcing them to lead the way and so sanitize a pathway for the troops, continued in 2019 with scant regard for international humanitarian norms.

CASOs have intensified, regardless of the coronavirus pandemic and according to a report by a human rights organization some 107 CASOs were conducted in the first half of the year 2020 alone.[10]

In a grim coincidence, even as I was writing this chapter, the long encounter of 9–10 April 2021, took place inside Jan Mohalla of Shopian town. Another encounter took place at the same time in Bijbehara. The encounters occurred soon after the police had forbidden journalists from covering gunfights and anything to do with what they term as law-and-order. The only accounts in the media of these gunfights are a few images of the Shopian mosque that was damaged and Tweets that surfaced after these incidents.

The troops' tactics of involving citizens is now enhanced with technology. A youth from Gopalpora tweeted he was pulled out of his home, given a mobile phone and ordered to make video calls to other homes so that army personnel could see what was going on inside.

'After the video calls I was taken as a human shield as [the] army barged into the homes. I was reciting Kalima thinking these were my last moments as I thought there might be someone inside any of the houses. Alhamdulillah, there was no one but it was another humiliating experience.' (sic)

A young lawyer from Shopian, Abdul, shared his experiences of being used during the operations. He told me, 'I had returned home from my father's apple orchards. Coming out of the washroom, I learnt a cordon had been placed that encompassed more than half the town.

'There was some noise outside so I stepped through the door with my young daughter in my arms, and found troops in the compound, who had scaled the wall to gain entry. They demanded to know why I had come out of the house. I said I was a lawyer, that's how I perhaps escaped a beating. But they wanted me to leave my daughter inside and accompany them on the search, as is common practice. I said I would but I wanted my daughter and wife safe at my uncle's place which was close by. I could not, I said, leave my wife alone and in fear.'

Abdul told me his chief concern was he did not want his wife to be subjected to the disrespect that is routinely meted out.

'They agreed and I accompanied them to my uncle's house first. As I led the way they gave me a constant flow of instructions. "Open the door. Don't open windows. Check the bathroom. Open the curtains."'

'I then saw my uncle being brought out, with a gun laid to his shoulder. The security forces agreed to let all the members of my uncle's family go to my house and keep my wife company.

'An army officer called out to the soldiers that they could also let me go back home since they already had five youths with them. We all stayed in one room, we could not sleep as the gunfight continued just a short distance away.' Next day they learnt an army officer had been wounded just close to the house.

When they went back to the uncle's house, they found charging cables and headphones missing along with edibles and even the dinner that had been cooked!

The incident left Abdul wondering on the concept of home and secure spaces that has so drastically shrunk in Kashmir. 'The assurance that my wife is safe at home sleeping in her room is not there. I continually worry.'

She too was in distress when he was told to accompany the troops and said, 'Oh, why did you have to come back home from the orchards.' Coming home can ironically be 'unsafe'.

All spaces for Kashmiris, whether outside or inside, have become frontiers. The concept of home as an inviolate space, of the right to privacy and where a family has its right to exercise control, has been subverted by militarization.

Quratulain Rehbar spoke to me about her growing up years in Pulwama where routine crackdowns left her confused about the meaning of such spaces. '*Mere kuch yaadein hain* (I have a few memories) when there were continuous crackdowns. If there were house-to-house searches the women would prefer to huddle together in one person's house. For me this was part of day-to-day life. Subconsciously I already had the understanding that the soldiers were someone you feared.'

Whilst she accepted *talashis* as a 'normal' feature of life she harboured intense feelings of anger that those who conducted them entered the home with jackboots. 'One day I burst out and told my mother *talashi karne pehle jootein kyun nahi utar teh* (before the searches why don't they take off their boots?).

'My mother told me '*Tumko nahi patta, aisa hi hota hai*' (You don't know it but that that's how it is done).'

Rehbar, now grown up, has realized how objecting to such searches can have serious consequences. She wrote the story of a woman, a Special Police Officer (SPO) who objected to paramilitary personnel entering her home with their shoes on and was arrested on charges of terror with a UAPA case filed against her.[11]

She considers herself fortunate that her family stays in the town and not the villages of Pulwama, where even after two decades there are still relentless searches and crackdowns.

'My *maamu* lives in Shopian near the Balpora camp. He has warned my brother, who also lives in Shopian, that as a safety measure he should delete nearly everything from his phone. Even ordinary news items or images of a gunfight or news of militants' deaths is viewed with suspicion.'

The Torchlight and Masculinist Military Gaze

'Imagine being fast asleep when you are awoken by sounds of commotion. A torchlight is shone on your face, you see uniformed soldiers gazing at you, with your own father having being chosen to lead them around the house. I had to desperately search for my headscarf and try hard to invisibilize myself.'

This was Shamin (name changed) talking about the gendered layers of a night raid, when home becomes part of the battlefield. Her comment on how she wanted to 'invisibilize' herself made me recollect the anguish of the elderly woman in Shopian, who was pulled out of her room without a salwar. A friend told me of a time when she had stopped changing into a night dress and used to sleep in her daytime attire. She didn't want to appear before troops in her night clothes.

Another woman, who began suffering anxiety attacks, said that in one of the raids the troops hadn't even bothered to pound on the door or try and ring the doorbell. They had climbed in through an open window and she now went about checking the windows at night.

In a research paper that looks at how lines between combatants and non-combatants are continually being blurred, Dr Samreen Mushtaq examines how public and private spaces are militarized and violence does not remain confined to the combat front but enters people's safe havens. Homes become frontiers where peoples' lives and spaces are subjected to militarized control that makes gendered constructs of identity especially prominent.[12]

One of the women she interviewed spoke of how in her village army soldiers came up to the windows to gaze at the women sleeping. She also notes how physical violence often occurred after troops had barged into people's homes under the pretext of a CASO or after a militant attack had taken place.

One of the most horrific incidents of the 1990s, highlighted the world over, was the Kunan and Poshpora case. The plea which is mired in the Supreme Court seeks accountability for the actions of a 125-man strong patrol of the Fourth Rajputana Rifles who, under the guise of a CASO, allegedly committed mass gangrapes on at least fifty women of the villages of Kunan and Poshpora.

It is alleged that on the cold wintry intervening night of 22 and 23 February 1991, instead of making a customary announcement of a CASO, the soldiers went from door to door, dragging the men outside. The light bulbs and lanterns were smashed and the women were alone at home. The village men were taken to makeshift torture centres in the *kuthars* (cattlesheds). They were ordered to sit in the snow, some people's heads were dunked in buckets of icy water from the stream, others were given electric shocks to the genitals. Torture and sexual violence was the bid to emasculate them, to make them feel vulnerable and helpless as screams rang out from the houses, where the women were gangraped. Among those raped in their homes was a deaf and mute girl, a pregnant woman and in some homes, children watched on screaming in sheer terror.[13]

Despite attempts to reopen the probe in 2013, the case has been embroiled in a legal labyrinth with stay orders. It has remained in the registry of the Supreme Court without being listed for hearing. More than thirty years have passed, some of the survivors have died but there has been no justice.

In the 1990s, women, especially those living alone, were forced to relocate because of continual threats and humiliation by the troops who would barge into their homes.

I heard one story from R. Begum (name changed), a member of the Hanji community or boat people as they are known because they live on or around the lakes. R. Begum's husband died when he was knocked down by a military vehicle whilst crossing the road and as a single parent she was left to fend for young children, including an adolescent daughter. The houseboat she lived on was in close proximity to the Nageen Club premises, which became a camp for the BSF in the 1990s. Late at night the BSF personnel, often in an inebriated state, would descend onto the boat under the guise of a search. The home environment turned so menacing and she feared so much for her daughter that she moved out and went to live elsewhere for a number of years.

Such intrusions into home spaces, triggering feelings of anticipatory violence, are part of the military's strategy whereby defamiliarization occurs, 'home' becomes the dreaded place.

The concept of home as a 'dangerous' place became clear whilst listening to stories of interlocking spaces. One became aware that for many civilians the proximity of militants in their surroundings could translate into many layers of fears. Crackdowns were more severe and relentless but could there also have been an added vulnerability emanating from militants?

I learnt of how a militant had been issuing threats when demands for financial support could not be met, and by hearsay, I came to know of the harassment of a young woman. Were there instances of unreasonable demands and acts of violence if these were not met, I wondered.

I spoke with a young Kashmiri lawyer, Mirza Saaib Beg, pursuing his studies in state formation, class struggles and sovereignty.

Militants, he explained, are not a homogenous unit. They do not have any proscribed behaviour or accountability but, because they are dependent on people's support, the militant leadership did try to lay down a code of conduct. Sometimes there were ad hoc justice and disciplinary processes for serious transgressions or to settle disputes.

He was emphatic though that the militants' demands for food or shelter cannot be compared with the state's forced entries into home and the CASOs. It is a false equivalence in terms of the extent and levels of violence.

A Poet Remembers the Flames

The Armed Forces Special Powers Act (AFSPA) not only empowers troops to search houses without warrants and by using required force, it also allows destruction of buildings or sites on the suspicion that a militant is hiding there. In the 1990s, this became a collective punishment for counter-insurgency forces, who would punish civilians believed to be sympathetic to militants and giving them refuge.

In one of the worst instances of this kind, on 6 January 1993, the BSF opened fire on passengers in a bus and set fire to most of the business establishments and houses of North Kashmir's apple town of Sopore. This reprisal came after militants had shot and killed BSF personnel and attempted to seize their weapons. According to an eyewitness, who later helped in recovery of bodies, some fifty-seven people died in that massacre of bullet wounds or burn injuries. Four hundred commercial establishments and seventy-five residential properties that included landmarks like the Women's' College and Samad Talkies were burnt.

Survivor Abdul Ahad Mir spoke of how he ran into a shop to escape the BSF firing and overheard two BSF personnel taking the decision to set the shop ablaze. The pile of clothing under which he was hiding caught fire and so did his clothes. He ran out with BSF personnel watching him and would have died but for a woman who splashed a pail of water that doused the flames. Years after his injuries healed, what remained blazed in his mind was the way BSF bystanders had mocked him in his agony.[14]

The stepping up of CASOs has seen a steep rise in the number of houses destroyed and cases of enforced homelessness. It is estimated that at least 105 houses were destroyed between 2015 and March 2018. Even when there were just two or three militants in a house, security personnel would deploy flamethrowers or improvised explosive devices that caused destruction of several adjoining buildings as well.[15]

A report on enforced homelessness quotes the experiences of people in whose neighbourhood houses were blown up. One woman, Mehreen, described the intensity of the blast. 'We could feel our home, half a kilometre away, shiver and shake. It was as if our house was scared too, just like us.'[16]

They feared the intensity of the blast could cause the teeth of a small toddler in the neighbourhood to weaken and fall out and inserted a soft piece of cloth into the mouth.

RTIs seeking details on the number of homes destroyed by armed forces revealed that when compensation was given, the amount was low and in some cases it was denied because the authorities claimed the family had voluntarily given shelter to the militants.

Natural loss and emotional distress is inevitable but on occasions, out of the wreckage and rubble of caved-in homes, a 'phoenix of resistance' has arisen. This was exemplified by the Nawakadal incident in downtown Srinagar where nineteen houses were razed after a gunfight on the intervening night of 19 and 20 May 2020.

The cordon was placed on information received about the whereabouts of Junaid Sehrai, a commander of the Hizbul Mujahideen and also son of the pro-freedom Hurriyat leader Ashraf Sehrai, and another militant. Many citizens in and around the Kanimazar area were forcibly evacuated before an improvised explosive device (IED) was used to bring down nineteen residential homes.

A researcher described for me the sight of gutted, half-blown homes in a congested locality, as people scrambled about trying to salvage possessions from among the rubble.

He also shared the narrative of Noor-ul-Anwar, who was forcibly evacuated and made to wait with security personnel in a Gypsy. Anwar had heard a soldier talking loudly on his wireless set. 'The official he was talking with had directed him to blast my house first. I pleaded to be allowed to take out important documents from the house but was not allowed and had to watch helplessly as my home was destroyed before my eyes,' said Anwar to the researcher.

Locals accused the forces of setting the houses on fire by sprinkling inflammable material even after the militants had already been killed and of blocking the path of fire engines that tried to enter.

The day after the incident, twelve-year-old Basim Aijaz was killed when the damaged wall of a house came crashing down. Two others who were grievously injured died some days later.

An initiative to rebuild the houses met with an overwhelming response and despite an attempt by the administration to block the account, the required target of funds was raised in just a few days. The sheer magnanimity of the people, during the strained times of Covid, put out a significant message of a shared suffering.

Another monument to resistance memory had been created two years earlier, when the ancestral home of Ghulam Mohammad Bhat, better known as poet Madhosh Balhami, was reduced to ashes in Balham, Pampore on 5 March 2018.

Balhami, the son of a saffron farmer, took to poetry as a form of surmounting grief when his parents died young. After he was beaten by soldiers of an army convoy who entered his village, his gaze turned intensely political. He saw his poetry as a way of documenting injustice and oppression in his homeland and often wrote elegiac verses on deaths of militants. He was imprisoned a few times but continued to write poems capturing all the nuances of resistance.[17]

One day militants rushed into his locality, asking him to leave, knowing a gun battle would ensue. Evacuating his house and sitting some distance away, Balhami saw the plumes of smoke rising from what was once home. It also contained thirty years of his poetic works. Three other houses besides his were burnt and the three militants killed.

A few days later, photojournalist Syed Shahriyar visited him and Balhami, using a piece of charcoal, scribbled on a surviving pillar of the house:

> *Bohot aaj tak lut chukay hai bharey ghar*
> *Abhi bawafa gardanein ka rahe hain*
> (Countless prosperous homes have been plundered. Now the loyals are being butchered.)[18]

Three days later, the local Shia community in keeping with the tenets of their faith, organized a mourning congregation, memorializing the burning of Karbala, the battle in which Hussain, grandson of the Prophet was killed. The mourners drew parallels between this historic battle, the gunfight at the poet's house and the sacrifice of Balhami's home. His fifty-five-year-old house became a shrine.

He told Shahriyar, '*Pehle yeh ghar mere liye bas ik makan tha. Ab yeh jagah mere liye ik aastan hai*' (It used to be just a house for me. Now this place is a shrine).[19]

The three militants were buried in a graveyard in the village.

Balhami later wrote: 'My thirty years of love for poetry and labour was reduced to ashes in minutes. But a poet remembers the flames. They are part of his folklore.'

Bullets Through Windows and Unfinished Doors

'It was around '91 or '92, about the time the Pandit houses around us were emptying out,' recalls Meenu, narrating an account of her close encounter with a flying bullet. Many of the elegant houses that the Pandits occupied were deserted as they left the Valley and the abandoned homes were taken over by squatters, either by militants who used it as a hideout or then by the BSF.

Meenu's home, set charmingly amidst a garden and nestled by tall mountains, in the heart of Anantnag, began to be encircled by the camps, with the steady build-up of the militarized matrix. Home began to feel the repercussions of the battle outside.

'I was in a festive mood for the impending Eid celebrations. Sitting in a room on the second floor of my home, I was doing my hair. I bent down to pick up a comb that fell from my hands on the floor, when a bullet went whizzing by. It had come in through the window.'

That simple act of dropping and retrieving the comb probably saved her life. A short while later there were two visitors to the house, officers from a BSF camp, who came in to apologize. The bullet, they clarified, was not targeted at her but sent accidentally because of cross-firing.

Twenty-four-year-old Fancy Jan of downtown Srinagar was not that fortunate. She was drawing the curtains on the first floor of her home to prevent the acrid smell of teargas shelling in the streets from permeating the room, when a bullet fired randomly by one of the troops in the streets below, came in through the windows and killed her. It was 2010. *Kani jung* (stone war) was being waged, and gun-wielding police and paramilitary forces chased the youths. The window had no glass panes as the house was still being built.

Incomplete houses and no windows. It reminds me of another story of an incomplete house and the shadowy war in Kashmir. I first heard it when I was a guest at the home of writer Arif Ayaz Parrey. His mother Mubeena, a school teacher, was talking to me about her pain as a mother for being unable to shield her children from the terror they were forced to witness in their village. I was introduced to one of Parrey's early poems which makes reference to a carpenter who was beheaded. The grisly incident conveyed some of the trauma that had permeated into the lives of children. The poem begins with Parrey's mother trying to offer him some comfort.

> Don't think about the war, pleads my mother
> her quivering voice a willow twig in August
> and midsummer drizzle hanging in her eyes...
> Don't think of the still-bleeding throat of the carpenter
> Whose headless body left the first floor of our house
> Without doors and windows for twenty years
> Don't think of the CRPF men who had shone a torch
> And torn him apart from the night of his wife...[20]

An essay he later wrote on the subject of beheadings and his early childhood memories, evolved into what he calls an 'archaeology of knowledge.' The essay, in turn, became the window through which I could glimpse the extent of brutality being inflicted on Kashmiris and how the concept of the right to life as enshrined in the Constitution, was being so flagrantly violated.

Parrey recollected the incident through the lens of childhood: 'I do not know all the facts about the incident, just that suspected militants had fired on a CRPF patrol which had probably lost or injured a couple of soldiers. The soldiers got down from their vehicles and dragged the victims from their homes because their lights were on, took them to the banks of the nearby stream and *khash.*'

Khash, he explains is the Koshur (Kashmiri) word for a decisive cut, violent and deadly, 'the point after which the subject is valid only as a body, not a person and which inescapably leads to *kal tsatun,* or beheading.'

The reference to having the lights on at home needs explaining to non-Kashmiris. Night curfews demanded you switched off the light. You would pay with your life, if you did not. It is an insight into how dangerously militarization had pervaded every aspect of life.

This recollection of the night curfew and no lights is also recalled in Farah Bashir's memoir. She informs, 'You couldn't switch on the television because it emitted light…When we were growing up we were scared of the light…'[21]

In Parrey's essay, the 'punishment' of *khash* was inflicted on three persons, for the 'crime' of having the lights on that night. One of them was Rahim Chhaan, the carpenter whom Parrey, then around five or six years old, remembers as 'a darkish, smallish fellow with sunken cheeks, bright eyes and the smile of a sunflower.'

'I remember him working on the frames of the second floor of our home in the corner room next to the only finished room on the floor. This room was later allotted to me,' he writes.

His memory of the carpenter is mingled with the aroma of pine, as he recollects the day Rahim had gathered him in his arms and laughingly explained that what Parrey saw on the floor was not bran that the cattle could feast on but sawdust.

He also remembers the wintry morning when he came upon his grandmother and parents in the kitchen cum eating area discussing the *khash* and its association with the CRPF in hushed conversation.

One of the victims was Abdul Ghani whose head was found 20 metres away from the body and people had to actually search for it. The horror of the discovery left an indelible mark on the collective memory of the village. It popped up in imagination when Parrey played cricket and went to retrieve the ball from the bushes. Only he 'saw' Rahim Chhaan's head instead.

Conscious attempts were made at erasure of memory, of not wanting to know more. But, Parrey writes, he also faced the dilemma of whether Rahim Chhaan should be reduced to 'just a name on a computer or piece of paper.'

'When the CRPF did him by *khash* on behalf of the Indian

State, what they actually wanted to do was to make him cease to exist. To make him a rumour; at best a good conversation.'

The beheadings, he realized, were done to 'instill disciplining fear in the Kashmiris to make them desist from participating in the demands for self-determination.'

This brought the comprehension that 'knowing more is a burden we must all bear.'

He felt the need to know more; and so from his mother he learnt that Rahim Chhaan had carved the window frames for three rooms and had promised to complete the remaining two. He had promised to make a kitchen that would never cease to amaze. The promise remained incomplete as did the house.

In a deeply moving conclusion, Parrey writes:

'So it came to pass that after Rahim Chhaan's beheading, all the rooms except mine on the first floor of our home remained doorless and windowless for twenty years after which we finally shifted into this new house. We had the windows for three rooms and we could have hired another carpenter to do the rest and the doors. We were not rich but we could afford all that, as the construction of this new house affirms. I have never asked my father why he did not get the doors and windows fixed. If I ask him, I'm sure he will make an excuse; he did not have the money; there were no good carpenters around; a new carpenter would not work on the unfinished business of a dead man, excuses I could simply show as absolutely ridiculous even in the most respectful, obedient-son tone. I think I have not asked him because sometimes understanding is much better than knowing.'[22]

8

Nyabar/Outside

A 'terrible beauty'. William Butler Yeats' lines acquire a particular resonance in Kashmir where the fabled landscape of lakes, rivers, glacial plateaus and meadows, fields and orchards speaks of the continuing occupation, a violent past and assumes an anthropomorphic quality.[1]

Driving into Hajin, the one-time stronghold of the Ikhwanis, on a spring day, I was struck by the splendour of the *yemberzal* or narcissus. It is one of the first flowers to blossom after the harsh winter and its profusion in graveyards carried a layered message of hope and regeneration.

Or the reminder that the dead must never be forgotten.

Graveyards in Kashmir are important sites of memorializing and play an important role in scripting counter-histories. The Mazar-e-Shuhada or Martyrs' Graveyard, came up in the traditional Eidgah playgrounds in downtown Srinagar, with what is believed to be the first grave in January 1990. The epitaph on the grave reads, Shaheed-i-Namaloom (Unknown Martyr). There are now some 1,000 people buried here ranging from small children killed during conflict to militants who died in battle. It also contains graves of renowned activists like Dr Ahad Guru and human rights defender, Jaleel Andrabi.

Kashmir's scenery, which adorns calendars and graces so many tourism websites, in reality is also a shroud for many unknown corpses. The Dal, with its picturesque shikaras and houseboats nurses its own deep secrets. Three youths, playing cricket in Kralsangri, the neighbourhood that fringes the lake, told me how bodies with visible signs of torture have been disgorged over the years. 'One was of a man, about thirty years old, with his face mutilated.'

The Jhelum waters, flowing calmly for the most part, swallowed up seventeen-year-old Osaib Altaf as he jumped into the river, on 5 August 2019. He was being chased by paramilitary forces from both sides of the footbridge that he and friends were playing on. Sand-diggers managed to save three other boys but it was too late for Altaf. His death, reportedly the first since the abrogation of Section 370 of the Indian Constitution, was officially denied but, as Kashmiris know, this was definitely not the first such 'drowning' in the Jhelum. Twelve-year-old Danish Sultan, of Noorbagh had jumped into the river in similar circumstances in September 2016. As had so many others.[2]

The river has become the witness. *Jhelum roya/Kashmir ke liye roya…* so go the lines of a music video by Mad in Kashmir, a team of talented young men in their twenties who came together. The video film, encapsulating private and public grief and yearnings was written and directed by Faheem Abdullah and Imbesat Ahmad. Junaid Rashid and Gufran Sheikh also collaborated in the video that recollects memories of the *sailaab* or flood of 2014 which engulfed Srinagar and left it devastated for several months.[3]

Researcher and poet Huzaifa Pandit explains the dialectics between the visual imagery and the lyrics. Images focus on a young boy's unresolved quest and private grief: the lyrics address the pervasiveness of death, literal and metaphorical, in the Valley. It reiterates that the Kashmiri self is forever implicated in the collective trauma of homeland. The *sailaab* is seen as a precursor to the terrible years of disenfranchisement and disappointment that followed.[4]

Whilst 'home' does not necessarily spell safety and secure places, *nyabar* or the outside can be so much more menacing, with an estimated 6.5 lakh to 7.5 lakh security personnel patrolling out there. Their counter-insurgency operations entail profiling and punishing the civilian population. Little distinction has been made between armed combatants and non-combatants. A pathbreaking report by JKCCS, entitled *Structures of Violence,* documents cases of 1080 extrajudicial killings and enforced disappearances, from among the estimated thousands that occurred. It tells a tale of violence and violations, concealment and revelation and establishes the truth amidst deniability.[5]

Like other boys, M of Manasbal (name withheld on request), discovered the dangers of the land, early in childhood, while venturing out to meet his sister. He and his brother were accosted by troops and told to ferry supplies to the top of a hill. 'We were young and as we struggled they realized that carrying more than six kilos was beyond our physical capacities so, halfway up, they told us to leave the loads and go.'

The troops were carrying out *begar* or forced labour which has a historical legacy. Begun under Sikh rule, it was intensified under the Dogras, who came to power in 1846. A particularly repressive form known as Gilgit *begar* was in use from around 1870 to 1885. The military garrison, set up at Gilgit to check Russian expansionism, required supplies and munition to be ferried from Kashmir and Kashmiri Muslim peasantry were forced to carry out this forced labour. Many died en route from cold or starvation.

As M learnt early in childhood, everyday landscape and familiar places had to be navigated with extreme caution because of the militarization. At a young age they had to figure out safer spaces for themselves.

This is because even when the security forces are not engaged in operations and are seemingly doing nothing, they are marking territory. It is manifested through the soldiers on the streets and in open fields, the innumerable army camps, checkpoints, watch towers, armoured vehicles, convoys, drones, surveillance cameras and so on. It is an abrasive ongoing exercise in subjugation and occupation.

The luxury of a stroll, running an errand and coming up against militarized structures, can be bruising as journalist Nisar Dharma describes in an essay on bunkers, written after the abrogation.

Accompanying his daughter Aishah to a stationery shop, his earliest memories of a bunker are stirred when she asks him searching questions on who lives in bunkers. He writes:

> 'Where do they cook and what do they eat?' Aishah's questioning resumes. 'Where are their families?'
>
> Warily, I explain how it is their job to watch us. That they have come from far-off places in India, places much hotter than Kashmir. That they are here just to make a living. I deliberately skip the intricate details, I omit how many of these men stationed in the Valley, homesick and missing their families, go to the extreme of shooting themselves dead.'[6]

Dharma's memory is jogged back to 1994 when, a few weeks before India's Independence Day on 15 August, the embankment of the Jhelum in Srinagar turned into a fortress. (It is routine for security to be tightened before Independence Day in Kashmir as a measure to 'ensure peaceful celebrations'. Additional troops are deployed.) One of the bunkers was right next to his home, he says. He describes the structure.

> 'Armed forces would erect these structures out of nowhere with jute and empty cement bags filled with mud and sand stacked up to form four walls: just enough space to accommodate one or two soldiers. The bunker would always have a small loophole at a shoulder height: a 'windowless window' to hold the gun's barrel.
>
> The loophole allowed one to glance at the soldier—anything more than that would have attracted his ire.
>
> Decades after India gave me this indelible memory, Aishah asks me about bunkers. The same bags filled with sand, the same 'windowless windows', the same barrels and a pair of eyes looking straight as us as they did 26 years ago.'

For Kashmiri women, the omnipresent 'pair of eyes' can be fraught with sexual overtones as a young Kashmiri woman, visiting Mumbai told me. 'I am struck by how young women in a metropolis walk with relative ease. We in Kashmir tread cautiously and instinctively avert our eyes when we go past a bunker.

'One day I was walking past the bunker in front of my house, one that I pass every day, when something glinted in the sunlight. I suddenly realized there was a mirror inside the bunker. This mirror enabled the guys inside to watch me and every woman who went by. It leaves me thoroughly creeped out,' she said.

Surveillance has now been heightened with the introduction of drones. They were deployed when people spilled out on the streets after Friday prayers were allowed at Jamia Masjid in 2020. In many locations of Srinagar, sophisticated CCTV cameras have been mounted on towers. Media reports say towers with facial recognition will soon be set up.

Whilst the technology for intense scrutiny has advanced, the practice is not new. In the highly militarized spaces of North Kashmir, the huge watch towers erected way back in the 1990s were responsible for a change in the construction of Kashmiri houses. The practice of outhouses was given up and toilets were built within the house so women would be spared this hostile masculinist gaze.

'Number Nine': Numbers Count, Not Names

Besides surveillance, Kashmiris undergo humiliating ordeals in everyday routines of being frisked or being stopped to show identity papers. The act of wearing a *pheran,* the Kashmiri long, loose robe, invites even more derision. A generation shares the memory of lifting up the *pheran* during a search. One meme I remember on social media, is of a smiling *kangri* seller, lifting his hands up, with the caption. ' *Joh mere dil mein hai woh aap nahi chheen sakte* (What is in my heart cannot be stolen).'

The collective humiliation of an entire population because of its geographic location is powerfully told in a nuanced report by journalist Majid Maqbool, after he visited a remote village in Bandipora. He writes how the most beautiful two-storey wooden house of the village now functions as a military camp, festooned with barbed wire interspersed with empty alcohol bottles.[7]

Any villager going in and out of the village must register at this camp and explain his reason for venturing out. Maqbool narrates how they gave a lift to an old man who had gone out. Clutching the hen he had bought, he stressed the word nine, number nine, to the soldier on duty. Only when the number was crossed out on the register, did the old man smile with relief. *'His number has been identified. He has been recognized.'*

The old man explained that the soldiers have assigned numbers to the villagers. *'If their name is on the register of the military camp, the villager exists. Numbers matter to the soldiers, names do not.*

'People have been reduced to numbers.'

The utter disregard and complete dehumanization of the people because of their proximity to borders, was vividly illustrated from the testimony of Qalandar Khatana of Hori Kalaroos, Kupwara district, one of the five villages in the remote highlands near the Line of Control. He has been featured in an award-winning Channel Four documentary and in a report on torture. I had also interviewed him.

A member of the Gujjar community, Khatana and his Gujjar community were viewed with suspicion by security forces, who would accuse them of guiding militants across the borders. Conversely, Kashmiris tended to be hostile towards them because they suspected them of being informers.

Khatana was unaware of these complexities, when, as a simple herder, he used to roam freely with his livestock at a time when borders were permeable and fluid.

'There was no one who could tell us where to go or not go. Then they began fencing our own lands, called it the border and clamped down on us ferociously, telling us we had transgressed,' he told me.

One night in the 1990s, BSF personnel from the Mori camp dragged him away and tortured him severely. He was sent, in turn, to various camps of the Special Operations Group and the BSF and was subjected to a series of torture ordeals. It culminated in the most barbaric act when bits of his flesh were cut and force-fed to him. A crude attempt was made to saw his legs off. 'When I regained consciousness I saw that various inmates of the torture cell had used bits of clothing to wrap my blood-stained legs.'

He was sent to the Kot Balwal jail where his wounds festered with maggot infestation and eventually both legs were amputated at the Badami Army Hospital. When he was finally released he went home, completely devastated, too frightened to make any complaint. Torture, as anthropologist Dr Mohamad Junaid explained to me, is used, not so much as a tool of interrogation but as psychosomatic warfare to send out a message to Kashmiris through broken and defiled bodies.[8]

Fight to Reclaim a Meadow

'Dissonance is produced by any landscape that enchants in the present but has been a site of violence in the past. But to read such a place only for its dark histories is to disallow its possibilities for future life, to deny reparation or hope—and this is another kind of oppression. If there is a way of seeing such landscapes, it might be thought of as occulting: the nautical term of light that flashes on and off, and in which the periods of illumination are longer than the periods of darkness.' This is what Robert Macfarlane poignantly reminds us: that 'landscape can offer the reassurance of nature's return.'[9]

One such occulting occurred when the nomadic and pastoral communities of Tosamaidan came together to fight against the tremendous suffering imposed on them by militarization.

A magnificent meadow at around 10,000 feet, surrounded by the Pir Panjal range and bounded by dense forests, Tosamaidan was long used as a pasture by communities such as the Gujjars, Bakarwals and Chopans. Folklore has it that in the days of the Mughals, this meadow was traversed by communities crossing over to the Valley of Poonch through the 13,000-feet Basmai Galli Pass.

One summer I journeyed to Khag, Sita Haran and Shungli Pora, whose communities used these grazing grounds. The mountains were covered by mist but every once in a while the curtain parted and I got glimpses of verdant green pastures dotted with flowers.

In a public garden at Khag, Mohammed Akram Sheikh, a carpenter by profession, and former sarpanch of Shungli Pora, rolled up his trouser to show me the scar on his leg from an injury sustained years ago in the meadow. He was drinking tea with a headmaster when a contingent from the Indo-Tibetan Border Police (ITBP) camp began firing exercises and a shell exploded close to where he sat. Timely medical aid helped save his leg from amputation.

He then told me how he had an older emotional scar also sustained in the meadow. In the 1990s, when he was in the second class, his older brother Abdul Karim, aged twenty-three, had brought him his school books and gone to tend to his cattle. A sudden burst of firing killed him on the spot. The grieving family was aghast when the Khag police refused to file an FIR and said they had no right to question the killing.

'Ek toh hamare hi mare, aur hum ko dabaya?' (A member of our family was dead but we had to be intimidated?)

The police dismissal and pressure tactics came about because Tosamaidan, the communities' grazing grounds for hundreds of years, had been leased in 1964 to the army as an artillery and firing ground, in total disregard of people's safety, right to movement and right to livelihood.

The annual melting of the snows that heralded the movement of communities to the alpine grounds with their herds, was now marked by the beginning of the army's firing exercises. Rocket launchers, grenades, mortar guns and the well-known Bofors guns were deployed for practice firing from one slope to another, leaving the meadow littered with hundreds of unexploded devices.

At Sita Haran, the sarpanch Ghulam Mohiuddin Sheikh,

whose wife was camping in their *dhok* (earth and wood dwelling) in the meadow, said how he grew up on the sidelines of death and restrictions. 'We, the local communities, would be stopped and frisked by the army whilst taking our cattle for grazing. If the women went out to collect firewood, they too would be detained and questioned even though this was our land. We were not the outsiders.'

Deaths occurred when shells missed target or when people unexpectedly came into contact with unexploded devices. Many were maimed: a woodcutter lost his hand when his axe hit a shell by accident, another lost his fingers digging for herbs. A shepherd watched in horror as sixty of his sheep were blown away in shelling. 'We had four killings from this village itself. Two women found dead in the forests probably because of contact with unexploded shells and two youths who died in firing exercises,' he said.

Data obtained under Right to Information (RTI) show that at least sixty-eight were killed and forty-three disabled over the years at Tosamaidan. The highest number—over thirty-seven—was reported from Shungli Pora.

The dead included seven-year-old Simran Parray, who came home one day in 2014, excited because she had found a bag. She tossed it around, not knowing it contained unexploded shells. The blast blew her body to pieces and tore away the leg of her five-year-old brother.

Ghulam Ahmed, a herder from Shungli Pora, told me how *taalim* (education) was particularly affected. School timings coincided with the boom-boom-boom of firing drills. The school building shook and children cowered in fright. Some suffered hearing impairment. Once a shell fell short of its target and landed near a school building in Chil-Bras. Houses in the villages of Drang, Khag and Sita Haran developed cracks and windowpanes were shattered.

The environment was severely damaged as the melting snows and heavy rains caused shells to be swept into the nullahs or glacial streams that are the primary source of water for Budgam. Bushes caught fire and huge craters formed in the fields.

Ghulam Ahmed says many species of birds—herons, jungle fowls, cranes—have disappeared because of the damage to the environment. Many medicinal herbs too seem to have vanished.

For years, the villagers accepted the killing fields as an unavoidable hazard. The world outside ignored their plight. There was ambiguity about whether they could apply for compensation for damage caused to livestock and crops because it had been designated a firing range. The absence of any guidelines under the Manoeuvres Field Firing and Artillery Practice Act of 1938 meant that no FIRs were filed for several years nor could action be taken for compensation.

It was only in 2013 that the villagers came together to form the Tosamaidan Bachav Front to fight collectively. The movement was initiated by Ghulam Rasool Shaikh, a doctor by profession.

He told me he first learnt of the presence of a firing range in Budgam when he went trekking in the region as a young man. 'Many trees had been felled. I was disturbed to learn that in this region of unsurpassed beauty there could be no question of eco-tourism because of the firing range.'

Later, working as a government medical officer in the mobile health services, Dr Rasool was shocked to learn about the number of widows in Shungli Pora, whose husbands had died due to the firing range. He was deeply affected when he came across a single household where three male members had died over the years.

Tapping into his experience as a pioneer in the Right to Information campaign in Kashmir, he used RTI networks to assess the effects of the firing range since 1969 and obtain data on deaths and disabilities, and details of the land lease given to the army.

People were afraid initially to give testimony against the army and articulate their opposition. A strategy was formed when the *panchayat* elections across Kashmir of 2010–11 were announced. Those who were strongly opposed to the firing range and wanted the meadow to be vacated were urged to stand for these elections. After their win, the *panchayats* helped create awareness on issues related to Tosamaidan.

Lubna Sayed Qadri, who has worked for years among the Bakarwal and Gujjar communities, highlighted the plight of the widows who had lost their husbands and were struggling to bring up their children. 'They would supplement income by seeking alms, sitting outside the mosques as is the customary practice. But they were inherently strong and we persuaded many of them to stand for *panchayat* elections. Now, they are articulate and argue forcefully on many decisions that have to be taken,' she says.

Once the Tosamaidan village committees were formed, over time, fifty-two *sarpanches* representing sixty-four villages signed a resolution against the firing range, and came together to form the Tosamaidan Bachav Front.

Local opposition was amplified with various environmentalists, members of the Kashmir Bar Council and various trade associations joining hands. A crucial discovery, through the RTI, was that the lease for the meadow came up for renewal every ten years and not ninety years, as the villagers had mistakenly believed. The year for fresh renewal was 2014. A vigorous campaign was launched to put pressure on the then National Conference government not to renew the lease. Protests were held at least twice a month in Srinagar with the local and national media focussing on images of those who had been maimed and stories of the dead.

Eventually, on 18 April 2014, the army vacated the meadow. The mopping up drive to remove the unexploded shells and sanitise the place was highly lauded in the media at that time. But the exercise seems to be less successful than its claims and a fresh drive had to be initiated after the death of a seventeen-year-old, Wajid Ahmed Ahangar, in August 2018 when an unexploded shell triggered a blast.

Issues that still need to be resolved are adequate compensation for loss of lives, for environmental damage and for the promises of state support for rural-based tourism in the villages around Tosamaidan. One local mentioned how compensation for death or injury was dealt with individually and arbitrarily by the army and that this has weakened the collective legal efforts for the community.

Mohammed Akram was clear the corporate tourism models of Gulmarg and Pahalgam would yield no benefits for the local population. 'Big tour operators lease the land, build huge hotels and gobble profits. We are left to work as labourers washing utensils and so on. The commercial model also wreaks environmental damage.'

Whilst some attempts on the rural tourism model have made headway, the overall grim situation in the Valley has had its impact. At a small eatery in Khag, the owner told me with a shrug, 'I built this terrace with a splendid view of the mountains, hoping I would get lots of tourists. So far the largest contingent of "visitors" have been army troops who come for cordon-and-search operations.'

Protests, Civilian Killings at Encounter Sites

The practice of hordes of villagers rushing towards the site of a possible gunfight when they saw the convoys approaching and of raising slogans or creating some kind of disturbance, saw a steep rise in civilian killings in 2017 and 2018. Although the concentric cordons restricted protests to as far as eight kilometres away, the troops would open fire on the unarmed civilians. There were also random reprisal killings of people, going about their business that day.

Whilst the army chief issued a warning, saying they would brook no interference by people in their operations, these deaths, referred to as 'targeted killings' are problematic in human rights discourses and international humanitarian law (IHL). The law declares that for a specific attack on a military objective to be lawful, it must 'discriminate between combatant and civilians, and the expected loss of civilian life or property cannot be disproportionate to the anticipated military gain of the attack.'[10]

Legal activists allege that the intent of security forces deployed during protests or near encounter sites, was not dispersal of crowds but shoot to kill and they say excessive force was used.

I learnt the details of one such civilian killing during a field trip in 2017. Earlier in that year, fourteen-year-old Amir Wani from Begumbagh, Kakapora, had been shot dead near an encounter site.

Accompanied by a researcher, I proceeded towards the house where the slain boy's mother gave me a quick embrace and disappeared. Bilal Ahmed, the elder brother, said his mother could not bear to talk about the killing, even after six months. 'We thought Amir had left for school as usual. I was in college when around 11 a.m. I learnt that protesters had gathered at Golipara, more than two kilometres away from Padgampora, where a gunfight was underway. The Special Task Force and police brought in from Awantipora opened fire on the protesting crowds and my young brother was among them.' Amir fell to the ground, said bystanders, and he was rushed to the primary health centre where he was declared dead on arrival.

'His body was brought back with a bullet that had gone through the neck and exited from the chest. The entire village was shocked that an unarmed minor was shot at close range in such a manner. Was it necessary to use such force against sloganeering?'

Summoned five months later before the police station, the family was told an FIR had been filed under Section 307 (attempt to murder). Curiously, in October they were told that a case was being prepared for ex gratia to be forwarded to higher authorities.

'It is amazing that, on the one hand, my brother is shown as accused and at the same time the police is recommending ex gratia,' said Ahmed.[11]

Eighteen-year-old Owais Shafi Dar was not even at a protest or with a crowd. He just happened to be at the 'wrong' place on the 'wrong' day. A newspaper cutting mentioned he had died of pellet gun injuries in Kakapora, Pulwama, on 18 August, when according to security forces, they had to deal with a 'mob'.

But when a researcher and I visited the home three months later, his father Mohammad Shafi Dar vehemently denied this official statement. There had been no protests in Pulwama that day and no crowds, he said. The mood of the CRPF forces who drove through the town in some seven vehicles after an encounter at Awneera, thirteen kilometres away, was clearly hostile and belligerent.

'There was heckling and booing and the forces must have been upset because they had lost some of their own personnel. When a particular CRPF vehicle neared Kakapora bridge, they came upon my son returning from the Jamia Masjid. He was alone and targeted with an entire cartridge of a pellet gun that lodged on the right side of his chest. Three shopkeepers were witness to the incident and rushed to his aid. But he died at the SMHS Hospital where he had been taken.' The protests and huge gatherings of people took place the next day when the funeral was taking place. Teargas shells were fired and two youths injured in the pellet gun firing. Mourning comes with its own risks.

The high number of civilian killings in public spaces drew international attention. The United Nations Special Rapporteur on extrajudicial, summary or arbitrary executions, sent official communications to the Government of India. It said that taking note of the high number of civilian killings since 2016, it was raising concerns about 'intentional, excessive or indiscriminate use of firearms' by Indian security forces and failure to conduct 'thorough prompt and impartial investigations' into these cases to uphold rule of law and non-reoccurrence of these violations.

The Government of India responded to the letter saying it took 'serious objection' to the mandate holders, referencing the Office of the High Commissioner of the United Nations of Human Rights and said it would no longer engage with any mandate holder on this issue.

Why We Rebels...

I come from the land of bloody crackdowns
where silhouettes of life rush to the playgrounds
['you sit your ass down, and don't make a sound
take off that pheran, you motherfuckin' clown']
—Words said by Indian Forces durin' a crackdown

—'Why We Rebels', sung by Rapper MC Kash

A Kashmiri friend, in response to my question on how his nephew, a few months old was doing, replied that he was a regular fellow. A real Kashmiri, throwing up his arms and shouting vociferously!

The pride in this description is justified given that Kashmir has a long history of peoples' mobilization, whether it is the shawl weavers' protest in 1865, the silk factory labour unrest in 1924, mobilization against Maharaja Hari Singh's autocratic rule in 1931, the demand for plebiscite from 1953 to 1975, the civilian uprising during the armed conflict of the 1990s and subsequent uprisings of 2008, 2009 and 2010. And of course 2016.

The sheer numbers on the streets—sometimes in lakhs—is a phenomenon that has been remarked upon by many anthropologists and political observers. In a region where the state exercises its bid to control spaces through curfews, checkpoints, restriction to mobility, punitive punishment and frequent imposition of Section 144, which makes assembly of four or more unlawful, the people responded spontaneously. They poured out onto the streets and through lusty sloganeering, defied the State.

The ability of the State to deploy emergency laws, bolstered by the military infrastructure, has robbed Kashmiris of the right to movement and access to many spaces. It often becomes challenging just to walk through the bazaars, to go hiking deep into the mountains, to loiter and, as a woman told me in 2010's curfewed days, even a walk can become a luxury. (It has taken the pandemic-induced lockdown for people in India, to understand the implications of such severe restrictions!)

Dr Mohamad Junaid points out curfews and such violent forms of control in Kashmir have turned practices of ordinary movement, mostly accomplished through walking, into a matter of existential concern as well as a crucial political problem.[12]

One of the ingenuous ways of exploring militarization and using poetic resistance through walking, came from someone who introduced himself as Cabbage Walker in the social media. He said he was taking a cue from the Chinese Han Bing series of 'Walking a cabbage in Beijing,' which made insightful comments on China's society. Kashmir's cabbage walker, dressed in a *pheran,* tied a cabbage with string and pulled it along the streets. He then posted images on Facebook. Keeping his real identity a secret, he said in an interview, posted on his Timeline: 'I walked my cabbage in Lal Chowk amidst armed personnel and they could have beaten me, shot me or taken me in for interrogation and whatnot and I was mentally prepared for all consequences.'

He wanted the absurdity of the act to draw attention to how violence has been normalized and how people have to be okay with the fact that guns will be pointed at them and they may well be killed.

Cabbage Walker declared, 'I as a Kashmiri am willing to recognize walking the cabbage as part of the Kashmiri landscape, but I will never accept the checkposts, the bunkers, the army camps, the torture centres, the barbed wire, the curfews, the arrests, the toxic environment of conflict and war as part of the same.'

Tehreek (broadly meaning movement), the incipient national liberation movement, also draws on bodily assembly as its weapon of resistance. Dr Mohamad Junaid, sketching the history of such resistance, writes how activists would send out a call for people to assemble at a public space, sometimes at a Sufi shrine culturally associated with Kashmiri identity, or then to walk towards historically symbolic places like city squares remembered as sites of past political events. On these occasions people raised rhythmic slogans for independence, they assembled and marched with bodies huddled together and through these acts of bodily defiance against spatial strategies of control, public space is collectively reclaimed.[13]

One year, a political leader urged nocturnal torch processions as a way to reclaim the night and 'remove the fear of soldiers'. In another instance the call 'UN Chalo' was made for people to march towards the office of the UN Military Observers Group in India and Pakistan, situated in the heart of Srinagar. Walking together becomes a way of assertion of freedom from military control.

Huzaifa Pandit, who holds a doctorate in the poetics of resistance, participated as a young student in some of the historic marches and rallies of 'Eidgah Chalo', 'TRC Chalo' and 'Pampore Chalo' during the uprisings of 2008 and 2010. An estimated three to six lakh people gathered for the 'Eidgah Chalo' in 2008 and Pandit recalls his surcharged emotions of being among that massive crowd, of belonging to something larger than one's own self. It was also an awakening of political consciousness.

He told me, 'Returning from the Eidgah rally in 2008, there was massive teargas shelling near Rambagh and I saw a boy falling down after being hit. I was then running for my life like the rest. Another time I saw a policeman raise his rifle to take aim. I folded my hands in plea and then fled.'

After all these years, he reflects sombrely how he escaped by the skin of his teeth, when so many didn't. A sentiment that resounds in his poem 'Cafés of Memory'.

> At an avant-garde café in uptown Pune
> the reserved tables celebrate
> a teenager's birthday in cosmopolitan English
> My nearly dead phone flares up with a call from home
> My mother laments in frayed Kashmiri:
> I am happy you aren't at home, two other boys
> Were shot dead today.

Pandit, who has also written a series of essays on forms of resistance, analyses the power of sloganeering. A slogan allows protesters to modify the meanings and forms of places, something the State is wary about. It implies the power to nominate and determine meaning and that accessibility has transferred from the State to the people.

That the act of sloganeering takes place in public, he explains, is an attestation of how symbolic associations with prominent places like Ghanta Ghar (the clock tower) in Lal Chowk or the UN can get built up over time and acquire a narrative infallibility that is impossible to erase.

A slogan is therefore an act of historicity, an act of collective dissent and an act of reclamation. As an illustration he takes up the slogan *'Jis Kashmir ko khoon se seencha/Woh Kashmir hamaara hai'* (The Kashmir you watered with our blood/That Kashmir is ours).

The slogan came about during the days of the plebiscite movement started by Afzal Beg, one-time lieutenant of Sheikh Abdullah. The operative word according to Pandit is *Jis (*That) as it opens up multiple imaginations of Kashmir. For the Indian State, Kashmir is sometimes paradise, or then a war zone, or then *atoot ang* or integral part of India. For Kashmiris it is *Maeej Kasheer* (Mother Kashmir). Pandit analyses in detail the emotive force of the word *seench* or watering, nurturing, ploughing and all the associations with the land. The tracing of the land through blood is a reminder, he observes, of the imaginaries in which a nation is conceived: sacrifice and bloodshed.[14]

Then there is the quintessential anthem of resistance that has rung out in every corner of the Valley and been engraved into its sociocultural history—*Hum kya chahate* with the resounding answer of *Azadi.* Heard in rallies across parts of India as well, more recently during the anti-Citizen Amendment Act (CAA) protests, the origins of the slogan are a point of contestation. Azadi, a Persian word, connotes freedom but depending on the context of its usage, it has acquired several layers as it calls upon people to struggle, to resist and fight against subjugation.[15]

In Kashmir, the words chanted like a divine verse, have become the focus of all forms of resistance—marches, rallies, funerals of militants. A journalist remarked that no matter what the protest, be it for more pay or a demand for electricity, it would ultimately end with the demand for Azadi.

Sarjan Barkati, a cleric from Shopian, shot to prominence in 2016 for leading the crowds in the Azadi chant and exploring more of its meanings. Using his hands to cup his ear, he would exhort the crowd with cries like *Yeh jabri kabja?* (this militarized occupation?) and the crowd would resoundingly shout back. *Na bhai na* (No, certainly not!).

The questions would continue in similar vein: *Yeh bullet pellet?//Yeh crakedown?//Yeh raat ka chhapa?//Yeh nakabandi?* (This bullet/pellet? This crackdown? These night raids? These checkpoints?) And with each query was a resounding '*Na bhai na.*'[16]

Gaining the epithet of 'Freedom Chacha', Barkati was arrested under PSA and spent some four years in jail before being released.

Another great bit of performative sloganeering came with 'Ragda, Ragda' during the uprisings of 2008 and 2010. Participants would form a rough circle and stomp their feet in synchrony, simulating obliteration. Believed to be inspired by the Palestinian *intifada*, it is said that a spirited transgender, Javaid Ahmed, popularly known as Jave Maam, came up with this stomping. It was during one protest in which he was leading the women of Maisuma to a feisty and fiery performance of protests. It then quickly became the rage.[17]

The women of Kashmir came up with another haunting leitmotif in 2019: *'Our days and nights have become one, No news of home!'*

Cut off from 'home' because of the siege imposed after the abrogation of Article 370 and living among people who could not understand their anguish, a group of young Kashmiri women adapted the words of 'Bella Ciao'. This Italian protest song, sung by workers in the late nineteenth century and by Italian partisans during the German occupation, has become the universal anti-fascist song.

Uploaded online, the song traverses a long history of oppression, marking particular days of commemoration from the 1931 rebellion onwards. It locates the varied markings on Kashmir's wounded, collective body—bullets, pellets, teargas, as also the chronicling of the 5 August 2019 siege, in just a few haunting lines.

'On one night, among the many long nights, we sat down to pen down our feelings and memories, as there was no space for us to vent our anger and sadness...So many countries around the world have their version of "Bella Ciao" to mark their protests against fascist forces...we penned down our thoughts which eventually developed into a Kashmiri adaptation.'

'We wanted to write our pain in Kashmiri, as we couldn't express it in any other language, we wanted to use raw Kashmiri words,' the women of the collective said in an interview. The song assumed particular symbolic overtones because it was uploaded on 23 February, marked as Kashmiri Women's Resistance Day as it is the anniversary of the fateful night when the women of Kunan and Poshpora were mass raped.[18]

The War of Stones and Friday Protests

If there is one element of Kashmir's resistance that has been in the glare of the arc lights of Indian media, it is *Kani jung* (war of stones) or stone pelting, as it is called. The phenomenon of Kashmir's youth taking to the streets to confront the militarized personnel and wrench back spaces, if only for short spells, sprang to the limelight in 2010. Young boys, some perhaps only eleven or twelve years old, faces covered with a range of masks or draped with scarves or using hoodies, pelting armoured vehicles and engaged in contest with armed-to-the-hilt security personnel, made startling visual content.

Accusations were hurled and continue to be hurled that the stone pelters receive slush funds from the Inter-Services Intelligence (ISI) in Pakistan or indirectly the Hurriyat; it was said that Narendra Modi's demonetization programme of 8 November 2016 was necessary to curb the activities of this force; it was similarly claimed that the abrogation of Article 370 led to fewer stone pelting incidents and so on. So many suppositions but with no real end to this ongoing phenomenon, it would suggest that *Kani jung*, like its early origins, is indicative of an ongoing confrontation between angry Kashmiri youth and occupiers. It is a battle for spaces. It is a statement against domination.

Historians say *Kani jung* was a common feature of political battles in Kashmir, going as far back to a time when urban youth threw stones at tax officials of the Dogra regime to protest heavy taxes on artisans and cultivators. The practice raised its head again during the 1990s when unarmed civilians confronted troops on the streets and lost some of its class stigma, gaining the name of *sangbazi*.

It accelerated in 2010, when youths were no longer willing to accept status quo and were incensed with the Machil killings and the death of young Tufail Mattoo. Protests and *Kani jung* or stone pelting became a ritual to be played out every Friday after prayers in downtown Srinagar, especially around the Jamia Masjid.

For years, photographers have gathered to capture the

performance with its stunning possibilities of dynamics. The youth, choosing to make their own statement, drape the chequered black and white keffiyehs, symbols of Palestinian solidarity or then choose green, or don different kinds of masks and bandanas. The first act is verbal baiting, shouting across to the armed personnel. The armed personnel are in their official combat gear with layers of protective clothing, helmets, face guards and protective shields. Their arsenal can range from catapults to teargas to pellet guns to bullets.

The stone pelting can lead to chases through the labyrinthine allies and crowded streets of downtown, where the youths are at an advantage because of the familiarity of terrain.

Sanna Mattoo, Tufail Mattoo's cousin, has covered many protests and spoke to me of the challenges. 'It's a very swift and hectic exercise, requiring dexterity and ability to make quick decisions in choosing angles or on which side the action is flowing. There is so much action going on. You can't shoot from a fixed position. *Kabhi iss side, kabhi udhar...*'

The entry of upcoming women photojournalists in hitherto male-dominated spaces, coincided with the entry of young women in the *sangbaaz* arena. College girls, distinguishable in their white uniforms, were seen kicking the armoured vehicles or joining male protesters in stone throwing in and around the Lal Chowk area in 2017. The images went viral and there was some heated debate on whether such forms of protests by women were acceptable. Zakir Musa, the militant who broke away from the Hizbul Mujahideen to form his own faction, issued a statement condemning women who came out on the streets without wearing a burqa. But, by choosing to ignore all condemnation and to assert themselves, the young women were demonstrating their agency. They were saying the streets of Srinagar have multiple languages and voices.

Walking near Regal Chowk one afternoon, I came upon some young women students, visibly upset after the protests had been pushed back by baton-wielding policemen. One of the young women had been kicked in the stomach, they said. Another woman was indignant that the media wanted to exoticize them and that bystanders hadn't joined in. Why were they out on the streets? I asked. They countered: What is the army doing in our colleges? Their question related to the incident in which soldiers in armoured vehicles had entered the Government Degree College of Pulwama in a naked display of force on 12 April 2017. Students, fearing some of them would be picked up, had protested; this had repercussions in Srinagar. The contestation of spaces and who controls them continues to be the flashpoint for sites of protests.

The young women's presence on the street brought back memories of the 1990s when women were very much in the forefront of protest. Anjum Zamrud Habib, an activist with the Muslim Khawateen Markaz (MKM) had told me of a time when women had hurled *kangris* at troops outside a stadium. They were protesting because youths had been picked up during a crackdown in the 1990s. She had been held and then later released.

Grief and Public Mourning in Resistance

The paragraph put out by a news agency in national newspapers on the killing of civilian Bilal Ahmad Khan on 4 August 2018, was sketchy. All it said was that a civilian was hit by a bullet at Ganawpora in Shopian district 'after the funeral prayers of a terrorist, who was among the four ultras killed in a gun battle with security forces at Killoora during an overnight operation.' (sic)

It added, 'Locals alleged that Khan was hit by bullets

fired by army personnel in response to stone-pelting by protesters.'

The very language in which the news was portrayed, designed to reinforce the nationalist narrative, raises questions. What was Bilal Ahmad Khan doing at the funeral prayers of a man labelled a 'terrorist' by the Indian State? Why were there stone-pelting protesters and army personnel at a funeral, in which this twenty-one-year-old youth had lost his life?

I joined a researcher who was collecting data on civilian killings that year and together we visited the slain youth's home in Pooja Berthipora, Keller tehsil, a few months later. For me this visit was important to gain some understanding of the nature of collective and public mourning in Kashmir and expressions of grief in the making of political resistance.

At the youth's home we were welcomed and Ali Mohamad Khan, the father, said Bilal and a younger son had both left home for the funeral prayers of the militant (whom he referred to as a *mujahid*). The younger son returned around 1 p.m. but when there were no signs of the elder youth, the father got worried and phoned him. The call went unanswered. A neighbour brought worrying news that there had been a killing after the prayers. A little later, the body of his son was brought home with a bullet wound in the chest.

From some bystanders, it was learnt that protests began after some security personnel had made a bid to snatch the militant's body. Thousands, who had collected for the funerary procession, protested and shots were fired into the crowds. A bullet hit Bilal in the chest. He was rushed to the Shopian hospital where he was pronounced dead.

The father, a baker by profession, told us two of his sons, including Bilal, had given up their schooling after he had suffered a heart attack and had back trouble. They were helping him to earn and add to the family's income. A fifteen-year-old daughter, who entered the room, sat briefly with us and then left quietly. The father said she had been deeply affected by her brother's killing, and had stopped going to school. 'We tried to send her to her aunt's place but she didn't want to go. She spends hours in the graveyard or then sits near the village stream, wrapped in grief.'

Would the family want to file an FIR, we asked the father? 'What hopes of justice since we are under occupation? It would be of no use to us,' he said. 'We have to accept this sorrow.'

I was left musing about a militant's funeral, the State's violent targeted response to public grieving and a family's intense private loss. What did these incidents tell us about the spaces for public and private grief in Kashmir?

The father of Bilal Ahmed had referred to the militant, whose funeral his son attended, as a *mujahid* (a warrior, one who practises jihad). In Islamic belief, one who has died on the battlefield is *shahid* (martyr). The traditional funeral prayers by which the living appeal to God for forgiveness and entrance to heaven on behalf of the dead, are deemed unnecessary for *shahids*. They are viewed as pure; during burial rites their bodies do not undergo the ritual of a purifying bath: they are laid to rest in their blood-stained attire. The funeral is seen as a celebration.

What is central to the understanding of the Kashmiri struggle though is that the religious is deeply intertwined with the political: jihad and *mujahid* have become vested with complex meanings. Jihad is no longer seen as a collective fight for the sovereignty of Islamic polity (*dar*) but, instead as a personal struggle for security of Muslim bodies against political violence, as Cabeiri deBergh Robinson, observes. This ethnographer and researcher, who spent years on both sides of the border studying the Kashmir conflict, explains in her insightful work, how modern jihad has forged an Islamic notion of human rights in Kashmir. Jihadi *tanzims* (militant groups) assert their right to represent Kashmiri political aspirations and have created a language in which *farz* (obligation) is paired with human rights (*insani haquq*). Those who sacrifice themselves in this struggle for justice are *shahids*.[19]

The funerals of these militants, viewed as *shahids*, is an interplay of traditional rites of celebrations along with social lived practices of grief and loss.

In the 1990s, funerals of militants became political statements with thousands and thousands gathering, jostling to get a glimpse of the *shahid*. Those who could not assemble on the streets, peered out of balconies, windows, clambered up rooftops or climbed trees to get a glimpse of the procession. Women too played a prominent role singing songs of praise (*wahnuwan*) recalling the sacrifice. Adopting a celebratory air, they would accord the status of a bridegroom to the dead militant, and would toss candy, rose petals and almonds on the body. But there could also be scenes of lamenting and sorrow as well as slogans for self-determination.

The largest funeral gathering in the nineties was that of Ashfaq Majeed Wani, age thirty, the first commander-in-chief of the JKLF. Thousands participated in the funeral procession and women sang 'Alvida Sane Ashfaqo'.

In recent times it is Burhan Wani's funeral that draws comparisons. On 9 July 2016, just as Eid celebrations were winding down, the news of his death in an encounter began circulating. Once it was confirmed there was a hushed silence in the villages around Tral, his home in South Kashmir. Later the loudspeakers from the mosques resounded with the cries of '*Burhan, tum zinda hai*' (Burhan you will stay alive). People began their journeys from all parts of Kashmir, some more than 100 kilometres away and even as far as Rajouri and Poonch, converging at his home in Sharifabad. They came in tractors, buses, motorcycles and then simply walked the last few kilometres as a massive sea of people. One correspondent wrote that the crowds were so dense that it took more than an hour just to walk the last kilometre. It is said there may have been two lakh mourners thronging for a last glimpse. Funeral prayers were recited at least fifty times so that the crowds could be accommodated.[20]

The killing of Kashmir's iconic hero and the tidal waves of emotion saw massive protests and uprisings that have kept Kashmir on the edge ever since. The State has criminalised the mere mention of his name in social media.

Erasure from social media is a relentless ongoing exercise but Kashmiris defy obliteration of memory. In a perceptive and insightful analysis, researcher Inshah Malik analyses the question often asked in mainstream narratives. Why do so many people choose to mourn for and are willing to die for a man the Indian authorities called a terrorist?[21]

Public funerals for militants challenge the State's narrative, she explains. The media and political class in defence of the State had created a distinction between who is to be grieved (soldiers) and who must not be grieved. Kashmiris reject such imposed political frames.

The politics of mourning, she notes, is a reclamation that signifies a contest for political power. Unprecedented grief for Wani did not simply raise questions about the legitimacy of the present form of Indian governance but presented a moment of moral challenge to India's basic claim to sovereignty in the region.

One of the most striking features of these public displays

of grieving is the way the personal spaces are also being carved out. The mourners for Wani's funeral included women, who traditionally are forbidden from attending final funeral prayers or prolonged displays of grief. It was testimony to the way Wani had captured the hearts and imagination of the people as well as a reassertion of the political aspirations of the people. It demonstrated too how women could outdo religious law, writes Malik.

At Tral, the slogan was *'Tera bhai, mera bhai, Burhan bhai, Burhan bhai'* (He was your brother, he was my brother. He was Burhan brother). Wani, says Malik, became a *boi* (Kashmiri word for brother), an emblem of identifiable masculinity. A brother who fought and lost his life in defending his homeland. An example of how militants become part of a larger family in the imagination.

The public claim on a body can become contentious though as during the funeral of Essa Fazili, a militant from Srinagar. Fazili, a former engineering student, is believed to have joined the Ansar Ghazwat-ul-Hind, a small group that, unlike the Hizbul Mujahideen, believes in the establishment of the Caliphate rather than the nation state. A scuffle broke out when groups of youths tried to drape a black flag on his body, even before the women, including Fazili's young cousins, had finished paying their last respects. Scuffles continued throughout the huge funerary procession in 2018, making for a sad reflection on the politics of grief.[22]

However, by and large, despite the milling crowds and the very public spectacle of grief, these funerals are marked by decorum and respect, as Mattoo testifies.

She is aware of the gender challenges in covering funerals where there may be issues of sensitivity regarding the presence of women during the *namaz-e janazah*. Mattoo says, 'There are occasions when the crowds have indicated that as a woman I should not proceed ahead. I respect their sentiments. At other times, as in the case of the funeral of Saddam Padder (the last of the associates of Burhan Wani), it was the crowd who helped me get as close to the body as one can so I could take pictures. It was immensely moving because there had been so many thousands, patiently waiting to get that last look. I see it as respect for spaces, a certain ethics, dignity in mourning.'

She recalls the huge sea of people who had somehow walked for miles, crossed barricades, just for that one glimpse, many of them weeping together. It was a time when people offered each other tea, when a sense of togetherness prevailed.

This was again a funeral in which both men and women participated and Padder's mother and sister fired a few shots in the air as a final gun salute.

Funerals of civilians killed by security forces are also very public affairs where emotions are especially volatile. This is because in Kashmir those killed in the course of the struggle are also considered *shahid*; even children are accorded the status of martyrs. In its broadest usage, a *shahid* is one who is a witness, and in the cases of those killed by violent events, they are seen as those who have 'borne witness to start of violence or the dissolution of a state of justice,' explains Cabeiri deBergh Robinson. 'It is the dead body itself that testifies to the state of improper order by which a death occurred.'[23]

Ashraf Mattoo, father of Tufail Mattoo, the schoolboy killed in 2010, told the media how the authorities handed back his seventeen-year-old son's body and told him to bury him but he refused, insisting on an autopsy. It was the first step in the long hunt for justice that he has consistently pursued.

Whilst his family was bringing Tufail's body home to be buried in the family graveyard, many members of the public persuaded the father to let them bury him at the Martyrs' Graveyard at Eidgah. 'Tufail was my son, but after he died he belonged to Kashmir,' Ashraf Mattoo said.

When I met him in 2017, he was attending a meeting of concerned civilians who had gathered to press for a statement to be given to the UN calling attention to the lack of redressal of gross human rights abuses. For Mattoo, the issue was not just his personal grief but a general concern for all children of Kashmir. 'If a boy returning home from school is not safe on the streets of Srinagar, then which child in Kashmir is safe?' he told me.

In a paper on familial grief and resistance, Gowhar Fazili, a professor in Sociology, writes on the struggle of Ashraf Mattoo for justice drawing upon his moral status as the father of a child wrongfully killed. 'He has acquired a fearlessness from the fact that he has already encountered the worst one can imagine and it helps him confront the system and speak to it unabashedly and from a position of authority.'[24]

The father has connected his personal suffering with those of others and this fight for a larger cause may also be one way of dealing with personal loss. The work here, notes Fazili's paper, is both political and psychic—the work to restore meaning to both collective and personal life, the sense of community and family shattered by the state of extreme vulnerability, violence and loss.

'His narrative and his struggle transcend personal loss and concern universal moral principles that demand attention from the whole world (universalization of suffering as a means to come to terms with grief).'

The State, which has become increasingly aware of the emotive power of funerals and collective grief, used the coronavirus pandemic as a pretext to prevent handing over bodies of militants to the families. They were buried in places far away from their native villages, thereby preventing public funerals. Even civilians killed in action are being denied this most basic right to mourn.

When Kashmir's most prominent and respected resistance leader, Syed Ali Shah Geelani, died at home in 2021, where he had been detained for years, armed police literally broke the door to the room. They snatched the ninety-two-year-old leader's body. It was spirited away in the darkness and buried in a local graveyard at 4 a.m. of 3 September. Hundreds of security personnel had already set up barricades preventing journalists and grieving civilians, including many of Geelani's relatives from participating in the funeral. As is now the norm, internet services had been suspended.

According to media reports, the family told the police they could not participate in this 'managed funeral'. 'Do whatever you want to do. You have power, you have authority, we have nothing.'[25]

9

Spaces of Dissent

How did political mobilization come about in Kashmir? Where were the spaces for intellectual growth and ideas, political discourses and the emergence of political identity?

Kashmir's political history is a complex and volatile interaction between external forces and internal struggles; of which an important milestone dates back to the 1930s. This was when Muslim intellectuals in Kashmir Valley began exploring avenues to be rid of authoritarian and oppressive governance under the Dogras. Under Maharaja Hari Singh, Kashmir had been impoverished by heavy taxation; forced labour or *begar*, which though banned was still prevalent. Agriculture was the chief source of livelihood for the Muslim majority but they did not have property rights. The state took half the share of the kharif crop. Landless labourers worked as serfs for absentee landlords. It was against this mounting socio-economic oppression that opposition to the Dogra rule began taking shape.[1]

Several intellectuals, who had returned from Aligarh Muslim University, were keen on the uplift of their community. Mobilization began with meetings initially organized in mosques, but slowly political consciousness spread from the intelligentsia to the middle classes and moved out from mosques to larger scale open meetings, culminating in the revolt of 1931.

Most interestingly, one of the spaces for this political awakening came through the concept of a reading room, which then evolved into the Kashmir Reading Room Party that nurtured the nascent aspirations of leaders like Sheikh Mohammad Abdullah, Ghulam Nabi Gilkar and others.

Over a lengthy conversation Zahir-ud-Din, the well-known journalist, lawyer and civil society activist who has tried to challenge blanket official narratives with that of local histories, sketched the humble beginnings of this movement. A reading room, he said, was conceived originally by two cousins—Moulvi Bashir Ahmad Vakil, a school teacher from Magarmal, a neighbourhood in Srinagar, drawing a salary of Rs 15 per month, and Munshi Naseer-ud-Din, former editor of *Al Barq*. With the idea of encouraging intellectual pursuits and discussions, they set up a room at Fateh Kadal, furnished it with a few chairs and brought in some old newspapers.

Zahir-ud-Din recounted an anecdote about how they even sought funds at the Eidgah during Eid to keep the venture going. Initial reactions were discouraging with people showing more interest in using the room for gambling and gossiping rather than intellectual intent, he added.

A concerted bid to get more serious-minded individuals was undertaken with the two cousins deciding to host the *rasam-e-qul* (death ceremony held after some days) for a woman related to one of their friends, Mohammad Sikander, a telegraph master. Invitations were sent out and during the gathering of some 200 people, plans to resist Dogra oppression were raised. Three persons, namely G.N. Gilkar, Mohammad Rajab, a former administrator of the Srinagar municipality and Mohammad Yahya Rafiqui formally joined the Reading Room at this event, which is believed to be 8 May 1930.

Gilkar, who had founded the All-Kashmir Muslim Uplift Association (in response to the All-Kashmir Pandit Uplift Association) had been instrumental in encouraging Muslims to seek education, by going into shrines and mosques and setting up night schools.

Since many of the members of this Reading Room Party were from the Qadiani sect (the Ahmadiyas), it was feared that they may not gain general acceptance from the public and so a decision was taken to appeal to Sheikh Mohammad Abdullah to join in. Born into a middle class family of shawl traders, Abdullah was among those who had received education outside Kashmir. He had a degree from Punjab University and did his post-graduation in physics from the prestigious Aligarh Muslim University.

Accordingly, an invitation was sent out even offering the Sheikh leadership but he refused, stating in reply to the postcard invitation, that as a school teacher of the government school, Bagh-i-Dilawar Khan in Srinagar, he had his limitations.

Gilkar and Mohammad Rajab then set up an underground political cell and Kashmiri Muslims were approached for support. Editors of newspapers from outside Kashmir like Sir Bannerji, editor of *Indian States*, London, Maulana Abdul Kalam Azad and members of the Pan-Islamic Movement were also contacted and a Kashmiri historian, Munshi Muhammad Din Fauq, agreed to edit special editions highlighting the miserable conditions of the Muslims. The editors of Muslim newspapers in Lahore were already on board. Printed in Rawalpindi, these newspapers were smuggled into Srinagar in trucks and cars.[2]

An enraged Maharaja imposed a ban on some of these papers like *Kashmiri Mazloom* and *Kashmiri Magazine* but Munshi Fauq went on publishing newspapers under different names.

Meanwhile an important development had taken place.

Sheikh Abdullah was transferred to a school in Muzaffarabad and he resigned in April 1931. He then joined the Reading Room and a month later there was a reorganization with Abdullah becoming President.

Since it was not possible to locate an anti-Maharaja office in one permanent site, the premises of the Reading Room Party kept shifting. It moved from various residences and once functioned out of the house of a businessman, Amma Lal Mattoo, who owned a tonga garage. Abdullah had also stayed on the top floor of this house.

The demand for more jobs for Muslims and a new political culture, spurred by the Reading Room Party, was backed by Mirwaiz Yusuf Shah of the Jamia Masjid and the Mirwaiz of the Hamdani Khanqah-e-Moula, a Sufi shrine, who traditionally were on opposite camps. A consolidation of forces was taking place, causing discomfiture to the government of the Maharaja.

The government pasted a notice on the door of the Jamia Masjid saying the religious premises must not be used for political purposes and the Reading Room Party held a meeting with Abdullah in the chair. It was decided to ignore the notice and even tear it down but it was Gilkar, rather than Abdullah, who elected to take on the task.[3]

Besides the Reading Room, there were others who provided spaces during the dangerous times of the thirties, added Zahir-ud-Din. One such space was provided by a bookshop, the Noor Mohammed Tajmal Kitab in Maharajgunj, whose owner Ghulam Mohammed Bhat was sympathetic to the movement. He had a great respect for the word and was keen to further education among the Kashmiris and would often travel to Lahore to bring back books in Kashmiri, Arabic and Persian. The bookstore still exists.

The intellectual ferment meant confrontation was inevitable.

The spark that ignited the revolt came in April 1931, when news came in from Jammu that during the Eid prayers a policeman had ordered the Imam to stop the Khutba (sermon). This created discontent in Kashmir; and on 4 July word spread through the city of Srinagar that an official had desecrated the holy Koran.

A public meeting was called on 13 July at the Khanqah-e-Moula, where Muslims, irrespective of their various schools of thought, gathered. Sheikh Abdullah addressed the crowds appealing to Muslims to demand their rights. He also made an appeal to the Pandit community to join hands in seeking redressal. But stealing his thunder was a Pathan named Abdul Qadeer, who made a rousing speech. Pointing towards the palace of the Maharaja, he called for the demolition of the 'edifice of injustice, cruelty and subjugation.'[4]

Qadeer was arrested, charged with sedition and lodged in Srinagar's Central Jail. Abdullah, Gilkar and others were detained at the Hari Parbat Fort or Koh-e-Maran. Qadeer's upcoming trial evoked huge interest and the District Magistrate, apprehending trouble, proposed it be carried out in the jail premises. Maharaja Hari Singh's appeal for people to stay away went unheeded and a large group of people gathered on the road leading to the jail compound. Slogans were raised and when people refused to disperse, many were arrested. One of the people, who stood up and recited the *Azaan* prayers loudly, was shot dead. This was followed by stone pelting and then firing took place in which twenty-one people died. There were more killings in the protests that swept the city in this first revolt against Dogra rule.

The dead, referred to as martyrs, were all buried in the compound of the shrine of Khwaja Bahauddin Naqshbandi. Commemorated as Martyrs' Day, 13 July used to be an official state holiday until 2019.

The people in Kashmir continued their revolt even with the

jailing of the leaders. They shouted slogans against the Maharaja from rooftops and observed a general strike for nineteen days.

Eventually the British colonial government of India exercising its prerogative as the paramount power, appointed a commission under an Englishman, B.J. Glancy, to examine the grievances that had caused the disturbance.

The Glancy Commission's report included 'a powerful indictment of the Kashmir durbar's partisan functioning in favour of its Hindu subjects to the neglect of Muslims.' Strikingly, the report had also invalidated the principle of 'first peoples' on the basis of which the Dogras and Pandits had imagined Kashmir as 'originally' Hindu. Some reforms were announced, including Muslim representation in the establishment of the Praja Sabha or Subject Assembly.

Perceptions of the 1931 revolt differ widely and there are contesting histories. Hindu Pandit organizations have called it communal in nature, calling 13 July a black day. They label it the first step in purging the region of the Pandits. For the common people of Kashmir, it was an occasion to memorialize those who had died in the expression of the collective pent-up anger and fight for justice.

Historian Mridu Rai notes how Glancy's report provided a corrective to the way in which the majority of Kashmir's subjects were marginalized. Through its recommendations it reinscribed Muslims into their history and region.[5]

She also points to the irony of the appropriation of Martyrs' Day by the National Conference, even as it eventually became a party of status quo and tightened its 'pact of convenience and dependence with Delhi.'

The latest act of trying to erase the memorializing of the Kashmiri people by scrapping the holiday and its nomenclature of Martyrs' Day in 2019 is in line with the bid to recreate and fictionalize a Kashmir in the imaginary of a hyper-nationalist state.

Despite contesting histories on the events of 1931, it is indicative of how the power of the word, the pursuit for political thought, the idea of a reading room went on to spur events that had far-reaching effects and which catapulted several political actors onto the stage.

Lal Chowk and Ghanta Ghar: Battle of Loyalties

Srinagar's Lal Chowk or the Red Square, named in solidarity with the Russian Revolution, from where Abdullah's National Conference functioned in the mid-1930s, may seem an anomaly when one has been talking about mosques and Sufi shrines as spaces for the struggle of Kashmiri Muslims. But it is reflective of the vibrancy of an era when diverse influences were shaping Kashmir's politics.

According to Zareef Ahmad Zareef, the noted poet, who is also a repository of many local histories, the area around Lal Chowk was originally a *shamshan ghat* or cremation ground for Hindus, known as Kavuj Bagh. The Kavuj, he explained, were those who burnt the bodies and were largely Kashmiri Muslims.

The transformation of name and identity from Kavuj Bagh to Court Road as the locality came to be known later, is intertwined with the history of Kashmir's judicial institutions. It was under the rule of Maharaja Ranbir Singh (1856–85) that chief courts or Saddar Adalats were set up and civil and criminal laws under the Ranbir Penal Code were compiled. This penal code remained in force until the scrapping of Article 370 in 2019.

In 1877, an institution known as Adaalat-ul Sudur (or High Court) was established and its powers defined. The administration of the present judicial system began from the premises of the old High Court Building which also housed the Saddar Courts until the disastrous floods of 2014 forced them to shift out.

Zareef Ahmad Zareef recounts the interesting anecdote of how a legal luminary, when questioned about the choice of a cremation ground for situating the judicial institutions, replied that it would remind those dispensing justice that one day they too would be interred or turned to ashes but that acts of justice would live on.

This was the history of how a cremation ground became the site for the establishment of courts and then turned into a hub of political activity. Lal Chowk's associations with the Russian Square came about as a consequence of the Leftists' influence on the National Conference. The Leftists included B.P.L. Bedi and his wife Frieda Bedi (parents of actor Kabir Bedi), who wrote the Naya Kashmir manifesto. It was Prem Nath Bazaz, a Left-leaning Pandit, who was responsible for convincing Abdullah into thinking about a secular force to challenge Dogra rule. Accordingly an Urdu magazine called *Hamdard* was begun by the two.

The momentous turn had occurred in 1939 when the Muslim Conference that Abdullah had founded along with Chaudhry Ghulam Abbas and Mirwaiz Yusuf Shah changed its name to the National Conference to reiterate a secular approach. It was around this time too that the flag was designed—a bright red with a white plough. The colours and symbol bear the striking imprint of Left ideals, especially the Russian Revolution.

Prominent Leftists of that era were from both communities, the Muslims and the Pandits, and they included names like Sajad Haider, D.P. Dhar, Somnath Zutshi, Pran Kishore, P.N. Jalali and the former Prime Minister of Kashmir, Bakshi Ghulam Mohammad. It is said that Sajad Haider and some comrades first unfurled a red flag at Lal Chowk.

In 1946 Rajani Palme Dutt, éminence grise of the British Communist Party, visited India, and in Kashmir met with B.P.L. Bedi. He attended the trial of Sheikh Abdullah who had been jailed by the Maharaja. As correspondent of the *London Daily Worker* he reported on the trial, proclaiming 'Kashmir Leader on Trial is Uncrowned King'.

Within a few months, Abdullah was at the helm of affairs with the hurried Accession signed by the Maharaja. The Maharaja had panicked following the advance of forces of Pushtun tribes from the North West Frontier, who poured into the Valley at the behest of the dissenting Muslims of Poonch who feared slaughter. Abdullah's National Conference moved out of Zaina Kadal into Lal Chowk. It was from here that an Emergency Control Room was set up and functioned.

Shortly afterwards Pandit Nehru visited Kashmir and huge crowds gathered at Lal Chowk, consisting of many National Conference volunteers who had worked as volunteers and patrolled Srinagar's streets during the Pashtun raids. Nehru unfolded the national flag from this venue and also promised the crowds there would be a referendum.

The Sheikh responded by quoting Persian poet Amir Khusro. '*Mun tu shudum tu mun shudi: Mun tun shudam tu jan shudi: Ta kas na goyad baad azeen, mun deegram, tu deeagray*' (You became me, and I became you, I am the body and you are the soul; henceforth, let nobody say we are separate from each other).

The actual spot that came to be known as Lal Chowk was in front of the Palladium Cinema and had a circular podium with a flagpost but these landmarks have since undergone considerable change. The Palladium was burnt down and is now the site of a military bunker. Ghanta Ghar, the famed clock tower, was built in the 1980s by Bajaj Electricals and at first had no real significance. It was Murli Manohar Joshi of the BJP who made it into a site of contestation when he tried to unfurl the Indian flag from its top in 1992. He had to hurriedly be taken away when a rocket fired by a militant landed close by.

Since then Ghanta Ghar has become the place where assertions of identity and political statements are sought to be made. People have made bids to plant various flags; it had to be swathed in concertina wire during the 2019 siege to prevent any statements!

In 2021, the clock tower was illuminated with the colours of the national flag in a build up to the Independence Day celebrations. But, hours later, the Shia community put up their own traditional banner in black, commemorating the sacrifice of Hussain ibn Ali, the grandson of Prophet Muhammad, during the battle of Karbala and a reminder of the fight for social justice. As a Shia youth told me, Hussain's life and fight in standing up against oppression takes on a particular resonance in present times.

The spatial expansions following the setting up of the National Conference office, also facilitated the mushrooming of various social and commercial activities.

Shops and establishments that had been set up flourished because of its central location. Zareef Ahmad Zareef recalls that whenever people from downtown wanted to purchase outfits for a wedding, the shoes for a bridegroom, a radio or a bicycle, they came to Lal Chowk. Pre-Partition, it was also the site from where bus services ran to Rawalpindi. Among the bus services, he could recall were the Nanda Bus Service and Radhakrishna Bus Service.

The political hubbub facilitated the springing up of many coffee houses and restaurants. The National Conference itself had first occupied the Punjab Muslim Hotel and the Kashmir Guest House.

Zareef Ahmad Zareef told me it was also the time when Lipton tea or the Indian-style brew made its appearance. Traditionally Kashmiris drink nun chai or salted tea.

One notable restaurant for animated conversations was the Coffee House, set up by the Coffee Board near Regal Lane where coffee and dosas were sold at nominal rates. Today the Khan News Agency occupies the spot. Its owner Hilal Ahmad recalls both Sheikh Abdullah and his son Farooq Abdullah picking up copies of various newspapers when it functioned as a stall on the road.[6]

Just down the road from Lal Chowk, on Residency Road, is Ahdoos, famed as one of the oldest hotels and restaurants of Srinagar. Overlooking the Jhelum, it attracted the lawyers and bureaucrats who used to meet for tea and conversation. During the 1990s, it was the only hotel functioning and hosted all outstation visiting journalists. Andrew Whitehead of the BBC, who purloined a hotel sign warning people not to drink, recalls it was the only hotel open when the others had shut down or been taken over by the army. 'Everyone knew where to find you.' Indeed, according to one media report, Whitehead once received a call at the reception desk with the caller identifying himself as AJ.

'AJ what?' It took a little time for Whitehead to figure out the call was from a militant organization, Harkat ul-Ansar, claiming responsibility for a blast. On Ahdoos' hundredth birthday, Whitehead hailed the hotel and restaurant as a survivor adding that in Kashmir, that is something.[7]

A few metres away from Ahdoos, opposite the Polo View, is Lala Sheikh, Srinagar's popular eatery, renowned for its chicken patties. Now divided into three sections, run by the great-grandsons of the founder, it is the first section that attracts the milling crowds, many of whom are journalists from the neighbouring Press Colony and newspaper offices.

Sitting down for a chai in the cavernous interior and facing the 135-year-old mirror on the wall, I was given several bites of fascinating history by journalist and friend, Nayeem Rather. I relished those along with mouthfuls of my chicken patty.

He told me that the restaurant, established in 1890 by Lala Mohammad Sheikh, became famous during the Second World War when British troops from the transient camp of the infantry at Naseem Bagh (now Kashmir University) would visit the Bund, the embankment along the Jhelum river that runs behind Lala Sheikh. Coming there for recreation purposes, they would then drop into the tea room but it wasn't for the chicken patties. In those days the rage was kidney *kanti* or the English equivalent that is fried kidney and toast and fish kebabs that were wolfed down with the cuppas.

Besides the chicken patties, Lala Sheikh is *mashoor* (famed) for the apocryphal tale of Mohammad Ali Jinnah being a guest. Popularly known as Quaid-e-Azam (great leader), Jinnah undertook his last journey to Kashmir in May 1944 and stayed about two months in Srinagar.

One of the great-grandsons running the teahouse, Altaf, said he believed the story was true because '*Yeh mein neh apne dada se sunnah hai*' (I heard about this from my grandfather).

What is in no doubt however, according to Zareef Ahmad Zareef, whom Rather has quoted in his article, is that in the forties a bunch of progressive writers—Dina Nath Nadim, Bansi Nirdosh, Akhtar Mohiuddin, Pran Jalal and others would gather at Lala Sheikh for discussions that could go on till midnight.

'Lala Sheikh has seen some of the fiercest literary and political discussions in Kashmir,' Zareef says. 'It is witness to our history, political and cultural.'[8]

In the 1950s and 1960s, the teahouse became the haunt of the National Conference party workers and supporters and, in the 1970s and 1980s, the clientele included famous singers and artistes from Doordarshan and Radio Kashmir which was located close by.

The 1990s were when, according to Altaf, *haalat bigar gaya* (conditions turned bad) but some of the militant commanders would drop by in the evening for a chai bringing along their guns which would be placed on neighbouring chairs, according to Rather. It was said that the JKLF leader, Yasin Malik, who hailed from the adjoining neighbourhood of Maisuma, would often send for tea from the tea room.

Today, the owners are still committed to keeping the rates affordable despite inflation. Its strategic location makes it an important haunt to stay abreast of fast-folding events in volatile times and gather information on whatever is happening.

Srinagar's vibrant coffee house culture and its political overtones came under state scrutiny, and in 2011, the government announced the opening of swanky branded coffee outlets, as a way of weaning away the student community from radicalized politics. The setting up of a subsidized branded outlet in the Kashmir University campus was sharply criticized by some members of the student community who objected to the university grounds being used for a commercial outlet. The outlet functioned for a few years out of Naseem Bagh, the part of Kashmir University that has some magnificent chinar trees, but it shut down after an accidental fire damaged the structure.

Whilst 'elitist' is the tag used for such branded outlets, anthropologists observe how the labyrinthine alleys and interiors of Srinagar and other towns with small eateries and tea stalls have provided spaces for urgent and charged-up conversations. Here, away from the main roads and highways manned by security forces, information is swiftly shared and flows into the community.

I personally experienced something of these shared intimate spaces when one summer morning, I stopped over at a small restaurant for chai. I sensed a palpable unease in the air. Nothing was being said but, unable to bear the unspoken, I asked a young man if there was going to be a *hartal* (a shutdown that is called for by the Hurriyat whenever there is a civilian killing). He looked up and said, 'No. But we hear Manan is trapped.'

He assumed I knew it was the militant Abdul Manan Wani, the PhD Aligarh Muslim University scholar, whose open letters to the Government of India had been made to disappear from social media (an 'enforced disappearance' as one scholar called it). The letters had kindled the imagination of Kashmiri youth, much in the way Burhan Wani's appearance on the social media and ingenious use of visual content had.[9]

As it happened, Manan escaped that day. He was killed some months later but I was witness to the way intense emotions can permeate the very air in such places and how despite so many curbs, this spirit cannot be completely trammelled.

Cinema Halls and Playgrounds: Venues for Secret Meetings

I asked Zahir-ud-Din about the 1980s, the period of intense political fervour, just before the 1990s, when surveillance and intimidation was at a high. How did people strategize for mobilization?

He spoke about the various ruses adopted when he was associated with student organizations. 'Cinema halls were still functioning and they were great venues for secret meeting. Naaz, with its separate cabins for families, was especially popular. You could go, sit in a corner and discuss something at length, especially during the seven to nine o'clock night shows when the audiences were not so large.

'I recall how for seven consecutive days we once sat down

for a film screening and tried to thrash out a problem. Of course I wasn't concentrating on the film, but then a friend told me it was a good one and I should definitely go on the eighth day just for the viewing! Meeting in cinemas was a gambit we could use through the late 1980s, 1987, '88 and '89. When the cinema houses shut down in the 1990s it was a big blow for us too!'

Another ploy adopted was for people to gather in a playground, perhaps a football field, and to sit around, maybe kick a ball around a bit, and then get into a huddle for an exchange of ideas. That was perhaps how many members of the Students Islamic League got together but by the time the 1990s came, the outside was no longer considered safe.

Barber shops and hairdressing salon that allowed people to sit down became the place to discuss politics, especially as many of them kept newspapers lying around.

Meat shops and especially bakeries were places that became conduits of information since it is customary for men to go in the mornings to purchase the fresh *lavasas* (Kashmiri bread) and also get a quick update on the news. Bakeries are small and transient spaces and escape surveillance; they can facilitate lively exchanges because of the constant flow of people.

Free and open spaces for longer spells of political discussions were the *waan pyend* or the front extensions of shops where men, especially the youth, generally congregate.

During curfews, there were ways of communicating with people in the neighbourhood through notes carried by the milkman to various households as Farah Bashir mentions in her book.[10]

Perhaps the most bizarre venue for a clandestine meeting and then the launching of an underground political party was a graveyard in Srinagar. An old-time activist of the 1990s, Noor Mohammad Katjoo, known as the 'Daredevil of Downtown' revealed to journalist Bilal Handoo, how in the late 1980s he met with Farooq Ahmad Khushru to begin local recruitment of youths for the forthcoming struggle. It was at the Malkhah, the largest graveyard in Srinagar, that it was decided to float a pro-freedom movement party known as Al Maqbool.[11]

Katjoo, in the same interview to Handoo, shares details of the manner in which plans were laid to use the Regal Talkies, a popular cinema theatre in Lal Chowk, as the catalyst for a mini rebellion against the Sheikh.

It was in the summer of 1985 and the film *Lion of the Desert* starring Anthony Quinn was playing at this theatre. The film, directed by Moustafa Akkad depicted the life of the Libyan Bedouin leader Omar Mukhtar who refused to surrender before the Italian army and colonial rule even though he is brought in chains. It had an impact on many Kashmiris, who believed Sheikh Abdullah had betrayed the peoples' aspirations by signing the accord with Indira Gandhi in 1975.

One day during the afternoon show of the film, the audience, mainly youths, began raising angry slogans against Abdullah, berating him for his capitulation and comparing him unfavourably with Mukhtar.

According to Katjoo, the reactions of the audiences were not as spontaneous as it was believed, but were part of a plan that had been hatched earlier. Many of the protesters had bought tickets and sat in the stalls and at a particular moment, began the slogan shouting. Outside they were joined by students of the Sri Pratap School and College and they all marched towards Ghanta Ghar, bringing down posters of Sher-e-Kashmir as Abdullah was once known. Amongst those in the crowd were Yasin Malik of the JKLF and others.

Katjoo says he had even brought along a photograph of Sheikh Abdullah to be burnt publicly. He obtained it by persuading a shopkeeper the previous day to let him have the framed photo saying that a brother was refusing to have his engagement ceremony without the Sheikh's photograph to grace the event![12]

Screenings of the film were discontinued. Years later, a member of the Islamic Students League called the Regal Talkies a building that held importance in the Kashmiri struggle. Cinema halls, however, began receiving threats from a lesser-known Islamic militant outfit known as Allah Tigers in the late nineties. They said showing movies was unIslamic. Many halls continued to struggle through the militancy years but Regal Talkies shut down when a bomb was hurled in 1999 that killed one person and injured others.

Cinema halls morphed into CRPF camps with drab netting draping their exteriors. Some even became torture centres and the Palladium was burnt down by militants, after which a CRPF camp functioned in the rubble.

In his epitaph to his city, Kashmir's iconic poet Agha Shahid Ali recalls :

> 'Dear Shahid, they burnt the Palladium;
> There the kiss each weekend at 7 p.m.
> Was enshrined, and we tried it, merciless
> to ourselves—we pulled the kiss off the screen...

And

> ...In Lal Chowk
> What's left to abolish? There is no horizon
> From the trees we are tearing flowers of smoke,
> No longer target for a kiss, but our lips open.[13]

Anchar's Legacy of Defiance

Lal Chowk has a chequered history but it is Anchar that proudly claims a legacy of defiance as Hayat Ahmed Butt, the man who led many of Anchar's spirited protests, told me.

This neighbourhood of Soura, a suburb of Srinagar, came into the arc lights of the media when videos depicting a procession of slogan-shouting people on 9 August 2019 was screened by BBC.

In the *sub kuch* normal *hai* (everything is normal) narrative, the Indian government insisted these Anchar protests did not happen but BBC, *Al Jazeera*, the *Guardian* and other media outlets showed otherwise, uploading the video. Subsequently, there were protests in September that took place after Friday prayers and the foreign media carried reports on it.

Anchar's inhabitants began to receive a steady stream of media persons and was variously described as 'Little Gaza', an 'oasis of resistance,' or then as a violent neighbourhood, in the grip of gun-toting militants.

In one piece, journalist Abhijit Iyer-Mitra, a fellow from the Institute of Peace and Conflict Studies (ICPR), stated Anchar was a place where its inhabitants know how to spin a yarn and market it. (The ICPR states it is an independent think tank and was founded by IAS officer P.R. Chari and Major General (retd) Dipankar Banerjee.)

In a triumphant burst of disinformation, the journalist announced there had been no pellet gun victims simply because he couldn't find any. This was around the time that attempts were being made to rubbish accounts of pellet gun victims that had begun surfacing after the enforced silences. Pellet gun victims, have always been hesitant about sharing information or even seeking medical treatment because they fear police action.[14]

When I visited Anchar, a few weeks later, in mid-October of 2019, there were security forces and their armoured vehicles on the main road. The woman who was escorting me, suddenly grabbed me by my arm and veered off this road into one of the bylanes. We were approaching the historic place of worship, the Asar Sharief Jenab Sahib, which contains holy relics and there were no visible signs of troops.

We were now in the 'liberated zone' of Kashmir's political imaginary. There were the distinctive imprints like slogans painted on gates declaring it to be LT HM Downtown. (LT stands for Lashkar-e-Taiba and HM for Hizbul Mujahideen).

Slogans of 'Azadi' and 'Chhota Pakistan' were scrawled across shuttered shops. In another spot there was a small photo gallery of militant '*shahids*'. Elsewhere a banner read 'Welcome Imran Khan.' The Pakistani leader's speech in the United Nations General Assembly was getting clear appreciation.

But there were also tell-tale signs of the grim struggle in the form of buildings with no windows. They had been boarded up with cardboard boxes or then draped with blankets to keep the chill out. Clearly, there had been night raids with wanton destruction and pitched battles had taken place with security forces.

I was also shown the tactics by which the Anchar residents resisted the entry of security forces into this zone. Trenches had been dug to halt vehicles; there were improvised barriers made of columns of bricks and stones that could also serve as the arsenal of the stone pelters.

I was taken to meet with Anchar's charismatic leader Hayat Ahmed Butt of the Jammu and Kashmir Muslim League, who had been freely meeting with media persons and addressing crowds.

I asked Butt what Anchar and its people stood for in this struggle. It drew a lengthy reply. 'We are *gayoor, deen-pasand log* (proud and honourable people who believe in law and religion), given to fighting for our rights from the time of the first agitation against *begar* or forced labour during the reign of Hari Singh,' he said.

Sketching the history of this locality, he demolished the suggestions that Anchar was just a media-created marketing ploy. He explained how it was in Soura, near the bank of the Anchar Lake that Sheikh Abdullah was born in a family of shawl traders. He nurtured this constituency and developed the first political party of Kashmir, the Muslim Conference, with its avowed intention to fight feudalism and work for the uplift of the Muslims oppressed by Dogra rule. When the Muslim Conference adopted a secular name and politics and became the National Conference, Soura was its hub and it was from here that the Reshumari Tehreek or fight for a plebiscite began. In 1969, the Abdullahs shifted out of Soura.

During the armed struggle, this National Conference bastion then became a base camp for the JKLF with its founders Ashfaq Majid Wani, Hamid Sheikh and Yasin Malik. In 1996, Yasin Malik announced the JKLF was eschewing the armed struggle to become a political party.

This shift towards an *awami tehreek* or a people's movement, said Butt, was reflected by the way the people in this locality participated in the protests of 2008, sparked off by the decision to give land to the Amarnath Shrine Board which triggered fears of a demographic shift, the 2009 protests when the bodies of two women, Asiya and Nelofar were found in suspicious circumstances in Shopian, and the 2010 uprising.

Demonstrating an ability for crisis management when the administration failed, it was the youths of Soura who rescued people during the 2014 floods. Volunteers paddled forth in small boats to various parts of the city. A community kitchen was set up in the adjacent Sher-e-Kashmir Institute of Medical Sciences (SKIMS) where food was prepared for doctors, patients, attendants and other medical staff.

The *ehtijaaj* (protest or dissent) that has rolled out from 2016 onwards has been amplified by the Anchar–Soura communities. The strong and articulate presence of women in the BBC video, is a demonstration of a well-knit community.[15]

I am reminded of how it was these women, who had staged one of the most potent images of resistance, lying down on the roads in front of the vehicles that were taking away their men and youths.

Butt was insistent that the Kashmiris were not begging but rightfully demanding what had been promised to them in Parliament. For those who had still believed in Article 370, abrogation meant that even this tenuous bridge with India had been severed.

It was the bid to try and stop prayers at the Janab Sab before Eid that drew a massive protest, he told me, with even the elderly joining in. 'We ensured security forces withdrew from our lanes and said the prayers, even as a helicopter and drones kept hovering above.'

The price of resistance for Anchar's working-class population had been considerable, we realized, as we interacted with the residents. Self-imposed shutdowns to protest against the government's actions are common in Kashmir but the one that followed the 2019 siege was prolonged. In Anchar, as in many working-class neighbourhoods, it was perceived as a strong statement of anger and an example of sacrifice for the cause. One young woman told me with some pride that her father was a driver of a Sumo. These shared services are the most common mode of transport in the city. 'The vehicle's battery is almost dead because he has not been able to ply during the *hartal*.'

Rumours that it was Pakistan's funding that enabled people to sustain the prolonged *hartal*, were scoffed at by Butt who dismissed it as propaganda.

'Our Islamic concept of *zakat* (a community wealth tax seen as a religious obligation) and *baitulmal* has put a system in place. Weddings are celebrated, our labourers can eat *gosh* (meat) and we help the *reddewallahs* (roadside hawkers). We funded the ticket of a woman who flew to Agra to visit her son in jail. This is because of our system—of *insaani jazba* or humanitarianism .'[16]

During our conversation, a youth came into the room, went to a corner and pulled out a small bottle of eye medicine which he inserted into his eye and then walked out. Here was a pellet gun victim. There were many more and later a youth mentioned he had sustained pellet gun wounds but did not go to hospital, knowing the surveillance is high. They preferred self-treatment rather than risk imprisonment.

Two days after my visit, security forces made an entry into Anchar and picked up Butt, placing him in custody. He joined hundreds of Kashmir's leaders, political workers and activists. Thereafter protests petered out.

One of the most powerful images of protest that had emerged from Anchar was that of a man who had ingeniously twisted barbed wire around his face to suggest a cage. Was Anchar, the symbol of defiance, now totally caged? Silenced?

Some of the most repressive laws and series of measures have been pushed through in Kashmir since the abrogation of Article 370. These range from a Forest Act that deprives hundreds of pastoral communities of their right to live in their ancestral homes; the sanctioning of mining leases to non-Kashmiris that threaten to destroy and ravage the land; amendment of domicile laws that allow a heavy influx of non-Kashmiris, especially Central government employees, to buy land and enjoy permanent citizenship; contract farming that threatens the livelihoods of Kashmir's large agricultural community and the new media policy which gives the state the right to determine what is news and to penalize those whom it claims are putting out fake news. Under this media policy, vigilantes can report and snoop on people on social media.

The goal, openly proclaimed by Hindu right-wing propagandists, is to bring about demographic change and turn the 68 per cent Muslim majority of J&K into a disempowered minority in their own homeland. The delimitation process is the essential step to permanently disallow even a remote possibility for reversal in the future.[17]

Kashmiris fear cultural annihilation. Will there be a *naqba* or permanent displacement, much like what Palestinians suffered? Will Kashmir lose its unique identity?

In my over decade-long association with Kashmir, never have I witnessed a mood so grim, so bleak. The ominous calm, the enforced silences don't provide neat answers.

Since the abrogation there has been a hardening of stance by both state and non-state agencies. There have been allegations of fake encounters and civilians killed in cold blood by security forces. There have also been killings of a Kashmiri Pandit pharmacist, a Sikh and a Hindu schoolteacher and some non-local Hindu labourers and hawkers. Police claim it is the work of a militant group called the Resistance Front and have said there are now hybrid militants or so-called overground workers, who live as civilians but are able to go after soft targets.

I recall Rodin's statues—'The Burghers of Calais'. In his work the artist rejected the prevalent theories of heroism as 'triumphal apotheosis'. He felt such glorification did not correspond to anything real. Instead, Rodin redefined heroism in his works to depict human beings in agony attempting to rely upon their dignity and self-control despite the presence of despair and fear.

Does such heroism prevail? In my mind several snap memories and conversations flit past. I recall the words of a Kashmiri friend, who is an engineer. 'I will not take up any government contracts, no matter how lucrative. I take up whatever small project I can get. How do I keep the spirit for freedom alive? I choose to believe in its possibilities. As long as it is in my mind, I believe I am free.'

I hear of the incident of a *reddewallah*, during the civilian shutdown or *hartal* of 2019. Bringing his cart out from a small alley, he tells his friend, 'I fulfilled my vow that I would participate for two months. The loss of income is my contribution towards the struggle.'

I remember too how I watched with amazement once as a man nonchalantly came up towards a soldier patrolling a street. He bent down, took out a piece of chalk from his pocket, scrawled the word 'Azadi' on the sidewalk, and then walked away, just as casually.

I read too with admiration at the way grieving families of two men killed in a fake encounter staged a sit-in. Relatives of Butt and Gul sat near the Press Colony in sub-zero temperatures, on the winter night of 17 November 2021, demanding the dead bodies. The authorities had switched off the electricity, but in solidarity, a gentleman switched on the headlights of his car to provide illumination. The incident attracted so much attention that the protest grew until the administration was forced to conduct an exhumation at the site where the bodies had been hastily buried. They were handed over to the families and a probe has been announced.

My most abiding image though comes from an autumnal October morning. It is 2019. The Ghanta Ghar is still covered with concertina wire. Armoured vehicles are parked at a site which has seen much history. It was here that the Palladium stood and Jawaharlal Nehru and Sheikh Abdullah pledged mutual allegiance. Later the cinema hall morphed into a bunker.

The shops have begun downing shutters; it is only 9.30 a.m. but the civilian protest or *hartal* is in force. Soldiers patrol the streets. Amidst all this a woman, oblivious to everything, hunkers down, scattering grain for the birds on the ground, doing something she probably has been doing all through the years.

Acknowledgements

I owe so much to the people and friends in Chhattisgarh and Kashmir. Without their constant encouragement and support this book could never happen.

The times are such that they will remain unnamed but never forgotten.

Notes

1. Forest

1. Kela, Shashank. *A Rogue and Peasant Slave: Adivasi Resistance 1800–2000'*, pub. Navayana Publishing.
2. Seal, Arunopol. 'Out of the Forest: the products, the people and their markets in Uttar Bastar', pub. Sahapedia. https://www.sahapedia.org/out-forest-products-people-and-their-markets-uttar-bastar, 14 March 2019.
3. Ibid.
4. Ramnath, Madhu. *Woodsmoke and Leafcups,* pub. HarperCollins Publishers.
5. Sundar, Nandini. *The Burning Forest: India's War in Bastar,* pub. Juggernaut.
6. Seal, Arunopol. 'Out of the Forest: the products, the people and their markets in Uttar Bastar', pub. Sahapedia. https://www.sahapedia.org/out-forest-products-people-and-their-markets-uttar-bastar, 14 March 2019
7. Ramnath, Madhu. *Woodsmoke and Leafcups,* pub. HarperCollins Publishers.
8. Abraham, Sara. 'Tribes, Rights and Justice in India'. https://againstthecurrent.org/atc176/p4418/.
9. Poyam, Akash. 'What's in a surname? Reflections on Adivasis' History of Northern Chhattisgarh', pub. *Round Table India,* 20 December 2016.

10. The terms 'Maoist' and 'Naxalite' are often used interchangeably in India. The terms 'Naxalite' and 'Naxalism' originated from the village of Naxalbari in West Bengal, where in 1967 far-Left radical communists supporting Maoist ideology began a movement. This spread to rural Central and Eastern India through various underground groups. All Naxalites are Maoists in India but globally, all Maoists are not Naxalites.
11. 'Chhattisgarh: A Resource Abundant but Turbulent Land'. https://shodhganga.inflibnet.ac.in/bitstream/10603/55404/11/11_chapter%203.pdf.
12. Sundar, Nandini. *The Burning Forest: India's War in Bastar*, pub. Juggernaut.
13. Sourced from 'When the State Makes War on Its Own People'. A report on the violation of people's rights during the Salwa Judum Campaign in Dantewda, Chhattisgarh. April 2006.'
14. Navlakha, Gautam. 'Maoists in India', pub. *Economic and Political Weekly*, June 2006.
15. Fact-finding Team: 'Attack on Vanvasi Chetna Ashram in Chhattisgarh', pub. Countercurrents.org. https://www.countercurrents.org/dobhal110609.htm, 11 June 2009.
16. Sundar, Nandini. 'Bastar, Maoism and Salwa Judum', pub. *Economic and Political Weekly*, July 22, 2006.
17. Sundar Nandini. *The Burning Forest: India's War in Bastar*, pub. Juggernaut.
18. Roy, Arundhati. *Walking with the Comrades*, pub. Penguin Random House.
19. Sundar, Nandini. *The Burning Forest: India's War in Bastar*, pub. Juggernaut.
20. Ghose, Dipankar. 'Chhattisgarh: At Salwa Judum camp, families forgotten for 13 years, untouched by poll campaign', pub. *The Indian Express*. https://indianexpress.com/article/india/at-salwa-judum-camp-families-forgotten-for-13-years-untouched-by-poll-campaign-5440861/, 11 November 2018.

2. Body

1. Ghose, Dipankar. '15 Maoists killed in Sukma encounter, another security operation underway', pub. *The Indian Express*. https://indianexpress.com/article/india/chhattisgarh-sukma-maoist-encounter-death-toll-arrested-5294310/, 7 August 2018.
2. Bhatia, Bela. 'Monsoon Massacre: What really happened in Nulkatong encounter?', pub. *The Caravan*, 1 January 2019.
3. Sethi, Aman. '35 killed as Maoists blow up bus in Chhattisgarh', pub. *The Hindu*. https://www.thehindu.com/news/35-killed-as-Maoists-blow-up-bus-in-Chhattisgarh/article16301608.ece, 18 May 2010.
4. South Asia Terrorism Portal India. https://www.satp.org/satporgtp/countries/india/maoist/timelines/2012/Chhattisgarh.html.
5. Poyam, Akash. 'Stepsons of the Soil', pub. *The Caravan*. https://caravanmagazine.in/conflict/in-battles-between-paramilitary-insurgents-victims-from-same-marginalised-group, 14 February 2020.
6. Salwa Judum order, https://hrln.org/uploads/2017/12/salwa-judum-order.pdf.
7. Case history: Front Line Defenders. https://www.frontlinedefenders.org/en/case/case-history-soni-sori.
8. A. Kritika. 'In the Gompad Trail: An account of 15 "encounter" deaths and bloodied facts in a haystack of security fiction from Chhattisgarh', pub. *The Leaflet*. https://www.theleaflet.in/in-the-gompad-trail-an-account-of-15-encounter-deaths-and-bloodied-facts-in-a-haystack-of-security-fiction-from-chhattisgarh/, 27 August 2008.
9. Subramaniam, Malini. 'One of Chhattisgarh's biggest anti-Maoist actions? Only civilians were killed, say Sukma villagers', pub. Scroll.in. https://scroll.in/article/891596/one-of-chhattisgarhs-biggest-anti-naxal-operations-only-civilians-were-killed-say-sukma-villagers.

10. A. Kritika. 'In the Gompad Trail: An account of 15 "encounter" deaths and bloodied facts in a haystack of security fiction from Chhattisgarh', pub. *The Leaflet*. https://www.theleaflet.in/in-the-gompad-trail-an-account-of-15-encounter-deaths-and-bloodied-facts-in-a-haystack-of-security-fiction-from-chhattisgarh/, 27 August 2008; Shukla, Kamal. 'A report on the Sukma "encounter"', pub. Ground Xero. https://www.groundxero.in/2018/08/26/sukma-encounter/, 26 August 2018.
11. Shaw, Padmaja. 'Villagers Say Chhattisgarh Encounter Victims Were Civilians, Including Children', pub. The Wire. https://thewire.in/rights/villagers-say-chhattisgarh-encounter-victims-were-civilians-including-children, 28 August 2018.
12. Alternative Law Forum, 'The Padayatra from Dantewada to Gompad: Liberating the Tricolour from the Clasp of Violence', http://altlawforum.org/pedagogy/the-padayatra-from-dantewada-to-gompad-liberating-the-tricolour-from-the-clasp-of-violence/.
13. Subramaniam Malini and Kamal Shukla, 'A Stark Nude Body Wrapped in Plastic, What Happened to a Young Woman in Chhattisgarh', pub. Scroll.in. https://scroll.in/article/810601/a-stark-nude-body-wrapped-in-plastic-what-happened-to-a-young-woman-in-chhattisgarh, 27 June 2016.
14. Manecksha, Freny. 'The Edesmetta Inquiry, and Adivasis' Odyssey to Justice in Chhattisgarh', pub. The Wire. https://thewire.in/rights/the-edesmetta-inquiry-and-adivasis-odyssey-to-justice-in-chhattisgarh, 13 April 2018.
15. Kaiser, Ejaz. 'Photo puts question mark on cops' claim of killing "Maoist" woman in gunfight', pub. *Hindustan Times*. https://www.hindustantimes.com/india-news/photo-puts-question-mark-on-cops-claim-of-killing-maoist-woman-in-gunfight/story-FeYPCYwAGaNClmQ9o6kE7L.html, 20 June 2016.
16. 'Tragic Case of Madkam Hidme's Encounter, Her Mother Lakshmi's Fight for Justice', Human Rights Law Network. https://2019.hrln.org/tragic-case-of-madkam-hidmes-fake-encounter-her-mother-lakshmis-fight-for-justice-continues/.

17. Baxi, Upendra. *The Future of Human Rights,* pub. Oxford University Press.
18. Sharma, Mohit. 'NHRC draws criticism over annual debate competition topic', pub. *India Today.* //www.indiatoday.in/india/story/nhrc-draws-criticism-over-annual-debate-competition-topic-1874915-2021-11-09, 9 November 2021.
19. The Bhima Koregaon case, as it has come to be known, dates back to events of 1 January 2018 when violence broke out at the site of a commemorative function held to mark the victory of Dalit Mahars and British troops over the Peshwas. Although the case was first filed against Hindutva leaders, Milind Ekbote and Sambhaji Bhide, the Pune police suddenly arrested a number of lawyers, activists and academicians, accusing them of inciting violence. Sudha Bharadwaj was among those held. They were accused of organizing the Elgar Parishad, a public event, the day before. The charges included that of having links with Naxalites and a conspiracy to assassinate the Prime Minister. The NIA has taken over the case and a total of sixteen people are being charged. Father Stan Swamy, a Jesuit priest of Jharkhand, died during custody.
20. Bharadwaj, Sudha. 'Gravest Displacement, Bravest Resistance'. https://www.academia.edu/16971927/Gravest_Displacement_Bravest_Resistance.
21. Boga, Dilnaz. 'India's illegal detention of juveniles rising, lawyers say', pub. New Internationalist. https://newint.org/blog/2015/06/05/indias-illegal-detention-of-juveniles/, 5 June 2015.
22. PTI. 'Hardcore Naxal commander Arjun killed in Bastar encounter', pub. *The Hindu.* https://www.thehindu.com/news/national/Hardcore-Naxal-commander-Arjun-killed-in-Bastar-encounter/article14572763.ece, 16 August 2016.
23. Burns, Anna. *Milkman,* pub. Faber and Faber.
24. Subramaniam, Malini. 'The killings of a teenage undertrial shows Bastar is a dangerous place to be young', pub. Scroll.in. https://

scroll.in/article/814621/the-killing-of-a-teenage-undertrial-shows-bastar-is-a-dangerous-place-to-be-young, 24 August 2016.

25. 'Bearing Witness: Sexual Violence in South Chhattisgarh', pub. Women Against Sexual Violence and State Repression (WSS).
26. Sinha, Tameshwar. 'Tribals dug 5 km road in Bastar', pub. Janjwar.com. https://janjwar.com/livelihood/tribals-dug-5-km-road-in-bastar-school-hospital-anganwadi-not-security-camps-in-our-villages-667050?fbclid=IwAR0eWIlqWr25hbjRytM6IMlZgKo-Od_Mnqnylh-CG__1nw_ZWwzwiZoPgXA.
27. Subramaniam, Malini. 'In Bastar journos force Maoists to roll back death threats', pub. Scroll.in. https://scroll.in/article/987628/in-bastar-journalists-force-maoists-to-roll-back-death-threats, 23 February 2021.
28. Sundar, Nandini. 'Mimetic Sovereignties, Precarious Citizenship, State Effects in a Looking-glass World'. https://www.academia.edu/7587675/Mimetic_Sovereignties_Precarious_Citizenship_state_effects_in_a_looking_glass_world.
29. Mishra, Ritesh. 'Dichotomy between Maoist surrender and rehab numbers', pub *The Hindustan Times*, Oct 20, 21. https://www.hindustantimes.com/india-news/dichotomy-between-maoist-surrender-and-rehab-numbers-101634754443964.html.
30. Maneckshа, Freny. 'What Drove an Adivasi Woman in Chhattisgarh to Suicide?', pub. Raiot. https://raiot.in/what-drove-an-adivasi-woman-in-chhattisgarh-to-suicide/.
31. 'Bearing Witness: Sexual Violence in South Chhattisgarh', pub. Women Against Sexual Violence and State Repression (WSS)

3. Court

1. The organisations are: Women Against Violence and State Repression (WSS), Coordination of Democratic Rights Organisations (CDRO) and the Jagdalpur Legal Aid Group (JagLAG). Adivasi leaders who intervened actively were Soni Sori and Manish Kunjam, Head of the All India Adivasi Mahasabha

and member of the Communist Party of India. They were aided and given a tip-off by intrepid local journalists.

2. 'Bearing Witness: Sexual Violence in South Chhattisgarh', pub. Women Against Sexual Violence and State Repression (WSS).
3. National Human Rights Commission India, Press Release. https://nhrc.nic.in/press-release/nhrc-finds-16-women-prima-facie-victims-rape-sexual-and-physical-assault-police.
4. Choudhury, Chitrangada. 'Over 50 days after Bijapur assault, two probes but no arrests yet', pub. *Hindustan Times*. https://www.hindustantimes.com/india/over-50-days-after-bijapur-assault-two-probes-but-no-arrests-yet/story-cguToagIvtRTMKOeT8Ri3J.html, 20 December 2015.
5. PTI. 'Chhattisgarh prisons the most crowded in country', pub. *The Hindu*. https://www.thehindu.com/news/national/other-states/Chhattisgarh-prisons-the-most-crowded-in-country/article16083422.ece, 27 October 2016.
6. In 2017, twenty-five CRPF personnel died after a Maoist ambush in Burkapal and thereafter, 120 villagers from various hamlets around the site were picked up and charged with various sections of the Indian Penal Code and also under the UAPA. The trial did not begin even three years after arrests as the police said it did not have sufficient staff to bring such large numbers to the court. The court on its part, refused to consider hearings for people being brought in batches. The 2020 lockdown has also been cited as another reason for tardy proceedings.
7. Pandey, Shikha, advocate and legal researcher, David W. Leebron, Human Rights Fellow, 2018. 'Anti-terrorism Courts and (In)justice: The Case of the National Investigation Agency (NIA) Special Courts in South Chhattisgarh, India', pub. *Socio-legal Review*.
8. Grover, Vrinda. 'The Adivasi Undertrial—A Prisoner of War', A study of undertrial detainees in South Chhattisgarh from the book *Contesting Justice in South Asia*, edited by Deepak Mehta, Rahul Roy, pub. SAGE Publishing India.

9. Manecksha, Freny. 'Evicting the Hope of Justice', pub. The Wire. https://thewire.in/government/evicting-the-hope-of-justice-in-lawless-chhattisgarh, 7 March 2016.
10. Scheduled offences are offences under other penal statutes that can also be investigated by the NIA, including inter alia, offences under laws dealing with national security and terrorism. The NIA Act creates special procedures that deviate from ordinary law on criminal procedure and this curtails several procedural rights of the accused.
11. Pandey, Shikha, advocate and legal researcher, David W. Leebron, Human Rights Fellow, 2018. 'Anti-terrorism Courts and (In) justice: The Case of the National Investigation Agency (NIA) Special Courts in South Chhattisgarh, India', pub. *Socio-legal Review*.
12. Ibid.
13. Amnesty International, 'India frees prisoner of conscience, Kartam Joga'. https://www.amnesty.org/en/latest/news/2013/01/india-frees-prisoner-conscience-kartam-joga/.
14. Purkayastha, Sharmila. 'Where is Sodi Shambo?', pub. *Himal South Asian*. https://www.himalmag.com/sodi-shambo, 16 October 2014.
15. Manecksha, Freny. 'Deconstructing the State's Narrative in a Bastar Fake Encounter', pub. The Wire. https://thewire.in/government/bastar-fake-encounter-crpf, 21 April 2017.
16. Manecksha, Freny. 'Adivasis establish their truth about the murder of 17 villagers in Bastar', pub. Raiot. https://raiot.in/adivasis-establish-their-truth-about-the-murder-of-17-villagers-in-bastar/, 7 December 2019. (Article has link for Kamla Kaka video).
17. *HT* Correspondents, 'Forces Hunt Down and kill 20 Maoists in Chhattisgarh', pub. *Hindustan Times*. https://www.hindustantimes.com/india/forces-hunt-down-and-kill-20-maoists-in-chhattisgarh/story-kZJKGD02AA7cKcJFqyCkiL.html, 30 June 2012.

18. Bharadwaj, Ashutosh. 'Top Naxals' are two 15-year-old toppers', pub. *The Indian Express.* https://www.im4change.org/latest-news-updates/top-naxals-are-two-15-yr-old-toppers-ashutosh-bhardwaj-15993.html, 2 July 2012.
19. Manecksha, Freny. 'Adivasis establish their truth about the murder of 17 villagers in Bastar', pub. Raiot. https://raiot.in/adivasis-establish-their-truth-about-the-murder-of-17-villagers-in-bastar/, 7 December 2019.
20. 'The Slaughter at Sarkeguda and Edesmetta: The Terrible Cost of an Inhuman Counter-insurgency', pub. Human Rights Forum. http://www.humanrightsforum.org/HRF_Inhuman_Counter-Insurgency.pdf, October 2013.

4. Jameen

1. Bordolai, Satyen K. 'Govt Rewarded the Maoist Who Shot My Father'. https://www.youtube.com/watch?v=EIt1nV3fKAI.
2. Poyam, Akash. 'A Man of the People', pub. *The Caravan*, 1 March 2021.
3. Kunjam, Mangal. 'A Peaceful Protest; A Massive Win', pub. Gaon Connection. https://www.gaonconnection.com/gaon-connection-9 August 2019.
4. Apurva, P. 'How the Arrest of Tribal Activist Hidme Markam Is an Attack on the Adivasi Community', pub. Yahoo News. https://in.news.yahoo.com/what-you-need-to-know-about-adivasi-activist-hidme-markam-044804885.html, 9 April 2021.
5. Mazumdar, Rakhi. 'In a first, SAIL offers to pay CRPF for its security', pub. *The Economic Times.* https://economictimes.indiatimes.com/industry/indl-goods/svs/steel/in-a-first-sail-offers-to-pay-crpf-for-its-security/articleshow/14379077.cms?from=mdr, 25 June 2012.

5. Siege

1. Dutta, Prabhash K. 'Kashmir: Why Centre is sending additional 38000 troops to J&K', pub. *India Today*. https://www.indiatoday.in/news-analysis/story/-if-situation-has-improved-then-why-send-38-000-troops-to-j-k-1576436-2019-08-02, 2 August 2019.
2. Nazir, Masoodi and Sharma Neeta. 'Amarnath Yatra Pilgrims, Tourists Asked To Leave J&K Amid Security Threat', report pub. NDTV.com. https://www.ndtv.com/india-news/amarnath-yatra-pilgrims-asked-to-return-from-jammu-and-kashmir-amid-security-threat-2079392, 2 August 2019.
3. Noorani, A.G. 'Murder of Insaniyat, and of India's Solemn Commitment to Kashmir,' pub. The Wire. https://thewire.in/law/murder-of-insaniyat-and-of-indias-solemn-commitment-to-kashmir, 13 August 2019.
4. Rehbar, Quratulain. 'Ground Report: Agony and Casualties in the Valley in the Immediate Aftermath of Shutdown', pub. The Wire. https://thewire.in/rights/jammu-kashmir-srinagar-article-370, 23 August 2019.
5. Dharma, Nisar. '"Moklovukh": Notes around my baby girl's birth', pub. Free Press Kashmir. https://freepresskashmir.news/2020/06/03/moklovukh-notes-around-my-baby-girls-birth/, 3 June 2020.
6. Varma, Saiba. ' Kashmir has become a zone of permanent, limitless war', pub. The Nation. https://www.thenation.com/article/archive/india-infrastructural-war-kashmir/, 4 September 2019.
7. Varma, Saiba. 'Resist to Exist', pub. *The Caravan*. https://caravanmagazine.in/conflict/resist-to-exist-chapter-one-assault-on-the-spirit, 23 August 2019.
8. Zargar, Anees. 'Shopian: 'Where Villagers Can't Sleep as They Hear People Cry', pub. Newsclick. https://www.newsclick.in/Shopian-Villagers-Sleep-Hear-People-Cry, 13 September 2019
9. 'The Human Rights Crisis in Kashmir: A Pattern of Impunity',

pub. Asia Watch, a division of Human Rights Watch and Physicians for Human Rights. https://www.hrw.org/sites/default/files/reports/INDIA937.PDF.

10. Hashmi, Sameer. '"Don't beat us, just shoot us",' pub. BBC. https://www.bbc.com/news/world-asia-india-49481180, 29 August 2019.
11. Hussain, Ashiq. 'Kashmir: Civilians allege army going door-to-door to collect their details, claim privacy breach, pub. *Hindustan Times*. https://www.hindustantimes.com/india-news/kashmir-civilians-allege-army-going-door-to-door-to-collect-their-details-claim-privacy-breach/story-VaKPLthWiwTNUN7CZfw9hK.html, 8 May 2017.
12. Manecksha, Freny. 'August siege: Notes on the Collective Punishment in Kashmir', pub. *Wande magazine,* January 2020.
13. 'Torture: Indian State's Instrument of Control in Indian Administered Jammu and Kashmir', Report by Association of Parents of Disappeared Persons and Jammu Kashmir Coalition of Civil Society.
14. Ghosh, Shrimoyee Nandini and Duschinski, Haley. 'The Grid of Indefinite Incarceration: Everyday Legality and Paperwork Warfare in Indian-controlled Kashmir', pub. journals.sagepub.com.
15. Ibid.
16. Manecksha, Freny. 'The Public Safety Act Is a Political Weapon For the Government in Kashmir', pub. The Wire. https://thewire.in/government/public-safety-act-kashmir, 28 December 2016.
17. Kathju, Junaid. 'Allow Kashmiri lawyers to defend Article 370, says Nazir Ronga, Post Release', pub. The Wire. https://thewire.in/law/article-370-lawyers-kashmir-supreme-court-nazir-ronga, 24 January 2020.
18. Maqbool, Majid. 'Judicial Harassment: British solicitors' body calls for release of senior J&K lawyer', pub. The Wire. https://thewire.in/rights/mian-abdul-qayoom-law-society-england-wales-letter-narendra-modi, 9 March 2020.

19. 'These are the 10 "Most Urgent_ Threats to Press Freedom in December 2019', pub. *Time*. https://time.com/5739491/threats-press-freedom-december/.
20. Nandy, Asmita. 'Sang *Hum Dekhenge* Enroute to Jail: J&K Journo Free After 9 Months', pub. *The Quint*. https://www.thequint.com/videos/kashmir-journalist-freedom-detained-psa-qazi-shibli-article-370-abrogation-interview, 1 May 2020
21. 'Imprisoned Resistance: 5th August and Its Aftermath', https://www.pucl.org/reports/imprisoned-resistance-5th-august-and-its-aftermath.
22. Davies, Marc Daniel. 'Internet Shutdowns Plunged Millions into "Digital Darkness" last year', pub. Bloomberg. https://www.bloomberg.com/news/articles/2021-03-03/internet-shutdowns-plunge-millions-into-digital-darkness, 3 March 2021.
23. Bhattacharya, Ananya. 'The 550-day 4G blackout cost Kashmir's economy $ 4.2 billion', pub. *The Quartz India*. https://qz.com/india/1970363/the-550-day-4g-blackout-cost-kashmirs-economy-4-2-billion/, 9 February 2021.
24. Zaid, Drabu and Hashmi, Aiman. 'SC Judgment on Internet Shutdown Ignores Both Rights and Remedies', pub. The Wire. https://thewire.in/law/sc-internet-shutdown-judgement, 13 February 2020.
25. Graham, Stephen, 'The politics of urban digital infrastructure'. https://www.youtube.com/watch?v=6aAAygjzZM.
26. 'Kashmir's Internet Siege: An Ongoing Assault on Digital Rights', Report by Jammu Kashmir Coalition of Civil Society.
27. Mehraj, Irfan, 'In Shopian a contest is on between militants and security forces to control the streets', pub. *The Caravan*. https://caravanmagazine.in/conflict/in-shopian-a-contest-is-on-between-militants-and-security-forces-to-control-the-streets, 26 September 2019.
28. Kak, Sanjay. 'The Fire Is at My Heart' in *Until My Freedom Has Come: The New Intifada in Kashmir*, edited by Sanjay Kak, pub. Penguin Books.

6. Hospital

1. Scroll Staff. 'Jammu and Kashmir: 2018 was the deadliest year in the state in a decade, says human rights report', pub. Scroll. in. https://scroll.in/latest/907778/jammu-and-kashmir-2018-was-the-deadliest-year-in-the-state-in-a-decade-says-human-rights-report, 31 April 2018.
2. Makhdoomi, Rumana, Dr. *White Man in Dark*, pub. Partridge Publishing, 2013.
3. 'The Crackdown in Kashmir; Torture of Detainees and Assaults on the Medical Community', February 1993, Physicians for Human Rights and Asia Watch.
4. Amnesty Report. https://www.amnesty.org/download/Documents/176000/asa200011995en.pdf.
5. 'Torture: Indian State's Instrument of Control in Indian Administered Jammu and Kashmir'; Report by Association of Parents of Disappeared Persons and Jammu Kashmir Coalition of Civil Society.
6. Iqbal, Javed. 'When 30 cops forced incompetent doctor to write autopsy report in custodial killing case', pub. *Greater Kashmir*. https://www.greaterkashmir.com/amp/story/kashmir/when-30-cops-forced-incompetent-doctor-to-write-autopsy-report-in-custodial-killing-case, 7 March 2018.
7. Batool, Essar, Ifrah Butt, Munaza Rashid, Samreen Mushtaq, Natasha Rather. *Do You Remember Kunan Poshpora?*, pub. Zubaan Books.
8. Report by Human Rights Watch.
9. 'Civil War and Uncivil Government': Report on Human Rights Violations in Kashmir', pub. Fact finding team consisting of Andhra Pradesh Civil Liberties Committee, Hyderabad, Committee for Protection of Democratic Rights, Bombay and People's Union for Democratic Rights, Delhi. http://www.unipune.ac.in/snc/cssh/HumanRights/02%20STATE%20AND%20ARMY%20-%20POLICE%20REPRESSION/E%20Jammu%20and%20Kashmir/06.pdf.

10. Habibullah, Wajahat. *My Kashmir. The Dying of the Light*, pub. Penguin Viking.
11. 'The Crackdown in Kashmir. Torture of Detainees and Assaults on the Medical Community', Physicians for Human Rights and Asia Watch. https://www.hrw.org/reports/INDIA932.PDF.
12. Vij, Shivam. 'Report #1 Attack and Killing on Pattan Hospital Premises', pub. Kafila. https://kafila.online/2010/11/15/report-1-pattan-hospital-attack-kashmir/, 15 November 2010.
13. 'Blind to Justice: Excessive Use of Force and Attacks on Health Care in Jammu and Kashmir, India', Report by Physicians for Human Rights, December 2016.
14. Ibid.
15. Ellen Barry, 'An Epidemic of "Dead Eyes" in Kashmir as India Uses Pellet Guns on Protesters', pub. *The New York Times*. https://www.nytimes.com/2016/08/29/world/asia/pellet-guns-used-in-kashmir-protests-cause-dead-eyes-epidemic.html, 28 August 2016.
16. Latif, Samaan. 'Doctors protest firing of shells inside hospital', pub. *The Tribune*. https://www.tribuneindia.com/news/archive/features/doctors-protest-firing-of-shells-inside-hospital-264083, 10 July 2016.
17. Ahsan, Sofi. 'Kashmir: Ambulance driver fired with pellet while ferrying patients to hospital', pub. *The Indian Express*. https://indianexpress.com/article/india/india-news-india/kashmir-ambulance-driver-fired-with-pellets-while-ferrying-patients-to-the-hospital-2986778/, 20 August 2016.

7. Home/Homeland

1. Bukhari, Parvaiz. 'A Nation Rendered Dumb', pub. *Adi Magazine*, Summer 2020. https://adimagazine.com/articles/a-nation-rendered-numb/.
2. Junaid, Mohamad. 'Laughter and leaked memos: Debating state violence at a Kashmiri baker's shop', pub. Association for

Political and Legal Anthropology. https://politicalandlegalanthro.org/2020/08/25/laughter-and-leaked-memos-debating-state-violence-at-a-kashmiri-bakers-shop/.

3. Haq, Sameer Ul. 'Why poet Iqbal was always concerned for Kashmir', pub. Kashmir Life. https://kashmirlife.net/why-poet-iqbal-was-always-concerned-for-kashmir-239677/, 12 July 2020.
4. Bose, Sumantra. *Kashmir Roots of Conflict, Paths to Peace*, pub. Harvard University Press.
5. Manecksha, Freny. *Behold, I Shine: Narratives of Kashmir's Women and Children*, pub. Rupa Publications.
6. Parrey, Arif Ayaz. 'Storm in a Teacup'. https://www.cupsofnunchai.com/storm-in-a-teacup-a-prelude-by-arif-ayaz-parrey/.
7. Ballinger, Pamela. *History in Exile: Memory and Identity at the Borders of the Balkans*, pub. Princeton University Press. https://www.jstor.org/stable/j.ctv301g0z.
8. Macfarlane, Robert. *Underland*, pub. Hamish Hamilton.
9. Geelani, Gowhar. *Kashmir Rage and Reason*, pub. Rupa Publications.
10. Jammu Kashmir Coalition of Civil Society: Biannual HR review.
11. Rehbar, Quratulain. 'For Defying Army Patrol, Kashmir Woman in Jail 44 days on terror charges', pub. Article 14. https://www.article-14.com/post/for-defying-army-patrol-kashmir-woman-in-jail-44-days-on-terror-charges, 28 May 2021
12. Mushtaq, Samreen. 'Home as the Frontier: Gendered Constructs of Militarised Violence in Kashmir', pub. *Economic and Political Weekly.* https://www.epw.in/journal/2018/47/review-womens-studies/home-frontier.html, 1 December 2018.
13. Batool, Essar, Ifrah Butt, Munaza Rashid, Samreen Mushtaq, Natasha Rather. *Do You Remember Kunan Poshpora?*, pub. Zubaan Books.
14. Zahir-ud-Din 'Flashback: Kashmir Story Since 1846', pub. Jay Kay Books.
15. Parvaiz, Athar. 'Kashmir Ceasefire Comes After 50% Rise

in Armed Encounters, Killings, During 2015–2017 Over 2012–2014', pub. India Spend. https://www.indiaspend.com/kashmir-ceasefire-comes-after-50-rise-in-armed-encounters-killings-during-2015-2017-over-2012-2014, 18 May 2018.

16. Mushtaq, Mariyeh. 'Enforced Homelessness: Collective Dispossession and Punishment in Kashmir', pub. The Kashmir Reading Room Report. https://jklpp.org/enforced-homelessness/.
17. Dar, Irfan and Farooq Gowhar. 'Madhosh Balhami: The Poet of Perseverance (Documentary Series), pub. Inverse Journal. https://www.inversejournal.com/2020/05/04/madhosh-balhami-the-poet-of-perseverance-episode-1-by-mohammad-irfan-dar-and-mohammad-gowhar-farooq/, 4 May 2020.
18. Shahriyar, Syed. 'Now the loyal are being butchered', pub. *Himal South Asian*. https://www.himalmag.com/kashmir-poet-ghulam-mohammad-bhat-madhosh-nalhami/, 2 May 2018.
19. Ibid.
20. Parrey, Arif Ayaz. 'A conversation with my mother on one of the last days of Ramzan', pub. *Wande magazine*,
21. Bashir, Farah. *Rumours of Spring*, pub. Fourth Estate, HarperCollins.
22. Parrey, Arif Ayaz Parrey, 'The Beheading of Rahim Chhaan and Two Others', pub. *The Kashmir Wallah*, 20 January 2013.

8. Nyabar/Outside

1. Yeats, William Butler. 'Easter Rising, 1916'.
2. Raina, Muzaffar.'Boy drowned, buried but not dead', pub. *The Telegraph Online*. https://www.telegraphindia.com/india/kashmir-boy-drowned-buried-but-not-dead/cid/1710066, 10 June 2021.
3. 'Jhelum' by Mad in Kashmir released on 18 November 2020, written and directed by Faheem Abdullah and Imbesat Ahmad with Faheem Abdullah as the singer/songwriter and Rauhan Malik and Ashish Joseph as the music producers.

4. Pandit, Huzaifa.'Top Music Videos of 2020: Of Songs and Grief', pub. *Kashmir Observer.*
5. 'Structures of Violence: The Indian State in Jammu and Kashmir', Report by The International Peoples' Tribunal on Human Rights and Justice in Indian-Administered Kashmir (IPTK) and The Association of Parents of Disappeared Persons (APDP).
6. Nisar Dharam, 'A new bunker on the way to school: Explaining to a child the military presence of India', pub. The Polis Project. https://www.thepolisproject.com/a-new-bunker-on-the-way-to-school-explaining-to-a-child-the-military-presence-in-kashmir/#.YMG8NvkzZPZ, 16 April 2021.
7. Maqbool, Majid. 'Village Number Nine', pub. Al Jazeera. https://www.aljazeera.com/economy/2011/8/1/villager-number-nine, 1 August 2011.
8. Maneckshа, Freny. 'Kashmir Man Who Lost His Legs to Torture in 1990s Keeps Up Fight for Justice', pub. The Wire. https://thewire.in/government/legs-cut-off-and-forced-into-begging-kashmir-man-recounts-severe-torture-by-security-forces, 14 June 2017
9. Macfarlane, Robert. *Underland*, pub. Hamish Hamilton.
10. 'Q&A US: Targeted Killings and International Law', Human Rights Watch. https://www.hrw.org/news/2011/12/19/q-us-targeted-killings-and-international-law.
11. Maneckshа, Freny. 'Civilian Killings in Kashmir, Despair Looms Large as Civilians Continue to Face Targeted Killings', pub. The Wire, https://thewire.in/politics/kashmir-despair-looms-large-civilians-continue-face-targeted-killings, 3 February 2018.
12. Junaid, Mohamad. 'Counter-maps of the ordinary: Occupation, subjectivity and waking under curfew in Kashmir', https://www.tandfonline.com/doi/full/10.1080/1070289X.2019.1633115.
13. Ibid.
14. Pandit, Huzaifa. 'Of Slogans', pub. *Kashmir Observer*, https://kashmirobserver.net/2020/09/24/of-slogans/, 11 June 2020.
15. Zargar, Haris. 'Kashmir's resistance anthem', pub. New Frame.

https://www.newframe.com/kashmirs-resistance-anthem/, 15 October 2019.

16. https://www.youtube.com/watch?v=XTjEQB2iBeE.
17. 'History of Ragda', pub. Made in Kashmir. https://madeinkashmir.org/history-of-ragda/, 14 May 2020.
18. Mushtaq, Samreen. 'Kashmiri Women's Songs of Resistance', pub. *Engenderings*, The London School of Economics and Political Science. https://blogs.lse.ac.uk/gender/2021/02/23/kashmiri-womens-songs-of-resistance/.
19. Robinson, Cabeiri DeBergh. 'Body of Victim, Body of Warrior: Refugee Families and the Making of Kashmiri Jihadists', pub. University of California Press.
20. Irfan, Shams. 'Scenes from Burhan Wani's Funeral', pub. The Wire. https://thewire.in/politics/the-funeral-burhan-wani, 8 July 2017.
21. Malik, Inshah. 'Gendered Politics of Funerary Processions: Contesting Indian Sovereignty in India', pub. *Economic and Political Weekly*, Vol. 53, Issue 47, 1 December 2018. https://www.epw.in/journal/2018/47/review-womens-studies/gendered-politics-funerary-processions.html.
22. Naqash, Rayan. 'From Srinagar, a new crop of militants who kill and die in the name of religion, not politics', pub. Scroll.in. https://scroll.in/article/872365/from-srinagar-a-new-crop-of-militants-who-kill-and-die-in-the-name-of-religion-not-politics, 8 July 2017.
23. Robinson, Cabeiri DeBergh. 'Body of Victim, Body of Warrior: Refugee Families and the Making of Kashmiri Jihadists', pub. University of California Press.
24. Fazili, Gowhar. 'Familial Grief, Resistance and the Political Imaginary in Kashmir', pub. *Indian Anthropology*, Vol. 46, Issue 2.
25. Irfan, Shams. 'How Syed Ali Shah Geelani's Body was taken from his Family, Buried in Haste', pub. The Wire, https://thewire.in/rights/how-syed-ali-shah-geelanis-body-was-taken-from-his-family-buried-in-haste.

9. Spaces of Dissent

1. Bhat, Ghulam Q., 'The Emergence and Development of the Muslim Political Identity in Kashmir 1846–1947', pub. *Journal of South Asian Studies.* https://journals.indexcopernicus.com/api/file/viewByFileId/927746.pdf.
2. Hussnain, Fida, Professor, 'The Genesis of the Reading Room Party', pub. *Greater Kashmir*, 14 March 2015.
3. Zahir-ud-Din, 'Bouquet', pub. Jammu Kashmir Coalition of Civil Society.
4. Bhat, Saima. 'The Hero of 13 July 1931', pub. *The Kashmir Walla.*
5. Rai, Mridu. 'Martyrs' Day: Memorializing 13 July 1931 in Kashmir', pub. Kafila. https://kafila.online/2011/07/13/martyrs%E2%80%99-days-memorializing-13-july-1931-in-kashmir-mridu-rai/.
6. https://www.findglocal.com/IN/Srinagar/232034690186775/Khan-News-Agency.
7. Behrawallah, Kritika. 'At Ahdoos, a platter of meat, a side of memories', pub. *Hindustan Times*, Jalandhar, https://www.pressreader.com/india/hindustan-times-28 June 2018. jalandhar/20180624/ 281968903415971.
8. Rather, Nayeem. 'Lala Sheikh: A Tiny Corner of Living History', pub. *Kashmir Today.* https://kashmir.today/lala-sheikh-a-tiny-corner-of-living-history/, 12 June 2020.
9. Hassan, K.W. 'The Letter That Vanished', pub. Raiot. https://raiot.in/the-letter-that-vanished/.
10. Bashir, Farah. *Rumours of Spring*, pub. HarperCollins.
11. Handoo, Bilal. 'Show Is Over', pub. *Kashmir Life*, https://kashmirlife.net/show-is-over-issue-48-vol-06-73252/, 16 February 2015.
12. Ibid.
13. Ali, Agha Shahid. 'The City of Daughter' from his collection of poems, *The Country Without a Post Office*, pub. Penguin.

14. Iyer-Mitra, Abhijit 'I went to meet pellet gun victims in Soura, the new epicentre of Kashmir's anger', pub. The Print. https://theprint.in/opinion/i-went-to-meet-pellet-gun-victims-in-soura-the-new-epicentre-of-kashmirs-anger/295950/.
15. https://www.youtube.com/watch?v=_JtibKy_xkk.
16. Manecksha, Freny. 'Anchar's Proud Legacy of Defiance', pub. Raiot. https://raiot.in/anchars-proud-legacy-of-defiance/, 28 October 2019.
17. Jaleel, Muzamil. 'From majority to disempowered minority: Politics of Delimitation in JK, pub. Free Press Kashmir. https://freepresskashmir.news/2021/07/07/from-majority-to-disempowered-minority-politics-of-delimitation-in-jk/amp/?fbclid=IwAR00vtjgka2eZpkop4s-RsBuwFJsxPxq9oViABEgsAyebReOhYKy, 7 July 2021.

Ingram Content Group UK Ltd.
Milton Keynes UK
UKHW011838270423
420877UK00004B/345